Buenos Aires

University Press of Florida ~ Gainesville Tallahassee
Tampa Boca Raton Pensacola Orlando Miami Jacksonville

Buenos

Perspectives on the City and Cultural Production

Aires

David William Foster

03 02 01 00 99 98 6 5 4 3 2 1

LIBRARY OF CONGRESS CATALOGING-IN-PUBLICATION DATA

Foster, David William.
Buenos Aires: perspectives on the city and cultural production /
David William Foster.
p. cm.
Includes bibliographical references and index.
ISBN 0-8130-1613-4 (cloth: alk. paper)
1. Popular culture—Argentina—Buenos Aires. 2. Buenos Aires (Argentina)—
Intellectual life—20th century. 3. City and town life—Argentina—Buenos
Aires. 4. Arts and society—Argentina—Buenos Aires. 5. Literature and
society—Argentina—Buenos Aires. 6. Buenos Aires (Argentina)—In art.
7. Buenos Aires (Argentina)—In literature. I. Title.
F3001.2.F65 1998
306'0982'11—dc21   98-23403

The University Press of Florida is the scholarly publishing agency for the
State University System of Florida, comprising Florida A & M University,
Florida Atlantic University, Florida International University, Florida State
University, University of Central Florida, University of Florida, University of
North Florida, University of South Florida, and University of West Florida.

University Press of Florida
15 Northwest 15th Street
Gainesville, FL 32611
http://nersp.nerdc.ufl.edu/~upf

Contents

Acknowledgments

I wish to acknowledge the support of the various Arizona State University research programs that have, for thirty years now, generously supported my work on Latin American culture. My research assistants for this project have included Gastón Alzate, Oscar Díaz, María Cristina Guzzo, Arthur Hughes, Darrell Lockhart, Francisco Manzo-Robledo, Kanishka Sen, and Camille Villafañe. Daniel Altamiranda provided me with a valuable critical reading of the manuscript.

All translations of quotations in Spanish are my own unless otherwise indicated.

A slightly different version of chapter 7 appeared in *Arizona Journal of Hispanic Cultural Studies*. Parts of the discussion on Talesnik's *La fiaca* in chapter 2 will appear in a volume edited by George Woodyard on Argentine theater in the 1960s. Chapter 3 will appear in a volume on Latin American culture studies, edited by Eva Bueno, to be published by the University of Pittsburgh Press. Some of chapter 4 appeared in Spanish as part of a longer study in *Tramas* (Córdoba, Argentina). The excerpt on Alicia Steimberg in chapter 6 is also included in a chapter on Jewish women writers in a book edited by Marjorie Agosin, to be published by the University of New Mexico Press.

Introduction

The challenge was clear. There was a complex and problem-filled interaction between the production of human geographies and the constitution of social relations and practices which needed to be recognized and opened up to theoretical and political interpretation. This could not be done by continuing to see human geography only as a reflection of social processes. The created spatiality of social life had to be seen as simultaneously contingent and conditioning, as both an outcome and a medium for the making of history—in other words, as part of a historical and geographic materialism rather than just a historical materialism applied to geographical questions.

—Edward Soja, *Postmodern Geographies*

. . . we need to conceptualize spaces as constructed out of inter-relations, as the simultaneous coexistence of social interrelations and interactions at all spatial scales, from the most local level to the most global. . . . in human geography, the recognition that the spatial is socially constituted was followed by the perhaps more powerful . . . recognition that the social is necessarily spatially constituted too. . . . The spatial spread of social relations can be intimately local or expansively global, or anything in between. . . . there is no getting away from the fact that the social is inexorably also spatial.

—Doreen Massey, "Politics and Space/Time"

After Argentina gained independence from Spain on July 9, 1816, the Porteño bourgeoisie began a development of Buenos Aires that,[1] despite the tyranny of the administration of Juan Manuel de Rosas in the 1830s and 1840s, led the port city to become by the end of the nineteenth century the major commercial center of Latin America and the major cultural center of the Spanish-speaking countries of the region. (For an excellent overview of Buenos Aires, see Walter; Kunckel discusses Buenos Aires in the context of Latin American metropolises; Romero and Romero constitutes the standard history of the city; see the essays in *Buenos Aires: 400 Years*; and see Sargent on Argentine cities).

Buenos Aires is the largest city of Spanish-speaking South America, the second largest after Mexico City (the hemisphere's true megalopolis). Because of its greater proximity to the United States, Mexico City may have diminished some of Buenos Aires's urban importance. The fact that Mexico City is also closer than Buenos Aires to Spain, the United States, and other Latin American cultural centers such as Havana and Bogotá has also given it an edge in publications and general cultural production that Buenos Aires now finds hard to compete with.

Nevertheless, since the return to constitutional democracy in 1983, the implementation of neoliberalist economic policies in the early 1990s, and Argentina's privileged and favored-nation status with the United States on the alleged basis of the two country's common European heritage (read: white society) and common economic goals, Buenos Aires has reconsolidated much of the importance it lost under the military dictatorships between 1966 and 1983. While there are different interpretations about what this means—the consequences of killer-shark capitalism versus a return to a legendary patina of social sophistication—Buenos Aires is no longer just the capital of one of Latin America's pariah dictatorships. The success of Alan Parker's film *Evita* is in part an index of the renewed importance and respectability of Buenos Aires, and it is important to note that the abundant exterior shots of the city—even when in reality many of them were shot in Budapest, where it was possible to capture the feel of the city in the 1940s and 1950s—should bring to international attention features of the so-called Paris of South America.

Buenos Aires occupies a major place in the social history and collective imagination of Argentina. True, one expects capital cities to enjoy this sort of importance; but there is something unique about the enormous weight of Buenos Aires vis-à-vis the rest of the country. A famous saying asserts that "God is everywhere, but He only holds office hours in Buenos Aires." This saying confirms the way in which, in the tradition of imperial politics to which Argentina is heir, all lines of power lead to the court, a conception within which the geographic and symbolic decentralization of financial and political administration is unheard of. It also underscores how, to evoke another characterization, this time taken from Ezequiel Martínez Estrada's 1940 essay, *La cabeza de Goliat* (Goliath's Head), Buenos Aires is truly a monstrous entity that overshadows the rest of Latin America's second largest nation. (See Rama for a major study on the intersection between the city and the ideology of cultural literacy. Although Buenos Aires is barely mentioned, *Rethinking the Latin American City* is a series of programmatic statements and analyses of the "Goliath's head" syndrome of Latin American urban centers.)

Both Brazil's historic capital, Rio de Janeiro, and the current capital, Brasília, are smaller and less important financially and culturally (and, therefore, politically) than São Paulo, the country's major city and nerve center. Mexico's capital, Mexico City, may overshadow the rest of the country as the world's largest city, but there are other cities like Monterrey and Guadalajara that have their own spheres of influence and identity as metropolises of national importance. By contrast, Buenos Aires literally impedes significance for any other population center of the country (for an overview of Latin American metropolises, see Kunckel). Córdoba and Rosario may be important industrial complexes, but they hardly wield comparative political and cultural weight,[2] and they, as much as the most rural outback of the country, have a persuasive right to complain about how the entire material wealth of the country and the cultural production that accompanies it are sucked into the black hole that is the city of Buenos Aires. (Concerning the study of Argentine culture from a perspective that is not Buenos Aires centered, see Kusch; see also Foster, "Prolegomenon.") In terms of the center/periphery relationship between Buenos Aires and "the provinces," non–Buenos Aires Argentina corresponds to what Shields has called "places on the margin." Buenos Aires was made into the Capital Federal with its own constitutional identity in 1996. Although it had been separated from the wealthy province of Buenos Aires as its capital with the creation of La Plata in 1880, it had no administrative independence from the federal government based there.

The creation of the Distrito Federal is a shift in the balance of power that will give separate political power to the residents of the capital and make them less dependent on the policies of the all-powerful federal government. The government's power was particularly felt during the neofascist military dictatorships, which exercised a baneful influence on cultural production concomitant with its overall tyranny in the affairs of social life.

From another point of view, the creation of the Capital Federal must be seen as another chapter in the symbolic stature of the city. It is, of course, for this reason that the term "Buenos Aires" will continue to be the preferred popular designation for a city that has played such a prominent role in the development of Latin American culture. (Despite the mail service's efforts to the contrary, Capital Federal is becoming the favored formal designation of Buenos Aires, which now refers to the province.)

Capital cities are usually strategically placed, and a major population center's emergence in a particular place is typically due to a number of economic and political factors. Whereas other cities seem to grow by accident, capital cities fulfill certain social designs. For example, Buenos Aires is one of a handful of major cities located on the coast. For reasons that often included protection from roving pirates, colonial centers tended to be located away from the coast, often with a satellite city that served such a function: Santiago de Chile and Valparaíso, Mexico City and Veracruz, Lima and Callao, Caracas and Maracaibo. However, coastal capitals could be fortified (Havana and San Juan, with the latter's forts, known as *morros* [pig snouts] for their location on promontories). Only Rio de Janeiro and Buenos Aires emerged as relatively unprotected coastal cities; Montevideo is more exposed than Buenos Aires, but it only came into existence toward the end of the colonial period.

Buenos Aires is, of course, located upriver from the Atlantic, whereas Rio de Janeiro is located right on the ocean (during the colonial period, protection was provided by development along an inner harbor) and Montevideo is at the confluence of the ocean and the Río de la Plata estuary and delta. Certainly, the relative insignificance of Buenos Aires throughout the colonial period explains why there was little to be lost in being so exposed to water traffic. Besides, Buenos Aires could only become a major port toward the end of the nineteenth century. Dredging projects at this time allowed boats to anchor on shore, something that had not been possible because of constantly accumulating silt from the vast fluvial system of which the Río de la Plata is the terminus.

Buenos Aires's location at the terminal point of a vast river network, and the fact that it is backed up against the vast plains of the Pampas, contributes immensely to its symbolism. Eduardo Mallea, an important establishment writer in the 1930s and 1940s, called Buenos Aires *la ciudad junto al río inmóvil* (the city next to the immobile river), and many have lamented that, if Argentina lives with its back to the rest of Latin America, Buenos Aires lives with its back to Argentina. It can also be construed that the "real

Argentina" begins at the Avenida General Paz, the thoroughfare that marks the boundary of the federal district like four sides of a rhomboid split open at one of their junctures along the edges of the city not marked by the waterways of the Río de la Plata (to the east and northwest) and the Riachuelo (to the south). (The concepts of Henri Lefebvre on the production of cultural space would certainly be useful in understanding how the totally artificial marker of the Avenida General Paz creates radically different cultural and spatial meanings on different sides; see Pile 145–69.) Writing in the context of a woman's identification with the city (see chapter 5), Alicia Dujovne Ortiz speaks of the relationship between Buenos Aires and its location:

> Could you build a circular city on the pampas, a kernel-city, a city curled up like a tightened fist? Apparently not, since Buenos Aires is the epitome of expansiveness: the city pours itself out like a liquid. A city without boundaries. Or rather, a port city; a gateway city that never closes. I have always been astonished by those great cities of the world that have such precise boundaries that you can say exactly where they end. Buenos Aires has no end. It needs a beltway around it [the Avenida General Paz] so you could point an index finger, trembling with uncertainty, and say: "You end there. Up to this point, you are you. Beyond that, God only knows!" Buenos Aires couldn't care less. . . . (118)

There are, as one might expect, many symbolic dimensions of the relationship between Buenos Aires and the rest of the country, in addition to concrete and material ones such as agricultural interests with corporate offices in Buenos Aires and the structure that relates all facets of government administration to the central government in the capital. I will refer in a moment to Ricardo Güiraldes's famous novel that provides an important ideological interpretation of the relationship between the metropolis and the countryside, and much of tango culture has its basis in suburbs of the city that subsequently become integral parts of the metropolis. Many members of the lumpen proletariat that Enrique Medina describes belong to what the self-styled European inhabitants of Buenos Aires called Perón's *cabecitas negras* (blackheads), a racist reference to the thousands of individuals with Indian and mestizo roots that Juan Domingo Perón brought from the far northern provinces during his first government (1946–52).

They were usually brought with free passage on the newly nationalized railways, ostensibly to constitute a labor force for his expansion of Argentina's industrial plant, but it was just as much a powerfully symbolic act of social aggression against white Buenos Aires, which had not yet even begun to get used to the presence of hundreds of thousands of "alien" Jewish immigrants. Indeed, Perón, although he was not free of the anti-Semitism of his day (the Argentine military from which he rose is to this day inhospitable to the nation's Jews), did much to promote Jewish commercial interests as yet another nontraditional sphere of political support to complement that of the general working class, the immigrant, and the *cabecita negra* support he also came to wield. The ideology of the *cabecita negra* has become an integral part of Porteño social life, and it has extensive cultural manifestations. Moreover, because of current economic circumstances, there continues to be a large migration into Buenos Aires from all over the country, making the basis of such an ideology part of a continuing demographic reality.

Thus, it is virtually impossible to speak of Argentine culture without reference to Buenos Aires. This is not only because the majority of publishing houses are located in the capital, as well as virtually all film and television production and original theatrical activity, but also because the overwhelming thematic content of that production refers to the city—its demographics as much as its symbolic dimensions. Nineteenth-century Argentine literature produced works like Domingo Faustino Sarmiento's *Civilización i barbarie* (Civilization and Barbarism), more commonly known as *Facundo*, on the life and times of Juan Facundo Quiroga (1788–1835), the eponymous caudillo from the province of La Rioja, and José Hernández's Gaucho epic, *Martín Fierro*. Nevertheless, both end up referring to Buenos Aires, in the sense that Sarmiento uses Facundo as a key to the barbarism of the Porteño dictator Juan Manuel de Rosas, and it is clear that the economic policies of the capital underlie the destruction of the Gaucho way of life that Hernández denounces in the first part of his poem ("Ida" [Departure]) and that he comes to view as both inevitable and necessary in the second part ("Vuelta" [Return]). But twentieth-century Argentine literature—the mythifications of Buenos Aires in the poetry and stories of Jorge Luis Borges; the representation of the lumpen proletariat in the fiction, chronicles, and theater of Roberto Arlt; the theater of Armando Discepolo; and one of the most important novels of the "boom" of

Latin American literature in the 1960s, Julio Cortázar's *Rayuela* (Hopscotch)—has essentially and insistently meant either the setting of culture
in Buenos Aires or, more directly, the representation of forms of life in that
city.

There exists a substantial bibliography on the city of Buenos Aires, and
many new titles have been published as the result of renewed intellectual
and scholarly activity since the return to democracy. James Scobie's research on the historical development of the city, academic material published on the occasion of the 400th anniversary of the foundation of
Buenos Aires (*Buenos Aires: 400 Years*), and the large number of photographic albums that satisfy as much a tourist interest in the city as artistic
interpretations are all indispensable sources for establishing a familiarity
with Buenos Aires. Although tour guides are not as common for Buenos
Aires as they are for, say, Mexico or the Caribbean, the Insight series
(Hoefer) has continued a tradition of coverage for the city that goes back
to the turn of the century, when the famed Baedeker series included a
volume for Buenos Aires as the only Latin American city so distinguished
(A. Martínez).

Despite this enormous abundance of scholarly and cultural material
on the city, to date no one has undertaken a specific examination of how
the city is given forms of cultural representation—nothing at least that
approximates Gomes's examination of Rio de Janeiro as a "cidade textual
moderna." There are, of course, essays on specific cases, such as Buenos
Aires in the works of Jorge Luis Borges (Paoletti) or Julio Cortázar (Roy-
Cabrerizo), as well as on specific urban groups, especially Italian immigrants (Onega; Foster, *Argentine Literature*, 53–56). However, no attempt
has been made to give an overall sense of Buenos Aires in broadly defined
examples of cultural production, especially in terms of genres that go beyond the strictly literary ones.

Since the first research twenty-five years ago by Edward Soja and others
on the modern city, there is an increasing sense of the importance of the
city as much more than just a place where people live. Rather, the city is
seen as first of all the defining locus of modern, and now postmodern,
culture, a perception that is tremendously important as a shift from the
ideology of rural settings as the font of national identity ("the call of the
land") and the interpretation of the city as a place where individuals lose
that identity. As opposed to a cultural nationalism that views both the

preservation of indigenous societies (for many regions, conceived as the basis for an authentic Latin America, although surely not in Argentina except for sporadic assertions) and a Creole Hispanic culture as only possible as far away as possible from the corrupting influence of the city, with its hoards of immigrants and the maelstrom of foreign influences. A paradigmatic literary version of this position is Ricardo Güiraldes's nostalgic novel of rural and oligarchic supremacy, *Don Segundo Sombra* (1926). But it is now possible to view the city as exercising a determining role in the creation of social subjects whose identification (positive or negative) with the city is a determining factor in the creation of an interaction between place and person that is crucial for any and all forms of cultural production, with culture understood here in its broadest, all-encompassing sense of human social enterprise. The city is no longer merely a way station, nor is it a profound curse: such views will, of course, have their reflexes in cultural production—specifically, in so much of the negative images of the plight of immigrants in a city like Buenos Aires—but they cannot transcend the view of the city as an aberration, as the delegitimation of any authentic national identity.

We are, then, talking about two essential principles here. First, the emergence of a view of the city as the primary and therefore fundamentally determining phenomenon of contemporary social existence and, second, of the city as the locus of subject formation, not an accident but a globalizing experience (see Pile for provocative proposals concerning the relationship between the city and subjectivity). The consequence of such views necessarily effects how the city is viewed in relation to cultural production, whether the latter is defined in terms of all manifestations of human social conduct or whether it is understood in the more limited sense of those phenomena to which an institutional definition of Culture is attached, a definition that may, in turn, move between mass, popular culture and elite or canonical, and, consequently, privileged forms of production.

The principal consequence of such a shift is that it can no longer be simply a matter of charting fixed images of the city in cultural works, images that are either iconically portrayed, as in photography and forms of illustration or in film and television, or ones that are metaphorically evoked, as in poetry and the novel (one does not mean to privilege any literalness about the form and poetic re-creation in the latter, but only to capture the way in which prevailing cultural ideologies usually view photography as more tangibly direct than poetry). Such images are useful and may be integral to the interpretation of specific texts: one would like to speculate on what sort of "typical" image of Buenos Aires might adorn the cover of an edition of *Rayuela*; although, to the best of my knowledge, no edition has attempted to resolve the matter of which view of the city to use (Forster provides such a survey of images in cultural production; see also Campra).

Concomitantly, a writer like Borges, whose life and sense of identity are so bound up with the city—which is quite ironic, to the extent that certain cultural nationalists have traditionally dismissed Borges as the paradigm of the "foreignizing" Argentine bourgeois writer—engages in various strategies, from directly recounting details of places and settings of the city (for example, "Fundación mítica de Buenos Aires" ["Mythic Foundation of Buenos Aires"], which Borges significantly sets as taking place precisely on the block in which he grew up at the turn of the century) to rather fanciful uses of the cityscape, as in the story "La muerte y la brújula" ("Death and the Compass"), where the references to geography of the city, no matter how verisimilar they may seem to be, do not jibe with its actual layout. But as interesting as these details may be, and particularly as satisfying as the outlines of the city may seem to be portrayed in Argentina's abundant cinematographic production, it cannot, in view of the considerable and crucial function of the contemporary city, be enough to construct an inventory of such images. Thus, a fundamentally different construction of the relationship between city and cultural production is called for. It seems to me that words written by Homi Bhabha regarding "writing the nation" are just as applicable to "writing the city," especially when, as in the case of the relationship between Buenos Aires and Argentina, for so many Argentines, Buenos Aires is essentially the nation:

> The people are not simply historical events or parts of a patriotic body politic. They are also a complex rhetorical strategy of social reference where the claim to be representative provokes a crisis within the process of signification and discursive address. We then have a contested cultural territory where the people must be thought in a double-time; the people are the historical "objects" of a nationalistic pedagogy, giving the discourse an authority that is based on the pre-given or constituted historical origin or event; the people are

also the "subjects" of a process of signification that must erase any prior or originary presence of the nation-people to demonstrate the prodigious, living principle of the people as that continual process by which the national life is redeemed and signified as a repeating and reproductive process. The scraps, patches, and rags of daily life must be repeatedly turned into the signs of a national culture, while the very act of the narrative performance interpellates a growing circle of national subjects. In the production of the nation as narration there is a split between the continuist, accumulative temporality of the pedagogical, and the repetitious, recursive strategy of the performative. It is through this process of splitting that the conceptual ambivalence of modern society becomes the site of *writing the nation*. (297)

To which we might add that the institutions of cultural production are not only reflexes of this writing of the nation and of the city, but that they are constructions of meaning, for it is herein that their eloquence and their efficaciousness lie as cultural constructs—they are forged from the "scraps, patches, and rags of daily life."

The essays in this volume model that very different understanding of the relationship between Buenos Aires and cultural production. Rather than examine the cultural production that evokes the streets and plazas of the city,[3] my goal has been to examine texts that portray coordinates of the subjective identity of individuals who inhabit, experience, resist, and create the human space known as the city of Buenos Aires. Toward this end, these essays do not inventory physical features, nor do they assess the accuracy of the details of the representation of such physical features. Cities like Buenos Aires produce particular forms of culture, and general forms of culture assume particular dimensions: "Sites are never simply locations. Rather, they are sites for someone and of something" (Shields, 6).

For example, one of the paradigms of Argentine culture is the tango, a conjunction of music, dance, and lyrics that would be inconceivable in anything other than an urban setting. The tango may have become internationalized, and it may have been appropriated in ways that are alternately "authentic" and "exotic" by other cultures (see Savigliano, *Tango and the Political Economy of Passion,* 169–206), but the tango remains firmly identified with Río de la Plata urban culture, whether Buenos Aires or Montevideo, and it remains firmly identified with specific social groups. The way in which the tango enacts forms of erotic behavior, the way in which it dramatizes forms of gendered sexual relations, and the way in which it is constituted by basic musical rhythms and dance structures all point to forms of culture and forms of the display of culture that have emerged and that continue to have meaning in an urban context in which immigrant culture (traced in the lyrics, for example, by poetic re-creations of urban slang associated with Italian immigrants), aggressive sexual display, and reference to concrete icons (streets, cafes and bars, tenements, dance-hall brothels) are insistently identified with the city, despite partial manifestations of these elements outside the metropolis.

Immigrant culture, the visibility of gay and lesbian culture in their modern and postmodern definitions, and women's movements (including the way in which individual women situate themselves vis-à-vis such movements) are all firmly rooted in the urban landscape. Certainly, immigrants are located elsewhere in Argentina. One of the first major works of Argentine-Jewish culture, Alberto Gerchunoff's *Los gauchos judíos* (The Jewish Gauchos of the Pampas), deals with immigrant agricultural settlements in the Argentine Mesopotamia northeast of Buenos Aires. "Jewish Gauchos" may be viewed as an oxymoron from the vantage of the Buenos Aires ghetto, but in fact the name refers to the project of locating Jewish immigrants in rural, agricultural communities, the domain associated with the Gauchos, much as occurred in the United States also at the end of the last century. The fact that in neither country have these communities lasted (although they do so longer in Argentina, where they are now dying out) speaks not only to the general population migration toward the metropolis, but also to the unreality of turning mostly urban Jews into farmers, a policy of imposed separatism on the part of immigration sponsors that was not free of a taint of racism. Reference might also be made here to Florencio Sánchez's famous play, *La gringa* ([The Immigrant's Daughter] written in 1904, a few years prior to Argentina's first centennial in 1910, and a major reference point for cultural texts analyzing national issues), in which the conflict between the Creole and the immigrant (this time Italian) is played out in a rural setting. Sánchez, most of whose works dealt with urban culture, used this play to express his endorsement of the official ideology underlying the encouragement of foreign immigration to Argentina: the belief that such immigrants would refresh the debased Hispanic stock of the population. Sánchez, very much in the nineteenth-century tradition of using women in allegorical roles (see Sommer), invests the Italian immigrant woman with the reproductive task of replenishing the rural stock.

Despite these examples, the vast bulk of Argentine literature associates immigrants with the city, both with certain areas of the city, whether identified specifically as ghettoes or not, and with the city as a whole, as in the course of history, where subsequent generations move up the social scale. It is an ironic detail of Argentine history that the majority of the military dictators of the recent period of neofascist tyranny between 1966 and 1983 were descendants of Italian immigrants, as of course was Perón. The current president, Carlos Menem, is the son of Syrian-Lebanese parents, but his roots lie in the western provinces, where many Middle Eastern immigrants settled because of geographic similarity to their homelands.

By the same token, the totality of Argentine cultural production dealing with lesbian and gay issues is centered in Buenos Aires. It is possible to find treatments of homoerotic themes (often defined in ways that do not match contemporary understandings of "gay," "lesbian," or "queer") in literature set elsewhere (for example, the fiction of Juan José Hernández in Tucumán, José María Borghello in Mendoza, Manuel Puig in a small Pampas town in the province of Buenos Aires); however, cultural production dealing with homoerotic rights ends up with a metropolitan basis, in part because the history of gay rights has been an urban history and in part because, significantly, the definition of gay rights is based on characteristics of urban life. Thus, it is important to note that Hernández, Borghello, Puig, along with others like Oscar Hermes Villordo (who refers to experiences in his native province of El Chaco), all ended up in Buenos Aires, only to write their literature on homoerotic themes there (Puig, however, became a well-known exile because of the openness of his writing during the military dictatorship), and published their works with Porteño presses. Hernández is the only one who has retained a premodern definition of homosexuality as something other than an identity and as part of the polymorphic, priapic eroticism of the male body (see Geirola).

Finally, and for many of the same reasons that gay and lesbian identities are constructed in the context of urban culture, women's movements are equally to be found virtually exclusively in the metropolis. Of course, a large part of feminist issues involves employment opportunities and remuneration equities, and such is far more possible within the structures of the liberal economics of the city than in the agrarian setting of the countryside, where often, as is the case in much of modern Argentina, there is a crushing equality for both sexes in peripheral provinces: economic stagnation and widespread unemployment.

What is at issue, then, is the way in which metropolitan life does not receive individuals who possess an already existent identity as immigrants, as gays, or as women. Rather, urban life constructs subjectivities that see themselves and are seen in these terms, and who conduct their life accordingly, resisting and redefining their sense of selfhood in the process. To be sure, individuals possess multiple identities: one may be a woman who comes from an immigrant household and self-identifies as a lesbian. As a consequence, we are speaking of multiple social lives with complex overlays and intersections, something that I have attempted to capture by building on recognized sociocultural categories and by establishing continuities between them, so that feminine social subjects are present in a discussion of women in urban space, while also appearing in treatments of the tango, gay visibility, and immigrants.

Immigrants appear in a chapter dealing with immigration, but they are also crucial to a discussion of the tango, and they form much of the lumpen proletariat that is examined in the chapter devoted to the dirty realism of Enrique Medina. Gays are integral to a treatment of homoerotic visibility in contemporary Buenos Aires, but homoerotic dimensions of the tango—or at least, the markedly homosocial basis of the tango—provide a different dimension of same-sex visibility. Marginal social groups are the basis of Medina's writings, but they appear also in a treatment of city and theater and always by implication when not directly evident in the middle-class world of Quino's comic strip *Mafalda*. Such an organization is important to any attempt to show how individuals participate in multiple, simultaneous, and serial subjectivities, and any adequate view of the urban life cannot reduce them to one crucial and all-defining identity.

Any attempt to examine satisfactorily the relationship between urban life and the formation of social subjectivities must analyze pertinent texts in some detail, with the result that the selection of such texts must be highly selective and, therefore, always relative in terms of what else could be examined. Many of the choices here will be controversial, not only because of what else could be discussed but is not, but also because of the decision to highlight certain forms of urban culture and to showcase certain artists. Two chapters are devoted to single individuals: Medina and Quino. Quino is undoubtedly a cartoonist with an international reputation, but focusing on *Mafalda*, a strip he only drew for a half dozen years and ceased to draw twenty-five years ago, not only means overshadowing his extensive non-*Mafalda* production, but it ignores the huge bibliography of graphic art produced in Argentina. Other graphic artists rightly complain that there are other Argentine cartoonists. And, Quino himself has not lived in Buenos Aires since he stopped drawing *Mafalda*, often lending his references to the city the same "archeological" cast found in the fictional writing from Paris on Buenos Aires by Julio Cortázar, a distance that, of course, provides its own advantages in terms of a productive ironic distortion of emphasis. For example, it is quite remarkable how Quino's work in recent years has begun to have a queer dimension about it, frequently colored by his underlying black humor, while no cartoonist in Buenos Aires, to the best of my knowledge, has yet to take such a step.

Enrique Medina continues to be a controversial writer, although English and French translations of his work have done much to mainstream them, to the degree that foreign recognition has always given Argentine writers a cachet of importance vital for local acceptance. Certainly, more than a decade of constitutional democracy has meant that his writings no longer go against the grain of official censorship (there was a time in the seventies and early eighties when virtually all of his books were banned). Reports and historical accounts from the late 1980s and early 1990s of state terrorism during the period of tyranny (see Foster, "Argentine Sociopolitical Commentary") confirmed how the seamy details of Medina's narratives were far from fiction (see the official government report, *Nunca más*). Rather, they anticipated the verifiable accounts of violent repression, while at the same time pointing out the continuities between the facts of such repression and abiding social structures that transcend a specific dictatorship and, indeed, serve to make tyranny possible (I point this out in my discussion of Medina's most famous novel, *Las tumbas*; see Foster, "Rape and Social Formation").

In other cases, the discussion centers on a limited selection of case studies. There are only two movies on gay visibility and none on lesbian life (although Raúl de la Torre's 1993 film, *Funes, un gran amor* [Funes: A Great Love] contains a subtheme of lesbian sexuality among prostitutes and is treated in something other than as a background stereotype). However, the wealth of materials from the theater on any urban group, as well as fiction on women's lives, hundreds of tango lyrics, and extensive interpretations of immigrant experiences, necessarily makes my selection of texts a quite personal one. Much Argentine literature of an urban nature has been translated into English—Puig and Cortázar join Borges in being the best-known authors—but there is also much that has not: tango lyrics do not translate very well and theater translations never seem to attract much interest. And while Quino has been translated into dozens of languages, I know of no English-language versions of his strips. My own translations into English of some of Medina's fiction is here a circular confirmation, since I cannot claim (except in the case of the published French versions) that someone else's translations validate my choosing him to best exemplify depictions in dirty realist terms of urban lumpen-proletariat life.

Nevertheless, as highly selective as some of the choices made here may be, I think the reader will come away with an accurate sense of what some of the major features of urban life are in Buenos Aires and how cultural production has engaged the process of subject formation within the context of that urban life. If there is validity of rejecting—or at least in attempting to go beyond—an approach that reviews the image of the city in cultural production, it is equally valid to question the usefulness of viewing the city as something created by cultural production. The city may not exist independent of its inhabitants no more than the inhabitants exist independent of the city. The circumstances of urban life constitute urban social subjectivities as much as the city exists by virtue of the lived experience of its inhabitants. It is precisely the synergetic relationship between these two propositions, rather than any one of them alone, that underpins the present examination of the urban culture of Buenos Aires.

One final note: This is in reality two books. The first is an examination, grounded on the theoretical bibliography relating to human geography and urban culture, about some—although clearly not all—major forms of cultural production that relate directly to the city of Buenos Aires. However, this is not an exhaustive coverage, and I leave to others what would be more properly a thorough survey of Argentine urban culture. The other book present here is more of a personal testimonial, and in this sense it is more an essay than a monograph, the fruit of more than thirty years of an intense relationship with the cultural production of Buenos Aires. In the case of this second book, two things have happened: (1) I end up examining in some detail what might be called "case studies" of cultural production. For example, rather than providing a survey of all of the range of Jewish literature relating to Buenos Aires, I focus on only certain texts. Since such a choice is always deeply personal, it runs the risk of being distorted when viewed from the perspective of someone else's choice of "casebook" examples. (2) My choice of cultural phenomena as much excludes as it includes. Sports are unquestionably a major form of cultural production that is not exhausted by reference only to Enrique Medina's novel on the boxer José María Gatica; but since I have not interacted with the culture of sports in Buenos Aires, I cannot really address this topic without a whole separate experience of fieldwork. The same is true of television—which is extremely important in Buenos Aires culturally, economically, and politically—and of popular dance and music. These are all topics left to other scholars, or perhaps to subsequent experiences that I may have in what I hope will be another three decades of cultural research in Buenos Aires.

chapter 1

Mafalda: From Hearth to Plaza

¡Así es la cosa, Mafalda!
—Title of Quino's second volume
of *Mafalda* comic strips

Mafalda, drawn by Quino (Joaquín Salvador Lavado), is undoubtedly the most famous comic strip to come out of Latin America (Quino's work is discussed inworks by Trillo and Saccomanno, 160–62; Rivera, passim; and Fossati, 44–45). While scholars may argue that other strips are more intellectual, more socially committed, more creative in the elements they use, there can be no disputing the enormous success *Mafalda* has had (see the interview with Quino by Ciechanower on the strip's history and impact). Quino seems to have written on the premise of Tolstoy's famous dictum: If you write about your own village, you will write about the world. Mafalda and her family and friends are not only indisputably Argentine, but also as specifically petite bourgeoisie as they are urban Buenos Aires. This specificity has not prevented *Mafalda* from being translated into more than two dozen languages; curiously, English is the one major Western language into which the ten original cartoon collections have not been translated. Moreover, *Mafalda* remains in print, available at virtually any kiosk in Buenos Aires and in bookstores throughout the continent.

What is especially surprising about this is that Quino ceased drawing *Mafalda* in 1973. The first appearance of *Mafalda* was on March 15, 1962; the last strip appeared on June 25, 1973. Despite the fact that previously ungathered material has been issued (*Mafalda inédita* [Unpublished Mafalda]) and the characters have been used for a limited number of special projects (such as a UNESCO pamphlet on children's rights, *Declaración de los derechos del niño* [Declaration of the Rights of the Child]), the ten original volumes (which are often issued outside of Argentina in a twelve-volume format) appeared during a very short period, 1966–73, and therefore the strip is permanently anchored in a very chronologically specific segment of Buenos Aires social history. In 1993, twenty years after Quino left Argentina for Italy (he continues to reside in Milan) and sent *Mafalda* "on vacation" (personal interview in July 1973), Ediciones de la Flor, *Mafalda*'s original publisher, issued *Toda Mafalda* (The Complete Mafalda). In addition to previously ungathered or partially published material, the volume contains a series of commentaries by other cartoonists on the strip, including their own artistic tributes to *Mafalda*'s abiding presence in Argentine popular culture. Earlier samplers of *Mafalda* were also published, including a Spanish volume (with the customarily black-and-white strips inexplicably reproduced in garish luminescent colors) that includes a brief commentary by the Italian semiologist Umberto Eco (for more extensive early semiological examinations of *Mafalda*, see Cirne; Cañizal). Eco notes:

> El universo de Mafalda es el de una América Latina en sus zonas metropolitanas más adelantadas; pero es en general, desde muchos puntos de vista, un universo latino y esto hace que Mafalda nos resulte mucho más comprensible que tantos personajes del comic estadounidenses; además, Mafalda es, en último análisis, un "héroe de nuestro tiempo," y no se debe pensar que ésta sea una definición exagerada para el personajito de papel y tinta que Quino nos propone. (iii)[1]

Quino continues to draw single-panel and narrative strips, which he gathers in essentially early volumes, usually around a unifying theme like *A mí no me grite* (Don't Shout at Me [authoritarianism]), *Quinoterapia* (Quinotherapy [medicine]), or *Sí, cariño* (Yes, Sweetheart [love and matrimony, which for Quino are definitely not the same proposition]). In recent years, his strips have become increasingly characterized by black humor, and there is a recurring incursion of previously unexplored topics. For example, the war of the sexes has segued into gender issues that have included an opening toward homoerotic questions, a notable taboo-smashing for a widely popular Latin American cartoonist. However, no matter

Mafalda, the most famous comic strip in Latin America, is drawn by Quino (Joaquín Salvador Lavado). Copyright by Quino/Quipos, Milan; reprinted by permission.

what change of direction Quino's drawings take, he will always be known as the creator of *Mafalda*.

For those of us who have written on the Mafalda character since the early years of her success (Foster 1974, 1980, 1989), it is not difficult to understand the basis of her enormous popularity. Working off the trope of "out of the mouth of babes," Quino endowed Mafalda with the right and the ability to say what others could not, either because they were constrained by their sense of adult-world propriety, because they were blinded by hypocrisy and self-righteousness, because they were disingenuous and self-interested, or simply because the burdens of everyday life had left them unable to perceive with acuity the world around them. Moreover, *Mafalda* was written during a time of military dictatorship in which there was considerable official censorship of social commentary and a general climate of repression (Samper Pizano, 9–11, provides a detailed correlation, partly tongue in cheek, partly in all seriousness, between the development of *Mafalda* and political events).

Ironically, Quino ceased to draw *Mafalda* with the brief return to institutional democracy in 1973, during which the ensuing explosion of opinion released by what turned out to be a transitory suspension of tyranny produced a lot of wrong-headed cultural commentary. (Hernández's *Para leer a Mafalda* is a particularly egregious example: "Mafalda no es una tira progresista, por el contrario, sus críticas se realizan dentro del límite tolerado por el sistema y no sólo no cuestinonándolo, sino ayudando a mantener con tus tímidos comentarios la farsa conocida comúnmente como 'libertad de prensa'" [13].)[2] Quino, feeling that he was unjustly attacked by the right for criticizing national institutions and practices, and by the left for being a commercial success during the dictatorship and, therefore, guilty of reduplicating bourgeois ideologies, took the decision to abandon the strip and, indeed, to abandon the country (personal interview, July 1973). Argentina returned to military control, with worse repression, in 1976; although it is noteworthy that cartoon-based publications like *Humor registrado* (Registered Humor) and *Superhumor* served as trenchant forums for political commentary, virtually the only ones to survive a systematically brutal censorship between 1976 and 1980 (see Avellaneda, 235, on the January 11, 1988, edict banning *Humor registrado*).

One could well attribute much of the success of *Mafalda* to the themes of daily urban middle-class life as viewed through the lens of children's perspectives. Adults, however, do appear in Quino's strip, unlike Charles Shultz's *Peanuts*, with which *Mafalda* is often superficially and distortedly compared, as if in order to legitimize its importance it requires affiliation with an American cartoon strip. Mafalda's father is an office worker, and her mother is a housekeeper (precisely at a time in which economic realities, much more than feminism, were beginning to make the traditional female homemaker a vanishing breed in Buenos Aires); she and her brother, who comes along midway through the strip's history, live with their parents in a residential high-rise in a neighborhood on the fringes of the Buenos Aires commercial core, probably Once, Almagro, or Flores. Quino, in the interview by Ciechanower, recalls how his strip began as part of a publicity campaign for household appliances directed at the middle class, and how when that campaign did not take off he converted *Mafalda* into a strip drawn for the middle-class readers of magazines like *Proceso*, the most "intellectual" news magazine of the period (Ciechanower, 63–64).

Mafalda and Guille(rmo) are surrounded by friends and playmates from similar backgrounds: Susana is from a bit more prosperous Creole family and always speaks with bourgeois pretentiousness; Manolito's father is a Spanish immigrant who owns a grocery store; Miguelito's grandfather was an Italian immigrant; Felipito is the paradigm of the boy next door and synthesizes Argentina neuroses. There are also adult neighbors, shopkeepers, schoolteachers, and assorted authority figures who are Mafalda's daily point of social reference. A strictly content analysis would show that Quino provides, in sociological terms, a masterfully complete image of Porteño urban barrio life in the mid-1960s and early 1970s, a period of considerable political and economic restructuring as a consequence of the agenda of military dictatorship that brought about a transition from the traditionally localist to the international marketplace, with often a strong clash between them.

The current neoliberalism of Argentina's economy and the concomitant internationalization of life in at least the middle-class sectors of Buenos Aires is, under democracy, a continuation of the policies of the juntas of the 1960s, with the only substantive difference being the disappearance of any attempt to mediate unchecked commercial expansion by the conventional moral codes the military sought to impose and maintain. Moreover, if there is anything archaic about *Mafalda*, the note of cultural nationalism in daily life—the lament of the disappearance of the familiar under the onslaught of imported merchandise and its accompanying social values—seems very much a lost value in the current business climate. For example, the corner grocery store owned by Manolo's father, which Manolo works in after the fashion of the family business, would likely have disappeared. But a detail such as this aside, much of Mafalda's world of twenty-five years ago remains very much intact in Buenos Aires.

What is particularly singular about *Mafalda*, what gives it a dimension that demands an analysis transcending a content analysis of surface details, is the way in which Quino has achieved a cultural product that models the inscription of children into the adult world. That is, without ever insinuating any sense of the "innocence" of the young, *Mafalda* demonstrates the interaction between fully socialized subjects (the adults) and those that are still on the margins of social institutions in their status as a general social class of children. This is why comparisons between *Mafalda* and *Peanuts* are especially inappropriate: Schultz believes in a prelapsarian innocence for children, and those children in his strips who reveal an adult loss of innocence (paradigmatically Lucy) are portrayed as cynical and materialistic, thereby establishing a sharp and essentially fundamentalist dividing line between two social hemispheres. By contrast, Quino ends up portraying the transitions between fully institutionally inscribed subjectivities and those in the process of becoming inscribed, along with all the ruptures, contradictions, reversals, and ambiguities of a world that cannot be easily segregated, as can Schultz's, into those who are innocent and those who have lost their innocence. In the process, Quino represents, through the figure of Mafalda and her companions, the complex processes by which one acquires an adult worldview in Argentina society. This is accomplished via her gaze, which defamiliarizes the world, and, in the process, denaturalizes the world controlled by adults. The acquisition of the world controlled by adults involves necessarily the interiorizing of an ideology that makes it seem to be natural and, therefore, not susceptible to criticism. This is even more so when that world is framed by authoritarianism in general and military tyranny specifically, as it was during the years of *Mafalda*'s production.

What I would like to discuss in this essay is how that adult worldview is formed in terms of a relationship with the city. Although other spaces appear in Quino's strips, there is a juxtaposition between the home, the space in which the child necessarily spends a major portion of youth, and, in addition to subcategories like school, commercial establishments, and the like, the broad sweep of the city outside the home. Significantly, the city in *Mafalda* is synthesized into two interrelated spaces: the street and the plaza. Streets tend to function in the citizens' imagination as limitless extensions of the city, even though they are necessarily more restricted for children, who are cautioned to stay close to home. But the plaza is a specifically "safe zone" of urban life, marked off by streets and set aside from the intense, often dangerous movement that takes place in streets. In both cases, these points of reference are unique in *Mafalda*. In the first place, Buenos Aires is particularly a city of plazas, which complement the many broad swaths of parks that enhance the livability of that city (see Armus on the history of the creation of the Buenos Aires plazas). In contrast to mid- and lower Manhattan, with its one mammoth Central Park and a scattering of tiny slices of greenery that are often more fillers in the geometry of urban design than specific set-asides (for example, Bryant Park, which fills up the back of the New York Public Library; Battery Park, which rounds off the tip of the island; or Union Square, which fills in the intersection of Madison and Fifth Avenues and Broadway), one cannot go for more than a dozen blocks in Buenos Aires in any direction without running into green spaces, which, to be sure, abound particularly in the middle- and upper-middle-class areas of the city.

Like the streets of Buenos Aires, the parks are relatively safe in terms of personal security, which is why in *Mafalda,* as in real life, both green spaces and sidewalks figure prominently as places where Mafalda and her friends congregate to observe and comment on the world going by. Schultz's children, on the other hand, congregate in their own houses and backyards, or in school yards; they are never seen out in the street or in public thoroughfares, reflecting the relative insecurity of these spaces in American life, even in the idyllic world *Peanuts* evokes. Charlie Brown's world may be free of crime and violence, but the world of the children who are his readers is not, and therefore the utilization of such spaces by children can hardly be suggested by the strip. Indeed, even the way in which Schultz's children, born of the suburban fifties, move alone outside the home may be problematic for many of today's parents, who are only confident if their children, when outside the home, are safely sequestered in a shopping mall (a post-1950s cultural institution that, by the way, also never appears in *Peanuts*).

Shopping malls did not exist when Quino began drawing Mafalda, although their forerunner, the British-style walk-through arcade (a *galería*) already existed and was, in fact, a common component of the ground floor of buildings erected in the 1960s. In any event, Mafalda and friends spend as much time out of doors as they do at home, and both street and plaza appear as frequent meeting places for them. And, as often as not, these meeting places are a counterspace to the home: a place where one can be free of the inevitable restraints of the hearth; a place where things occur that are not explicitly accounted for at home; a place where there is interaction between children that is free of the impediment of controlling adults; and, above all else, a place where there is a process of assessment and interpretation of what is said at home and what is discovered to be the facts of a considerably, but, of course, not completely, unconstrained world as it is modeled by the urban cityscape.

Therefore, there is an element of subversiveness in *Mafalda* that is one of its unique characteristics and a basis of its popularity at different times in Argentine social history. Of course, by comparison to the leftist demands for an aggressively subversive, iconoclastic culture, and by comparison to right-wing interpretations of what constitutes subversion/perversion, *Mafalda* is hardly a threat. However, the way in which Quino came to believe that he was the unfair victim of denunciations from both sides is perhaps a rather eloquent index of the fact that *Mafalda* was articulating a form of critical commentary that had little interest in conforming to the dogmatic agenda of either stance. Instead, it was aimed toward the loosely structured sense of discontent and frustration of the millions of readers who had little direct stake in either the rigors of a revolutionary culture or the draconian principles of moral renewal.

One particularly significant rhetorical strategy employed by Quino is Mafalda's walks through the city. In four or five panels we see Mafalda contemplating the world around her: the so-called natural word, the built environment, the display of commercial activity, human interrelationships, the emergence of some new phenomenon in the urban mosaic. As Mafalda walks along, she comments to herself in ways that are alternately pithy, bemused, ironic, and at times almost cynical (in the English sense of nonidealistic, rather than the Spanish sense of immoral) about what she sees. Often there is only one final comment that makes a conclusively interpretive statement, a comment that is spoken to herself or, at times, to one of her friends she happens to meet. Mafalda is not the only one to engage in this sort of commentary. On occasion we see her as the addressee of a comment, sincere (by Felipe or Miguelito, for example) or dramatically ironic (typically by Susanita, but also by the protocapitalist, Manolito), coming from one of the other characters. In these cases, Mafalda is a witness, and the exactness of what is said creates a sense of understanding between Mafalda, who is here the receptor of others' comments, and her friends. This is even the case when Mafalda's look of perplexity or dumbfoundedness reveals the incorrectness, the deviant nonsharedness, of Susanita's comments, which are frequently parallel to those of adults, her parents included, that Mafalda finds so baffling. There are even those occasions in which some adult, usually Mafalda's father, who, contrary to one reading of the codes of Argentine masculinism, is often as uncomfortable as his daughter with the demands of the establishment. That is, although there is an allowance for nonconformity for the man who feels that a decadent or sold-out establishment violates his masculinity (the case of the betrayed macho of many tangos or even of the military man who attributes to himself a legitimate right to reshape the establishment in a more authoritarian, masculinist image), there also exists a deviance from the masculinist imperative to accept things the way they are, to go along, to get along, to conform to the rules of the *barra* (gang). It is this latter deviance that the military saw in "hippies," "communists," and "faggots," and toward which Quino's dreamy-eyed Felipe or often childlike Papá de Mafalda incline.

Furthering the disruption of a conventional social semiotic of conformity, Mafalda's outspokenness contrasts sharply with the outspokenness of Susanita. Susanita is unreserved in her critical commentary, but with the license extended to women by the masculinist voice irately dissatisfied with the lack of rigor and order in society, of those who make pronouncements of the sort that "we need a strong hand around here." This is, to be sure, a reactionary voice, since it compares lived experience with some sort of abstract norm of a time when things were better, more comprehensible, more structured. Susanita's critical stance contrasts with Mafalda's, but not so much because the latter's comments do not likewise refer to an image of a lost better world (this is especially true when Quino has her evoke the sort of leftist cultural nationalism common in the 1960s, whereby import substitution could only be understood as the loss of what was authentically Argentine). Rather, the difference lies in how Susanita repeats received wisdom and therefore can only echo what adults say (even if what she is echoing is being said by adults outside the strips, such as the voice of authority and bourgeois propriety being spoken at the time by the official discourse of the military junta), as opposed to how what Mafalda articulates strives in some sense to be a counterpoint to received wisdom, an original interpretation that has not been uttered previously. This is why, even when Mafalda may actually point toward something that could be called traditional, such as the appointments of pre-1960s barrio life, she does so in a way that is refreshingly different from official discourse. The fact that Quino accomplishes this with the wit and humor appropriate to a *comic* strip is one of *Mafalda*'s guarantees of popularity.

For example, there is a strip from volume 6 (Lavado, *Toda Mafalda*, 356) in which we see Susanita talking, in turn, to Felipe, to a cat, and to Miguelito as they walk down a street. The top two-thirds of each panel is covered by a tiny illegible script that represents Susanita's monologue. All three of her interlocutors are dizzy from the onslaught of Susanita's speech; the cat is stretched out flat as though it has been run over. In the fourth and final panel, Susanita laments to Mafalda: "¿Te conté que mi problema de incomunicación es no poder incomunicarme?"[3] The effect of the strip is to give a graphic representation of the overwhelming nature of the communicated discourses of society, of the way in which one and all are crushed by/under the weight of the society spokespersons' mass of text—both spoken and written, in ways both multiple and overdetermined. Susanita has constructed her identity as an enthusiastic collaborator of these discourses, and she feels it her duty to generously communicate them to one and all. It is only when she sees that they numb rather than convince that she has a fleeting moment of self-reflection, which never lasts from one strip to the next.

Susanita's diatribes and ready clichés serve to highlight the perceptiveness of Mafalda's comments. In one of the strips that feature Mafalda's excursions in the street (Lavado, *Toda Mafalda*, 9:527), she hears the sounds of colliding vehicles, represented by the onomatopoeic script "¡YÍÍÍÍÍÍÍÍÍÍÍÍK! ¡CRASH!" As Mafalda stops to view the crash, represented

outside the frame, dialogue globes symbolically representing the altercation of the two drivers float above her head. As she continues on her
way, she muses: "yíííííííííík-crash: preposición inseparable que suele an-
teponerse a ciertas expresiones idiomáticas."[4] This pedantically amusing
assessment of details of urban life contrasts strikingly with Susanita's dia-
tribe, which appears to have nothing to do with anything, which is why we
are not shown what she is saying, and which, rather than interpreting the
lives of others, serves instead to oppress them, as is evident in the space the
representation of her monologue takes up in the strip and the dazed reaction to it of the two humans and one animal. Mafalda, on the other hand,
undertakes to explain the world to herself. In the process, she interprets
the idiosyncrasies of others in an attempt to stand outside herself and
internalize what she observes. This is represented in the strip when she
stops walking and stands still to witness what is going on. As she proceeds
on her way, she provides an assessment for herself, a silent commentary of
what she has seen. That her commentary is silent is circumstantial, a consequence of her walking alone; certainly, in many strips Mafalda vocalizes
her comments to her companions, other children, adults, or even animals
and inanimate objects. However, in this case, her silent commentary, a sign
of inner reflection, contrasts sharply to Susanita's sustained and apparently
meaningless chatter.

Readers have argued that Mafalda's comments are often too precocious
and imply knowledge that is not reasonable for her age. Certainly, in the
strip just described, Mafalda ends up sounding like a grammar book, hardly
the discourse model for even the most precocious children. But of course,
such comments miss the point of any cultural production that pretends to
do anything other than entertain at the lowest common denominator. *Mafalda* is not a strip about Porteño children, no matter how their social status
may be defined. It is a text that provides a vehicle for interpreting Argentine social history, and its frequent topicality underscores how it is meant
for Mafalda to view and comment on specific circumstances and incidents
of the day. Toward this end, there is a necessary rhetorical construction of
the dialogue of the strip's characters, a construction that is understandably
heightened in the case of Mafalda because of the centrality of her position
as heroine.

Although Buenos Aires is hardly a blighted city as megalopolises go, it
is an ingrained part of modern culture to complain about the deterioration

of urban space. *Mafalda* is filled with strips that engage in this sort of commentary. Quino seems to have been particularly interested in this topic in the early years of the strip, when, under the effects of the military coup of 1966, a stagnant economy dictated the deterioration of the metropolitan infrastructure, whereby the prosperous Buenos Aires of the early 1960s was quite noticeably down at the heel. In volume 3, Mafalda, in one of her many incursions into the street, overhears two old friends greeting each other, apparently after several years' separation (Lavado, *Toda Mafalda*, 3:203). As one of them utters the cliché "¡Es que el mundo es un pañuelo!"[5] Mafalda is left to muse (again, typically, as she walks), "Habrá que quejarse al lavadero entonces."[6] The idea of the world as a soiled handkerchief is undeniably vivid in signaling the omnipresence of urban grime. In the same volume, there is a strip in which Mafalda's mother is fitting her for summer clothes for the family's year-end vacation (one of the collection's many indicators of the very different economic circumstances in Argentina thirty years ago: the family can afford a summer vacation, but store-bought summer clothes, if available at all, are outside their reach). Mafalda is standing on a cushion as her mother fits her, and she can see the expanse of the urban landscape outside the room's window.

Urban apartment dwellers, if they are fortunate enough to have any kind of view other than air shafts (called *pozos* [wells]), usually have a view of apartments similar to their own. One counts oneself lucky to look out on a plaza or a park, and only the most expensive apartments have anything near a sweeping view of the cityscape. Against the modest view of Mafalda's apartment, her mother describes the Arcadian beauty of the countryside where they will vacation. When Mafalda asks her who made such splendors, her mother answers, as one might expect, with the attribution to God's handiwork, whereupon Mafalda looks out the window at the smoke curling up from the buildings (this was before trash burning was banned in city buildings in the 1970s) and observes wryly that the construction of the city must have been awarded to a different contractor.

One of the most brilliant strips dealing with the urban landscape and Mafalda's consciousness as a lens for the discovery and interpretation of Argentine social reality also involves the vacation motif. In the strip, Mafalda and her family are returning home from the annual summer vacation. As her parents doze, Mafalda stares out the window of the moving train. Since the trains connecting Buenos Aires to surrounding areas necessarily pass through slums, which customarily take root alongside the tracks as fillers around industrial areas served by the cargo component of the rails, Mafalda looks out the window at a typical shantytown, a *villa miseria*,[7] with its poorly clad and malnourished inhabitants (Lavado, *Toda Mafalda*, 2:124).

This discovery is significant for Mafalda, and we witness her wide-eyed reaction. Undoubtedly, she has heard or read one of the favorite slogans of the military and its supporters that challenged the views of left-wing critics of the period: "In this country, no one dies of hunger." Such a slogan, based on the premise of Argentina's unique Latin American status because of its inexhaustible prosperity, is just the sort of thing Susanita might typically echo. And, indirectly evoking Argentina's legendary prosperity, which made it one of the first countries in Latin America to have television (beginning in the mid-1950s), Mafalda had settled in to see the countryside through the rounded square of the train window as though watching a television screen as they appeared at that time: "Mirar por la ventanilla del tren es como ver al país por televisión."[8] However, after viewing the "program" of the shantytown, she revises her comment: "¡Lástima que la televisión tenga mejores programas que el país!"[9] There is a play on words involved here: *programa* as the entertainment productions of television and the word as it refers to official economic policy, which, as is always the case of right-wing military governments, serves to emphasize class differences. Mafalda's family may have continued to be beneficiaries of the strong middle class that existed in Argentina at mid-century, but many of Quino's readers knew that the underpinning of that class was to become increasingly precarious, as in fact the past thirty years of Argentine economic history has demonstrated. Finally, there is considerable irony in Mafalda's last comment, since it was common for artists and intellectuals of the period to have signed on to the emerging critical denunciation of television, often characterized as depending for its programming on foreign, mostly U.S., imports. There was, to be sure, excellent local programming, such as Juan Carlos Gené's famous dramas for television, *Cosa juzgada* (Case Closed [published under the same title]). In the absence of any official support for cultural production, and a policy of moral and political censorship, the paradigm for foreign programming discouraged critical experimentation within whatever commercial parameters might have been available to it.

The motif of the train window as a view on a social reality unavailable to Mafalda during her excursions through the city's streets or through her apartment window is repeated the following year in volume 3 (Lavado, *Toda Mafalda*, 3:208). This time, the poverty Mafalda sees is not the marginal urban slum, but rather the extremely limited circumstances of noncity dwellers, which can be taken, in part, as a commentary on how Buenos Aires is a black hole that sucks in whatever resources and wealth the country possesses. Mafalda comments ecstatically on the idyllic setting of the farmland and marvels at the image of cows grazing in the field, until she sees the shack inhabited by the farmhand's family. She remarks, "¡Oh! . . . ¡Y esa pobre gente! . . . ¡Qué ranchito miserable! . . ."[10] The final panel moves back inside the train, as we see Mafalda being admonished by an older adult, and her father looks on with chagrin. The older man, with the stereotypic visage of a flinty-hearted banker, wags his finger at Mafalda and informs her, "'Pintoresco,' nena, 'pintoresco.'"[11] The interplay between "miserable" and "pintoresco" marks the difference between the child's honest assessment of economic circumstances in the agricultural sector and the businessman's disingenuousness motivated by interests higher than those of critical analysis. The fact that he lectures Mafalda underscores how Mafalda must learn a lesson about social reality, one that leaves her in the final panel with a dumbfounded expression on her face.

Quino, like many creative talents of his generation, was concerned with the importation of foreign products and customs endorsed by the military and its commercial backers, an importation that took place through the medium of television and allied forums. Although the late 1960s had a relatively small import sector compared to the massive flooding of foreign imports on the marketplace under the neoliberal economic policies of the 1990s, given the traditional features of Argentine life fostered by the cultural nationalism of Peronismo in the late 1940s and early 1950s and its attendant policy of encouraging local industry and the parallel but very different resistance to foreign business by the left of the period, any foreign products assumed an iconic status of major proportions. Quino ties this to the question of schooling, the process of preparing the individual for civic and economic life, in the form of a frustrated homework assignment.

Felipe, who is constantly beset by attacks of hysteria, surely a form of nonconforming masculine behavior that signals his inadequate assimilation to his world, meets Mafalda in passing on the street. Mafalda asks him if he has done his school assignment, a composition on national independence (Lavado, *Toda Mafalda*, 7:386). Felipe replies that he hasn't yet and that he decided to go out for a walk to see if something would inspire him. But, as the strip places the two children in a wide-angle shot of the city, he says he hasn't had any good ideas yet. The wide-angle view, reinforced by Mafalda's wide-eyed amazement, captures the cityscape dotted with foreign names, either foreign products or imitations of foreign products: "Boutique Petty," "Shopping Center," "Grill Trattoria 'Il Buon Pranzo,'" "Beautiful 'Velvet-Skin' Night-Cream," plus seven other examples. Notably, not all the designations are English based: *boutique* is a French word, and *Petty* appears to be an English variation of French *petit(e)*; *grill* is English, but *Trattoria 'Il Buon Pranzo'* evokes Italian, which has historically been the second language of Buenos Aires since the onset of massive Italian immigration in the 1880s; *velvet-skin* and *night-cream*, on the other hand, reveal the often solecistic use (because of the misplaced hyphen) of foreign words and phrases in such advertising.

Numerous strips make use of language play, such as the one cited above regarding the car crash. Particularly entertaining are those that revolve around school, since the education establishment is an official institution for the formation of citizens, and its ideology—or the interpretation of its ideology—can be useful for understanding the social dynamic. For example, there is a strip in volume 5 in which Mafalda is standing before the class alongside the teacher's desk in a traditional authoritarian testing situation (Lavado, *Toda Mafalda*, 5:303). She is conjugating the verb *confiar*. When she has finished doing so successfully, she turns to the teacher and startles her by saying, "¡Qué manga de ingenuos! ¿No?"[12] Not only is this sort of comment inappropriate for this testing situation—verb forms rather than the description of national character—but it involves a form of interpretation, an impertinent type of negative criticism, that is impossible in a traditional teaching environment, especially in 1969, when the volume was published and Argentina remained under military dictatorship. Mafalda's pithy comment may be read as less an attack on Argentine naïveté than on an educational philosophy that creates a learning environment in which such things cannot be said, precisely because the strip assumes that its readers has no confidence in the political system under which they are living and likely even less in self-interested military leaders who have no reason to believe their own ideological slogans. In effect, the verb *confiar*, despite Mafalda's perfect conjugation of it, is totally deponent in the society she inhabits.

In contrast, Susanita's endorsement of the status quo is illustrated in a strip from volume 7 (Lavado, *Toda Mafalda*, 7:378). The teacher, using a less authoritarian technique, calls on students to give the tense forms of various verbs. After receiving two successful responses from other students, she asks Susanita for the future perfect form of the verb *amar*. Susanita, with the beatific glow of one who has absolutely no doubt about the correctness of her reply, answers "¡Hijitos!"[13] What is particularly symptomatic about her reply in terms of evoking an establishment code is not that she dreams of having children, which is, after all, not in itself categorically patriarchal. Rather, it is the use of the diminutive, an inflection that invests the word with superficial romantic emotion, thereby making it resonate with the language of establishment commonplaces.

Schoolhouse images and the underlying ideology of language use are, to be sure, metonyms of urban reality, since it is that context which underlies the response of teachers and students as the actual stuff of their daily experiences outside the institutional confines. In closing I would like to refer to a strip from volume 6 that gives an interpretive opportunity to Mafalda's often bewildered and befuddled father, his reactions to the world around him *and* to his daughter's attempts to understand that world, as he faces the urban jungle (Lavado, *Toda Mafalda*, 6:246). The first four panels of the strip show Mafalda's father getting ready to leave for work. In each panel he executes one step of his morning routine, which is ad-campaign perfect: "Una afeitada perfecta." "Una camisa impecable." "Un café delicioso." "Un rubio excelente."[14] However, in the final panel, as he tremblingly opens the door of his apartment building, we contemplate with him through the glass panels of the entryway the frenetic everyday swarm of the city he is about to join. Before stepping across the threshold, from the secure domain of the perfection guaranteed by advertising into the real-life jungle of the streets, he says to himself: "Y aquí es donde la cosa deja de ser como en los avisos."[15]

It is this sort of perception about the difference between masquerade—whether derived from conventional wisdom, official ideology, or advertising fantasies—and the material reality of the world that drives the humor of *Mafalda*. Although I have chosen not to do so here, one could scour the ten volumes of strips, approximately two thousand of them, and construct a sociologically accurate image of urban life in Buenos Aires for both the half dozen years in which they were drawn and, in many aspects, for the quarter of a century since Quino stopped drawing them. The palpable urban reality of the *Mafalda* strips is indeed striking and, when joined with the clever and often biting humor in which Quino frames the process of its discovery by Mafalda and her companions, and through them also certain adults' rediscovery of the world, it is one of the features of the work that has guaranteed its abiding popularity.

chapter 2

Theater and Urban Culture

One of the privileged aspects of theater as a cultural product is the relationship it has to a direct modeling of lived experience. Certainly, film and television also provide such modeling, but they involve an electronic/technologic mediation between the viewer and the circumstances of lived experience, while one associates with the theater in its many forms the presence of a live enactment of individual and social life. Thus, no matter how abstract or experimental theater becomes in its own forms of cultural mediation, it continues to involve the actual presence of the human body, and from that body one can extrapolate all the myriad circumstances of lived experience in which the human body can participate—that is, the full range of material life.

Historically, the theater has always attempted to reconstruct the spaces of actual lived experience on the stage and to give the impression of the body of the actor in its intimate interaction with those spaces. Moreover, the ideology of realism has dominated modern theater and, in the case of Latin American theater, has been crucial to the emergence of national theater movements. For example, in the case of Argentina, which has always had in Buenos Aires one of the great centers of theatrical activity on the continent (see the excellent survey "Argentina"), it would be inconceivable now to think of the definitive emergence of the dominant bourgeois theater establishment without the realist works of Florencio Sánchez. All theater languages in that establishment refer, in one way or another, to the model of Sánchez's dramatic oeuvre (see Cruz; Ordaz).

It would likewise be impossible to speak of culture in Buenos Aires without mentioning the theater. Indeed, theater has for some time been the one form of Argentine cultural production that has received the greatest amount of academic attention, far outstripping the scholarly work de-

voted to film and even surpassing critical writing about narrative, the paradigmatic modern literary genre. Theaters in Buenos Aires are both concentrated in a formally recognized theater district and yet scattered around
the city, either as part of alternative, experimental, or traditional venues
located outside of what historically has been the theater district. Theaters
in Buenos Aires are equally commercial, independent, state-agency affili-
ated, and university based; there have also been theaters attached to private entities, such as cultural projects (the famous Instituto Di Tella in the
1960s), banks and similar institutions (the theater within the Banco Patri-
cios at its branch on Callao and Sarmiento), and businesses (the theater
space that is part of the Hotel Bauen). And, of course, there are theaters
specializing in diverse forms of theatrical activity. It is no exaggeration to
say that, per capita, Buenos Aires has more theatrical activity than any
other Latin American city, as can be judged from examining the listings in
the daily newspapers.

However, my interest here lies not with the presence of theater in
Buenos Aires, but with how the theater is a cultural forum for the enactment of interpretations of the urban life of Buenos Aires. From an immediately superficial point of view, Buenos Aires must necessarily be present
in an insistent way in theater spectacle. To the extent that modern theater
is predominantly the representation of bourgeois life in its urban contexts,
one would expect to find in any registry of plays and their themes a continual presence of the city, its social types and the indexes of them provided
by lived environments, costume, and structures of interpersonal interaction. Indeed, the greatest synecdoche of a society or of a social subgroup is
virtually inescapably present, even when the substance of a play may not
be directly identifiable as social interpretation. I refer to language.

Sociolects are so distinctive for a people that they become immediate
markers of identity, even when other markers are not directly transparent
in meaning. Since the Hispanic stage does not customarily make use of a
unique stage Spanish, nor is there any privileged prestige dialect, theatrical representation virtually never makes use of a linguistic register that
masks the origins of the actors. To be sure, individual actors may engage in
a number of training exercises that modify the sociolect with and within
which they were raised, in an attempt to become more "sophisticated" or
"professional" in a vague and uncodified way. They may choose to mask
their class origins by attempting to imitate the speech of, say, a more edu-

cated class, something like immigrant and working-class La Boca to elite Barrio Norte. They may choose to mask their provincial origins, since cosmopolitan Buenos Aires is clearly where the social and cultural action is. Or, more drastically, they may choose to mask their Argentine origins, opting for either the imitation of Peninsular Spanish (presumably an urbane Madrid register), although it could also be some other Latin American dialect or some degree of a denatured Pan-American Spanish that makes it all but impossible for the untrained linguist to identify actors' places of origin.

The latter option, that of masking nationality, is probably never chosen, although one could wonder what happens when actors work outside their country, where either long absence (such as during Peronismo or subsequent military dictatorships) or production demands attenuate regional differences. This is the case of someone like Libertad Lamarque, for example. No matter to what extent the stage dialect she used in her Argentine productions differed from colloquial patterns (I would suggest that they did so only in an overlay of what was considered to be sophisticated diction in the 1930s and 1940s), her long tenure in Mexico, with employment in film, theater, television, and singing, required her, if not to become Mexican (although she certainly played a number of roles as Mexican women), to at least mask her Argentine origins. One exception, of course, is when she portrayed an Argentine. When she sang tangos for the Mexican market, she gave them a *bolero* flavor, but at least she sang them with a recognizably Argentine diction.

Language is an overwhelming social index, and the fact that theater is principally a spoken cultural medium means that cultural identity enters in by the mere articulation of dialogue in the theater (see Foster, *Espacio escénico y lenguaje*). Resonances of lived material experience are practically always heard in an individual's spoken language, experiences that are as much personal as collective. Witness, for example, what happens with the interplay of *tú* and *vos*, the latter understood not only in terms of the personal pronoun, but also as specific verb forms that may be used with the pronoun *tú* (as, for example, in the Chilean *tú hablái, tú tenís*). The *voseo*, in either its Argentine manifestations or in those of other Latin American regions, is so powerful an index of sociolectical and geolectical issues that its mere presence evokes an array of spectator responses, as does, concomitantly, its absence. Thus, foreign works translated into Spanish can be performed with the *tú* pronoun, but when an Argentine dramatist like Griselda Gambaro decides to use the *tú* rather than the *vos* in certain works from the 1960s, the result is extremely jarring (see Foster, "El lenguaje como vehículo espiritual en *Los siameses* de Griselda Gambaro"). By the same token, when an Argentine work is performed, say, in Mexico, it is of interest whether it will be performed with the *tú* pronoun or with *vos*. When Roberto Cossa's *La nona* (see below) was performed in Mexico City in the 1970s, not only was the *vos* changed to *tú*, but also virtually every other trace of Argentine Spanish was either neutralized or Mexicanized. The only linguistic element of Cossa's original text that was retained was the title, but it was necessary to explain to the audience in an opening voice-over that *nona = abuelita*.

The sense of Buenos Aires's presence is particularly strong in works where the sociolects of the city, from the moment a character speaks, announce categorically the urban nature of the work. Such works include Cossa's *La nona*, Ricardo Talesnik's *La fiaca* (The Dumps), Oscar Viale's *Chúmbale* (Sick 'em), Jacobo Langsner's *Esperando la carroza* (Waiting for the Hearse [Langsner is Uruguayan, but his work is set in one of the lower middle-class neighborhoods of Buenos Aires]), Nelly Fernández Tiscornia's *Made in Lanus*, and Ricardo Monti's *Una noche con el Sr. Magnus e hijos* (A Night with Sr. Magnus and Sons), among many, many others. This is not to say that these works are especially colloquial in the particular social registers they employ. Most of them are, in the sense that lower-middle-class characters are involved, usually characterized by essentially colloquial forms of speech in all circumstances. However, this is not always the case, since Monti's play involves characters who move between everyday colloquialism and formal registers, while Langsner's play involves examples of social mobility and the attempts at idiolectical modification this implies. Nonetheless, the extensively overdetermined nature of Buenos Aires Spanish is always immediately recognizable in such works. It may be indefensible to say that Argentine theatrical works are more colloquial than, say, Mexican or Chilean or Brazilian ones are, but the extent to which non-Argentines are so quick to recognize—and often to disparage—what are taken as the specific markers of "Argentine" (usually Buenos Aires) Spanish is a rather special case in the ideological debates surrounding Latin American Spanish.

The extent to which language has such power as a sociocultural index means that it is, in effect, a metonymy of a spectrum of phenomena. Each phenomenon is indexical, metonymic, but never with the same power that language possesses. Thus, there is a tendency for other features to complement language, rather than for language to reinforce other elements. Details of decor, dress, even plot itself seem so often to confirm the precise point on the sociocultural barometer marked by language that the latter may need only be schematically represented. Language, however, is, with the exception of absurdist or minimalist theater, always fully represented in the dramatic text, a fact that in itself is an eloquent demonstration of the determinative status of language.

Roberto Cossa's *La nona* is one of the most important plays to be produced during the period of the dictatorship, more so because it was a hit during the draconian *guerra sucia*,[1] which unleashed state-sponsored terrorism in the late 1970s against real and imagined guerrilla insurgency. The ideology of the *guerra sucia* brought with it a considerable amount of general societal repression and an attendant climate of fear. Official acts of censorship were complemented by a self-censorship on the part of writers and artists that resulted in a drastic drop in the amount of cultural production. Therefore, Cossa's work, which has come to be read as an allegory of the dynamic of the *guerra sucia* as well as a chronicle of the devastations brought about by the economic policies of the military, was an act of courage, since one never knew how official sectors and their supporters would react to cultural works that could come to be viewed as critical of the regime (Previdi Froelich). Ambiguity and confusion worked together, however, to mean that critical works did survive, while it also meant that relatively tame or innocuous works could end up being treated harshly.

There is, however, nothing tame or innocuous about *La nona*, which was so successful it performed for two consecutive seasons, 1976–77. Nona is an ageless crone of a grandmother—one character puts her age generally at a hundred—who eats her family out of house and home. In the neogrotesque fashion of much of Argentine critical theater (Kaiser-Lenoir), the production is dominated by two sounds: Nona eating (which is amplified as the crunching of a cockroach), and Nona going to the bathroom, represented by the Niagara-like flush of an old water-chest toilet. Nona is nothing more than a hugely efficient alimentary canal. She lives with two grandsons and a granddaughter and the wife and daughter of one of the grandsons. The family is a model of the struggle for survival, which is eventually unsuccessful, undermined by the relentless feeding of Nona. By the end of the play, although Nona survives, one son has had a heart attack from overwork and the other has committed suicide. The two women have gone to live with relatives in another city, and the granddaughter has fallen into prostitution. The dissolution of the family is a reflex of the killer-shark economic exploitation that took place during the dictatorship, and it is a figure of the effects of the intransigent authoritarianism represented by the older woman during a regime that defended the importance of patriarchy and hierarchical power, which the apparently senile Nona manages so efficaciously.

Because of the configuration of this family, there is a dual dimension to the urban colloquiality of their speech, which manifests both the lower-middle-class Spanish of their social standing and the *cocoliche* that derives from their immigrant origins.[2] Nona, who is from Catanzaro in Regio Calabria in dirt-poor southern Italy, undoubtedly belongs to the first immigrant generation from right before the turn of the century, when millions of Italians came to the Americas with the dream of *hacer la América* (to make it in America), which here means Argentina as much as it does the United States. Although Nona speaks more properly in Italian, *cocoliche* is a third language between Spanish and Italian. Since these two languages are historically close and usually mutually intelligible, Italian immigrants were able to make themselves readily understood, thereby losing initiative to learn Spanish. However, over time, Italian spoken by immigrants (most of whom were illiterate but made efforts to learn Spanish) was directly and indirectly influenced by Spanish, and *cocoliche* emerged as an interlingua. *Cocoliche's* deficiencies with regard to Spanish and Italian made it available for comical purposes, much as the English of Yiddish speakers in the United States (for example, "Throw mama from the train a kiss"). However, as early as the second and third decades of this century, *cocoliche* was used in dramatic texts as a metonym of the immigrant pathos, and Armando Discépolo made it one of the essential elements of his grotesque and expressionistic works (Foster, "Lenguaje y espacio escénico: El italiano en dos textos teatrales").

A phenomenon like *cocoliche*, even more than the colloquial registers of Argentine Spanish mentioned above, is considerably more pregnant with the "feel" of lived urban experience. Not all Italian immigrants ended up in the city, and not all of those who came to reside in cities were concentrated in Buenos Aires, but both propositions are true for the vast majority, and today a quick examination of the Buenos Aires telephone directory reveals just how marked by Italian that city is. *Cocoliche* brings to the stage a dense signifier of a particular type of lived space, of a collective experience, one manifestation of which is enacted by the setting of the stage and the people who inhabit it. The kitchen, where the action of Cossa's play takes place, is a microcosm, various degrees removed, of the Italian household, the Italian neighborhood, Buenos Aires as a city crisscrossed by the manifestations of Italian culture, and Argentina as an immigrant country. Ultimately, it is also a microcosm of a generalized sense of the abstract Italian that, through the unique history of Italy, exists as an emigrant culture.

But primarily what is brought onto the stage is the sense of Buenos Aires, the sense of a harsh, unyielding, and unforgiving immigrant society where there is no escaping the realities of existence, viewed as the timeless realities of lower-middle-class life and/or viewed as a metaphor of a specific circumstance of Argentine social history, that of the so-called Proceso de Reorganización Nacional of the 1976–83 dictatorship, which, and this would be Cossa's point, did more to destroy Argentine society than to reconstruct it. In Cossa's *La nona* (The Granny), the characters' hardscrabble speech—and one could choose almost at random from the text—has nothing to evoke but this fact.

Nona. Bonyiorno.
Carmelo. ¡Nona! ¿Qué hace levantada?
Nona. Vengo a manyare el desachuno.
Carmelo. ¿Qué desachuno?
Nona. El desachuno. E la matina.
Carmelo. ¿Qué matina? Son las diez de la noche.
Nona. [*Enojada.*] Ma, ¿y la luche?
Carmelo. [*Mira a Chicho.*] La luche . . . ¿Qué luche?
Nona. [*Más enojada.*] ¡La luche! ¡Il giorno!
Carmelo. Es la luz eléctrica, Nona. Mire . . . [*Levanta la cortina que da al patio.*] ¿No ve que es de noche?
Nona. Ma . . . tengo fame.
Carmelo. Hace quince minutos que terminó de comer.
Nona. ¿Quince minutos? Con razón. ¿No tené un cacho de mortadela?

Carmelo. Es la hora de dormir, no de comer. ¡Va . . . ! Vamos a la cama.
Nona. [*Se sienta a la mesa.*] Ma . . . ya que estamo. El desachuno.
(Cossa, 115–16)[3]

One of the primary characteristics of the Argentine neogrotesque theater is this: the black humor that mixes the gritty details of survival with the
comic. Nona's family is determined to keep her from eating because their
meager resources are inadequate to meet her constant demands to be fed.
In the attempts to deflect her from eating, there is a funny exchange about
light and her conviction that it is reasonable to want to eat again, even if it
is not time for breakfast, because it has been fifteen minutes since dinner.[4]
Nevertheless, such humor does not "humanize" the text or make it more
immediate to the audience. Rather, the humor is part of the colloquiality
of the text and, therefore, part of the raw sense of the city that this work,
and others like it, transmits so admirably. Such humor does not exist in a
vacuum; consequently, it is not harmless or innocent. Rather, it is part of
a discourse text, part of a social fabric, and it is always at someone's expense
(here at Carmelo's expense, because Nona is playing dumb to get her way),
always part of a power play designed to enhance survival. The comedy in
purely comic terms may serve to gloss over historical contradictions, but in
its grotesque embodiment it effectively evokes, quite to the contrary, the
grim material conditions of urban life: "*Nona*. ¡Ma va fangulo! Dame papa
frita" (124).[5]

Ricardo Talesnik's *La fiaca* (1967) belongs to the period of the first
neofascist dictatorships in Argentina. While it is true that it is less darkly
grotesque than Cossa's *La nona*, it is also true that the earlier Onganía
regime did not possess the same apparatus of repression that was put into
effect after the March 1976 coup. Nevertheless, Talesnik's play—and it is
worth noting that both *La nona* and *La fiaca* were made into successful
movies that maximized visually the representation of urban space[6]—is also
concerned with the dynamics of the economic system, in this case how
there is no possibility of opting out, since the phenomenon of hunger is an
irrefutable mechanism that ensures the historical necessity of exploitative
work. As it is experienced by most individuals, work may be profoundly
humiliating, degrading, and dehumanizing. But if hunger were not worse,
Talesnik's Néstor would in the end prevail. But he does not, even if Néstor
does awake one day and announce that he will no longer go to work.

Despite the consternation of his wife, his mother, his colleagues, his supervisor, the company physician, and the world at large, he steadfastly and stubbornly maintains his position. Néstor is unable to theorize about his decision: he is neither an intellectual nor an ideologue, he simply cannot take the meaninglessness of work any longer. Yet he must fail, not so much because he is unable to forge a viable practice of leisure or to recover the lost innocence of the prelabor aimless activity of children, but because of the historical necessity of work and the way that necessity undermines any attempt to provide meaning to aimlessness and leisure. In the end, as though pursuing a carrot on a stick, Néstor accepts a sandwich in exchange for returning to work. One of Talesnik's powerful theatrical strategies in the play is to reduplicate the audience in the person of Peralta, a colleague who enthusiastically endorses Néstor's rebellion but is in the end frustrated by the collapse of the project. Like the audience, who is asked to sympathize with Néstor's defiance, Peralta goes along with his friend. But also like the audience, which must abandon the theater to go home and sleep and get up the next day to go to work, Peralta can only be frustrated over the necessary end of both the act of rebellion and the privileged place of the play that models it.

In this way, Néstor's apartment is as much a microcosm of the spaces of the Argentine middle class as it is a free zone engaged in a subversion of the demands of that class, where the historical necessity of work is ideologized as a transcendental human virtue that confers identity and dignity on those who subscribe to it. The articulation of the ideology of work is conducted principally through a language of pseudoformality. It is a pseudoformal language in that it expropriates, if only precariously, various types of non-colloquial discourse that provides rhetorical clichés for defending its principles. For example, Néstor's mother, fulfilling a traditional maternal role of being the repository of conventional societal values, takes over for her daughter-in-law and admonishes Néstor:

> *Madre.* [*Después de mirarlo y sacudir varias veces la cabeza. Ad-monitoria.*] ¿Esto es lo que yo te enseñé? . . . ¿Eh? ¡Contéstame! [*Néstor juguetea con un extremo del cubrecama.*] ¡Tantos años de lucha! . . . ¿Y para qué? ¿Para que me pagués de este modo? ¡Faltando al trabajo como un vago de este modo? ¡Faltando al trabajo como un vago cualquiera! [*Néstor no contesta. La madre se mira con Marta, quien le hace señas para que siga.*] (Talesnik, *La fiaca*, 67)[7]

Stills from the
film version of
Ricardo Talesnik's
play *La fiaca,*
starring Norma
Aleandro and
Norman Briski.
Courtesy of Ri-
cardo Talesnik.

The mother's words here and throughout this scene (and later those of other characters) echo a vast reservoir of commonplaces regarding responsibility, loyalty, application, seriousness, respect, and the like, concepts that, in order to be effective in countering the realities of lived experience, where someone like Néstor feels in his gut that work is nothing more than a demeaning exploitation, must cast themselves in high-sounding terms that can only be transmitted via a noncolloquial language that places them in a timeless realm beyond the grasp of everyday experience. Since everyday experience contradicts them, they must be protected from everyday experience. And since colloquial expression is an integral part of everyday experience—indeed, it is the primary expressive vehicle of everyday experience—bromides about the dignity of work must be cast in non-everyday, noncolloquial language in order to invest them with a serious formality required to make them credible—or, at least, what is required to enable the attempt to make them credible. A subset of this pseudoformal language of ideological conviction is professional jargon, which is immediately evident in the speech of Jáuregui, the "representante del Departamento de Relaciones Humanas de Fiagroplast":

> *Jáuregui.* [*De corrido.*] ¡Por favor, señora! . . . La ciencia de las Relaciones Humanas nos permite conocer a fondo los problemas, inquietudes y aspiraciones del obrero y el empleado. Es una actividad que nos obliga a penetrar en todos los aspectos de su personalidad y, en consecuencia, a comprender todos los errores, fallas y desviaciones que, como seres humanos, padecen normalmente. De esta manera nos hacemos partícipes, establecemos una relación más cálida, menos comercial. Conseguimos que cada obrero, cada empleado, se sienta parte de la empresa. Para ellos, Fiagroplast no es una abstracción, algo frío, lejano . . . no. Se sienten protegidos, amparados . . . y sienten a la empresa como algo propio, casi como un segundo hogar . . . [. . .] Un empleado ejemplar como su marido debe ser considerado muy especialmente. Fiagroplast no puede abandonarlo en una situación tan anormal, tan [*No recuerda.*] . . . crítica. El objeto de mi visita es orientarlo, ayudarlo, recuperarlo para su bien personal y el de la comunidad toda. (86)[8]

Although such language exists in the realm of the city and, in fact, constitutes one dimension of its ideological continuity, since, of course, in this case work is what keeps the city going and Néstor's rebellion is a direct challenge to the continued existence of the city, it is not the medium of expression of individuals like Néstor. This is so in the sense that Néstor may consume such language passively, because it is all around him, operating by osmosis, but also actively, as in specific circumstances in which he is called to stop and listen to it, as in the case of the speeches of the mother and Jáuregui. But it is never the language individuals like Néstor or Peralta are likely to produce. To be sure, all social subjects sustain the ideological apparatus, as much as they are obliged to live by it. But what I am trying to get at here is that someone like Néstor is only able to stage (even if eventually ineffectively) his rebellion, because, unlike his mother and Jáuregui, he has an insufficient commitment to sustain the concept of the value of work. Jáuregui has commitment because that is his job, and his mother has it because it constitutes the only basis of her identity as an efficient trainer of her children as new social subjects.

By contrast, Néstor's language and that of his allies is markedly collo-quial, and in this they are true children of the city. Colloquiality, of course, is the mark of all spoken language, and thus occurs in all constructed social environments. But the specific colloquiality that Néstor speaks is that of the city. Through the lens of his speech an image of the texture of the city emerges that Talesnik would ask us to accept as accurate. The very title of the work announces this fact. *La fiaca* means "the blues," "the blahs," a sense of not giving a damn, of listlessness bordering on anomie. It, too, is a word drawn from Italian. However, it is important to note that it is not an example of *cocoliche*. Rather, *fiaca* is dialect (probably northern Italian), and it exemplifies the enormous reservoir of Italian words that has been incorporated into Argentine Spanish through the channel of Italian immi-gration (see Meo Zilio and Rossi). These words have become standardized in Argentine Spanish, and thus cannot be said to be Italian or to exemplify *cocoliche*, and there are numerous registers of them under the broad head-ing of *lunfardo* (there are numerous publications, often typically popular in nature, like that of Gobello; see also Terrugi; Villanueva; Pezzoni and Freyre). In proper historical terms, *lunfardo* is the coded speech of the Italian underworld in Buenos Aires at the turn of the century, and like all such argots it is both protean in nature and extremely flexible in its forms. However, a basic inventory has become fixed, in large part because of the way in which the Gardelian tango expropriated *lunfardo* and the way in which, as a part of local colorism during the 1930s and 1940s, it became synonymous with urban culture. Indeed, there is a certain tendency to use the term *lunfardo* to refer to all urban colloquial speech, even when its elements (mostly lexical items, but some morphosyntactic processes and metaphoric patterns) do not historically derive from immigrant Italian dialects. In fact, Talesnik has had a successful career in recent decades as a stand-up comic whose routines are built in large measure around urban colloquial speech (see, for example, *Talesnik en camiseta*, a reference to a quintessential comic strip of the local-colorist period that focused on lower-middle-class themes, *Buenos Aires en camiseta*). Most recently, Talesnik has worked as a writer for an enormously successful television program in which colloquial speech figures prominently. It is worth noting in passing that Talesnik himself is of Jewish origins, a fact that underscores how *lunfardo* long ago transcended ethnic boundaries in Buenos Aires.

If the title of Talesnik's play sets the tone of the action via a colloquial expression that, in fact, summarizes its theme, the play concludes with an obscenity; obscenities, of course, are paradigmatically colloquial: "*Peralta.* [*Infantil, desilusionado.*] Ta que lo parió . . . " (Talesnik, 118).[9] Although this expletive sentence is not exclusively Argentine, it is typical of the colloquiality of Buenos Aires. In this way, it is clear that what is being staged in Néstor's and Marta's apartment is the crucial issue of work and that that issue is commented on by an interplay between the gritty colloquial language of the public places of Buenos Aires and the vacuousness of the ideological justifications of work. A corollary consideration is the long-standing belief that urban work is always devalued because it is part and parcel of the dehumanization of modern life in the city—this by contrast to traditional, and therefore "real" and authentic work in the countryside, especially when performed for the direct sustenance of the individual and the immediate family unit. However, one can find little reason to endorse such a romantic view of non-urban life, particularly since urban versus non-urban production of capital is part of a single process, and self-contained survival is virtually nonexistent in the modern world. See, however, Néstor's paean to self-employment (Talesnik, 102–3).

But there is another more immediate way in which urban life is present in *La fiaca*: Néstor's references to recovering the carefree existence of a child, marked by life in the streets of the barrio, silly games, and soccer play in the plazas and vacant lots (Archetti comments very lucidly on the permissible boyish irresponsibility permitted by soccer culture):

> *Néstor.* ¡Fiagroplast no existe, Peralta! ¡Hay un potrero! . . . ¡está lleno de pibes jugando a la pelota!
> *Peralta. [Gritando.]* ¡El potrero no está más! ¡Los pibes son tipos como nosotros! ¡Están todos adentro, trabajando! ¡Y yo no estoy en mi lugar!. . . ¿Qué digo, Vignale? ¡Me van a echar . . . ¡me van a echar!
> *Néstor. [Desperado.]* ¡No seas maricón, Peralta! ¡Quedate a jugar conmigo! (83–84)[10]

Fernando Ayala's film is able to represent these activities (for example, the game of "Chancha" [83]) and to depict these spaces with, in one case, Néstor and Peralta actually playing ball. In the play, they remain simply evoked, but as icons of an urban childhood that Néstor would wish to be able to recover fully in the suppression of any memory of the curse of work that marks his life as an adult.

At the end of the play, as Néstor begins to cave in under the combined assault of his wife, his mother, and Fiagroplast's *señor gerente*, the latter addresses Néstor with the usual clichés of a superior:

> *[Las mujeres, al notar el tono cordial y amistoso del gerente, se han acercado con más seguridad. Néstor intenta pararse, hablar, pero no puede.]*
> *Madre.* Mírelo, no tiene palabras. (116–17)[11]

With Néstor unable to speak, no longer able to articulate any sense of *fiaca*, his repudiation of work, his vision of a lost urban childhood (all in a distinctive colloquial register), all that is left are the manifestations of the official discourse, and the play is over. Peralta, of course, has the last word, a vulgar expletive, but it is a meaningless gesture of defiance the expression of obscenities usually is, even as it is the last shred of urban colloquial speech left.

A radically different theater language is represented by Roberto Bartís's *Postales argentinas (sainete de ciencia-ficción en dos actos)* (Argentine Postcards [Science-Fiction Operetta in Two Acts]). Bartís may with considerable justice be considered the most important voice in Argentine theater to have emerged during the period of redemocratization that began in

1983. As both a dramatist and a director, Bartís has been instrumental in bringing to the Argentine stage innovative ways of representing interpretations of social experience that leave behind the critical realism that dominated Argentine theater from the late fifties on through the period of military dictatorship, having as its last major exposition in the Teatro Abierto collective movement that defied censorship by staging cycles of trenchant one-act plays. Working off, however, the language of the neo-grotesque that was a component of critical realism, Bartís exemplifies a much more abstract theater in which the dramatic work involves less ingenious representations of scenes of immediately recognized social experience (everyone has a grandmother with some characteristics of Cossa's Nona; everyone has at one time or another said the very same things Talesnik's Néstor says) than extremely elaborate conceits in which certain underlying ideological principles are embodied in fugue-like sequences that defy allegorical reductionism and conventional narrative interpretations.

Yet it is significant that *Postales* evokes in its subtitle the tradition of the *sainete*. Although the *sainete* has its origins in the Spanish nineteenth-century lyric operetta genre of the *zarzuela,* in Argentina it became a melodramatic vehicle of the local-color representation of the texture of urban life, especially as it related to lower-class immigrants. Alberto Vacarezza's *Tu cuna fue un conventillo* (1920) is a paradigmatic example, especially in its conjugation of the multiple voices of its numerous characters. *Sainetes* like this are a veritable babel of dialects of different immigrant groups, all jumbled together in the commons of the ghetto. For Vacarezza and his colleagues, such a commons and the intersecting patterns of personal and social interests it stages are dramatic figures of the unique urban life of Buenos Aires at the turn of the century. While there are elements of pathos and the grotesque in the *sainete,* it is, however, basically a form of theatrical realism. And while Bartís is not concerned with continuing the tradition of realism in the theater in his works, by evoking the *sainete* he would seem to wish to underscore, nevertheless, the way in which he is still constrained by a principle of the interpretation of daily life.

In a quite oxymoronic fashion, Bartís juxtaposes his evocation of *sainete* with *ciencia-ficción,* which serves here less to signal what is customarily understood by science fiction (which, of course, is well known to involve allegories of the historical world) than to emphasize the limitless expressionism with which he is working. Jorge A. Dubatti notes in his running marginal commentary to the printed text that "Buenos Aires, y otras ciudades argentinas [. . .], son en sí mismas un vasto teatro, un escenario gigantesco" (5). Dubatti is not referring here to the venerable Shakespearean trope that "All the world's a stage," but rather to how, since the return to constitutional democracy in 1983, the public spaces of the city have been used for the staging of theater in the streets, plazas, shopping centers, and even in the subway (see Carreira). But the point is not just the theatrical performance outside traditional stages, but also the converse manifestation: the more specific enactment of the street on conventional stages. A work like *Postales argentinas* marks this sort of dramatic Moebius strip where the clear demarcation between the stage in the city and the city on the stage is lost.

Postales argentinas—the title is significant for the way in which it recalls a genre of postcards devoted to cityscapes and urban scenes—is a series of tableaux constituting a series of lectures in the year 2043 based on manuscripts from our day found in the by-then dry bed of the Río de la Plata. One ought to bear in mind that the broad river was a dumping ground from the air for the still-live bodies of political dissidents during the dictatorship. So when the river eventually dries up, the historical remains of the period will be revealed as fossils of a tyrannical political process. Thus, what is represented on the stage is a futuristic model of *"Buenos Aires en el 2043, una ciudad devastada,"* which, as in all science fiction, is to be read as a figure of the present moment of the spectator. Héctor, the main character, opens the work with the following:

> [*Escribiendo con un metro amarillo de ferretería sobre un pedazo de diario e intermitentemente mirando a su alrededor.*] 45 años hoy, atravieso un Buenos Aires que emite sus últimos estertores. En las esquinas, las fogatas de los sobrevivientes iluminan los esqueletos rancios de mis vecinos de antaño. Hay viento y hay cenizas en el viento. Todo parece recordarme una ley de la sangre: debes escribir. (Bartís, 6)[12]

Héctor carries with him a basic tool for the measurement of space and, while he speaks about the need to comply with the imperative to write, he is essentially surveying his world in a literal sense: a fin-de-siècle Buenos Aires that is on the verge of collapse. In the process, what he will discover are the traces of a social dynamic that, like his mother, has been relegated to an old trunk while still exercising a powerful force to define subjectivity and to impose an order of meaning. The mother evokes her son's father and establishes a correlation between the absence of the father and the destruction of the urban order, a correlation that, given the Lacanian understanding of the law of the father in Argentine culture, is crucial to interpreting the dominance of authoritarianism in that society:

> [*Entrando en un éxtasis ambiguo, deja las cartas, se recuesta y mira adenlante.*] ¡Tú padre! ¡Oh, tú padre! ¡Cómo te quería! Fue el hombre más bueno que jamás se haya conocido. Para él no había ni sábados ni domingos, su bondad no condescía con el almanaque. [*El se queda dormido, la madre golpea sobre la mesa para despertarlo.*] Siempre estaba dispuesto a levantarte sobre sus hombros y llevarte a dar una vuelta por la barraca. ¡Oh, su amor, abismo sin medida! Otros tiempos . . . [*Música de bandoneón.*] Las calles tenían la luz y la fragancia del sol y las uvas madurando en cada esquina, cantaban los ruiseñores su canto mejor y al viento las campanas cantaban su amor. (10)[13]

The text moves between the nightmarish image of the city in ruins and an idyll that is both patriarchically authoritarian and nostalgic: the mother's sigh of *"Otros tiempos"* is as much a sentimental lamentation for a bygone Arcadia that never existed as it is for the efficient neofascist tyranny of an ordered world: a unified image of paternal power and idyllic perfection. Idyllic perfection may be a chimera, but paternal power certainly did exist and continues to do so, if only in the "diluted" form of democracy and the grotesque expressionism of a world of irremediable chaos that remains underlain by authoritarianism (if only evoked nostalgically). Therefore, it is understandable that the spectator may find the latter far more legitimate and recognizable. These are Héctor's words that close the play:

> [*Con ella (Pamela Wilson, la bella florista) en brazos.*] ¡Qué hermosa está Buenos Aires! ¡Negra! ¡Negra y brillante como un presagio de la muerte! [*Deja a Pamela en el piso.*] Aquí estamos, viejo Puerto de La Noria, como ayer, descubro ahora a punto de morir, todo. Adiós Pamela, mi pequeña muchacha, mi ilusión, no haberme dado cuenta antes que te amaba . . . Adiós, madre, dondequiera que esté tú espíritu

imbatible . . . Adiós, Buenos Aires, la reina de la Plata . . . Buenos Aires, mi tierra querida . . . Adiós muchachos compañeros de mi vida . . . Adiós, cosas muertas . . . Parto hacia ti, anaranjado mar de Buenos Aires [*Hace un bollo con sus papeles, lo arroja, mima con su cuerpo la caída.*] (23)[14]

Héctor's eulogy to Buenos Aires is, as will be quickly spotted, a series of commonplaces, one of which is the opening line of S. M. Contursi and H. M. Rodríguez's 1926 tango, "La cumparsita" (the gang), introducing, along with the *sainete,* another popular culture genre that depends heavily on evocations of the city. As I will argue in the next chapter on the tango, this genre embodies in song the masculinist city. Indeed, Bartís's play has several other references to the tango, including Héctor's opening speech, which is introduced by "Música de bandoneón" (6).

Clearly, Bartís's play is far removed from conventional postcard, local-color images of Buenos Aires. If there is no validity in the nostalgic recollection of an ordered and idyllic city that never existed, there is still a powerful validity in the remnants of patriarchal authority that can be discerned in the city in its final decay. The interest of the text lies in measuring the continuities between the Buenos Aires of the spectator and the Buenos Aires of 2043, and in the realization that they may well be one and the same city. The highly stylized, abstract, and expressionistic routines that make up the work are, then, driven by the need to reinforce and over-determine the way in which, in spite of everything else, the essential structures of hegemonic urban society remain intact: "¡Soy Héctor Girardi! ¡Soy un argentino!" (20).[15]

This discussion of the presence of Buenos Aires in the Argentine theater has not endeavored to examine attempts to re-create the city through sets with sounds, lights, and movement; however, this can, in fact, occur, as in Francisco Javier's marvelous dramatic interpretation of Calé's famous comic strip from the 1950s and early 1960s (see Prado), *Buenos Aires en camiseta,* at the Teatro Cervantes during the 1995 season, where the hustle and bustle of the city, including the representation of a *colectivo* (bus), is enacted on the stage. Such an attempt is of interest in part because of the technical problems it involves. However, my interest here has been to show how urban-life practices are staged in theatrical works, practices in which particular details of language and imagery evoke the urban social context in which individual lives take place. The urban social context is a complex and burdensome one, as commonplace after commonplace about the city tells us. How, exactly, that burdensome complexity is staged in theatrical works is what this chapter has sought to describe in an effort to understand what details of dramatic language are especially effective as conduits to a spectrum of shared experiences about the city. Two of these works accomplish that through an iconic use of urban language, while Bartís's *Postales argentinas* makes use of highly expressionistic metonyms of the city to underscore the meaning of its science-fiction melodrama.

chapter 3

Tango and Urban Sexual Regulation

Porque el tango es macho.[1]
—Popular saying

If there is anything that is known about Buenos Aires, it is that it is the home of the tango. It is impossible to consult a respectable guidebook about Buenos Aires without the tango being featured as one of the greatest tourist attractions of the city.[2] Although the tango is accompanied by music, it records the tradition of the dance as poetry before it ever becomes orchestrated and choreographed. While one may quibble with the way in which the tango is characterized—especially since such images tend to congeal the tango in very traditional dimensions, such that contemporary innovations are lost—and with the ways in which it is thought to be appealing to a universalized international tourist audience (particularly problematic is the sensuality of the tango, a characterization from which the elements of macho domination, including sadomasochism and anal and clitoral sex, are expunged), there can be little question that it is an icon for the city, as much as is beef or the putative European base of Porteño culture. Furthermore, the fact that such characterization tends to homogenize these three icons in their failure to separate the very real cultural bases of each one (respectively, rural Creole in the case of beef; urban immigrant, typically, but hardly exclusively, Italian, in the case of the tango;[3] and ultramarine French and English in the case of Europeanization), they each serve to enforce the other as somehow quintessentially Argentine (on the recurring themes of the tango, see Corbatta; Sabato).

The tango is correlated with the city in such tourist—and semiofficial images—as a juxtaposition between dance poses and the backdrop of the cityscape, either viewed panoramically (Avenida Corrientes) or as specific locales (the multicolored mosaic of wooden houses in the alley Caminito in the waterfront district of La Boca), as though somehow the tango synthesizes the driving (masculinist?) energy of the "city that never sleeps" or how, beyond the Porteño facade of sophistication, the hard-edged brutality (masculinist?) of the tango were the "real" essence of Buenos Aires (see Matamoro on the relationship between the tango and Buenos Aires; Lara and Roncetti de Panti provide the best overview of the tango from a literary point of view). Such propositions assume that the much-maligned massive lower-class Italian immigration of a hundred years ago has somehow given the city a defining cultural product to which there is a universal subscription. Alternatively, such correlations imply the proposition that, while one will not find wildly dancing tango couples in the streets, in the plazas,[4] or on strategic corners in the shadows of famous monuments, somehow the entire city is imbued with the tango, and synecdoches and metonymies of the tango can be profitably sought in the commerce of everyday urban life. After all, one way of describing an allegedly particular Argentine tendency to give darkly melodramatic interpretations of sociopolitical events is to speak of "el tango nacional."

Such highly generalized and superficial interpretations of cultural phenomena always carry an element of truth, and they are often important pedagogical tools, especially when absolutely so little is known about the cultural practices of a society. However, they are likely to have little to do with a theoretically grounded attempt at deep cultural interpretation, and indeed the latter may have little to do with something like the tango. That is, some form of cultural theorizing, with a specific application to Buenos Aires, may find the tango to be irrelevant or marginal, at best, finding, in fact, that phenomena not usually featured in tourist guides are more useful. This is certainly so if the tango has become essentially a fossilized cultural form, kept in existence for reasons of romantic nostalgia or tourism, but with little adherence among primary or emergent cultural practices. All societies have a reserve of such fossilized forms that somehow echo a sector of nationalistic myths without having much of a sustained or productive meaning in practices outside the confines of romantic nostalgia. Concomitantly, there is a Buenos Aires imagery that defines itself in terms of the tango: the tango is Buenos Aires, and Buenos Aires is the tango, such that certain tangos are the city's theme songs.

I do not wish to imply that the tango does not have current meanings for Porteños and other Argentines, nor that it is so much bad-faith pap for naive tourists. Of course it is not. But what does need to be questioned is the extent to which tourist guides and semiofficial images privilege the tango as dance and overinvest it with transparent meanings regarding national essences, whereby the city figures the tango and the tango models the city back. Such a form of juxtaposed mirrors is not likely to render much that is useful for a principled discussion of the interaction between urban space and cultural production because it is based too unthinkingly on the proposition of culture as reflection (such that the brassy music of a Sousa march captures perfectly the brash nature of turn-of-the-century American ruthless capitalism) and on the mechanistic notion that certain societies will inevitably generate certain types of cultural genres, to the effect that the violent nature of Argentine social history accounts for the bleak pessimism of so much of Argentine literature.

An alternate way of examining the relationship between cultural production and urban space is to undertake less of a study of the images of the city in a segment of cultural production than to investigate the way in which the latter proposes a specific interpretation of urban life. In such a case, it is not directly material if such an image does not match dominant or prevailing views of the city. Quite the contrary, such an interpretation may end up creating a particular view of the city that, while unique and unacceptable in its inception, may come to constitute a prevailing understanding, much like Dickens's portraits of London's backstreet life or Twain's American regional backwaters. Dickens's portraits are now considered to be quintessential London, and where would the American mythic landscape be without Twain's Hannibal?

A reading of tango lyrics, in addition to correcting the overemphasis on tango as dance (and the equally distorting practice of simply reading the lyrics as content statements that support interpretations of the tango as dance primarily conceived of as social ritual), must attend to the principle that culture is a socially symbolic act, a semiotic proposition, in that it is a reading of the social text. Such a reading, far from providing an easily readable interpretation of what then becomes an obvious social truth (the artist comes along and sees for us what our limited, untrained vision was not previously able to see, but what we can now see with the clarity art provides us), creates, conditions, imposes, and forces problematical meanings that are every bit as opaque as the social or historical circumstances they pretend to elucidate. It is reasonable to believe that many of the fabrications concerning Buenos Aires either do not match patented interpretations or have, in fact, been suppressed by the latter because they provided problematic or dangerous counterevidence to those interpretations (this seems to be especially true when sadomasochistic humiliations, based on classicism, sexism, and homophobia, of interpersonal behavior in public or semipublic spaces are involved: "Con una mueca de mujer vencida / me dijo '¡Es la vida!' Y no la vi más," by Alfredo Le Pera and Carlos Gardel,[5] "Volvió una noche," in Albuquerque, 248–49).

One could argue that few of the tangos actually involve the evocation of urban public spaces. Indeed, if the mainstay of the tango centers on the melodramatic recollection of betrayal in love (typically, of a man, the narrator, by a perfidious woman [Foster, "Narrative Rights"]) and if the tone is essentially confessional (basically directed toward the imagined audiences of the song; at times toward another male interlocutor; at times toward the woman herself; and at times a combination of two or three of these possibilities through direct and indirect quotation within the text), then private spaces would seem most to be at issue. However, personal dramas, particularly romantic entanglements, usually end up involving the public sector in significant ways. Current feminist theories may hold as an axiom that "the political is private" in an attempt to understand how private lives are in fact defined by political ideology. This is true, as I hope to demonstrate, for the tango, and to it one would add the inverted proposition, "the private is political," to the extent that the private becomes (re)enacted in public domains as part of the process of legitimizing the right of the narrator of the tango to engage in a lament for his suffering and the denunciation of the one who has brought it about.

The tango, leaving aside individual artists' renditions of specific texts (and this is undoubtedly a whole other area requiring investigation), is resolutely heterosexist. Despite the curious historical fact that the tango may have been originally danced among men awaiting turns with prostitutes in turn-of-the-century riverfront brothels in Montevideo, Buenos Aires, and other cities along the Río de la Plata network, there is no trace of homoeroticism in any of the texts of the canon. The tango is heterosexist, at least, to the extent that it portrays exclusively heterosexist relations and that it shows individuals attempting to fulfill and comply with a heterosexist norm of male behavior. Nevertheless, as Savigliano argues, "Tango is not about sex—at least not about heterosexuality—it is about love, but love and sensuality . . . are queer preoccupations" (*Tango and the Political Economy of Passion*, 45). That is, the misfit between lived experience and the heterosexist ideal to which the tango alludes provides for precisely the pathetic conflict for the macho recounted in the lyrics (for an anthropological interpretation of sex roles in the tango, see Taylor, "Tango"). What is curious is that, in the conjunction of dance and lyrics, the latter may refer to this tragic conflict, while the dance itself may enact the masculinist domination lived experience tends to belie. The pathos of the lyrics segues to what Savagliano calls the queer precisely because of the impossibility of maintaining the heterosexist code. She asserts elsewhere that:

> Tangos are male confessions of failure and defeat, a recognition that men's sources of empowerment are also the causes of their misery. Women, mysteriously, have the capacity to use the same things that imprison them—including men—to fight back. Tangos report repeated female attempts at evasion, the permanent danger of betrayal. The strategy consists basically in seducing men, making them feel empowered and safe by acting as loyal subordinates, and in the midst of their enchantment of total control, the tamed female escapes. The viscous power crystallizes. (209)

It would be interesting to inquire into reinterpretations of the tango by the current, very active Buenos Aires gay and lesbian scene, most of which, however, seems tied to the culture identified with the international gay rights movement rather than with a phenomenon like the tango, which is, after all, associated precisely with the brutally enforced homophobia associated with the cultural sectors identifying with it.

The heterosexism of the tango has two principal implications for its narrative rights. The first is that it will explore insistently the dynamics of the relationships between the sexual genders. Like compulsory heterosexism in general, such an exploration will be underlain less by the privilege of romantic love than by the imperative for it. Romantic love is not a choice, but it is an obligation, whether as part of an ideology based on the need to perpetuate the species (although couples in the tango rarely have children or, at least, they are rarely talked about [it would seem that love goes awry before the reproductive imperative can take place]) or as part of a need to affirm sexual allegiance. Such a need, under the broad aegis of masculinism, is always an imperative for men, for they must demonstrate not only that they are "real" men, but that they are not queer. This does not mean to imply that a woman's femininity is never called into question in societies associated with the tango; it only means that the tango never makes an *issue* of femininity or a woman's ability to give her man children. Virtuous mothers are fairly common in the tango (Alfredo Le Pera and Carlos Gardel's "Silencio en la noche," for example) and bad women who run out on husbands, homes, and children may be mentioned, but there never seems to be any interest in decrying barren women.

Thus, the jilted lover's pathos-drenched lament has a primary, generalized effect of demonstrating the authenticity of his male identity: the repeated pursuit of women, whether or not specifically the Don Juan syndrome, which is more closely associated with sexual insecurity, demonstrates the appropriate quality of a man's sexual needs, even if fate and women make it impossible for him to hold a partner. To perform as an appropriate heterosexual is part of a public/publicized demand. The public domain is filled with confirmations of the exclusive legitimacy of heterosexuality. Such is the case with the way advertising displays increasingly dominate public spaces with the immense spread of commerce that began during the heyday of the tango. The tango repeatedly models the fundamental social conjunction of the man and the woman, and the family that is presumed to result from that conjunction. To be sure, culture generally models the pairing of man and woman to extents that result in multiple overdeterminations of this social model, which the tango, like other examples of cultural production, merely repeats as the degree zero of the personally and socially natural (see Savigliano concerning the sexual economics of the tango).

The second implication is that the demonstration of proper heterosexual urges takes place—must take place—in the public domain. Certainly, the tango itself is often performed in a public space. Although it may be consumed in private—what one might expect to be the case with recorded, sung lyrics, or the dance when executed as part of a house party—the tango is most often associated with large-scale public display: Gardel's movies, concerts and exhibitions, radio and television transmission, and café, cabaret, and plaza performances. One could argue that the public display of the

Tango dancers in "Dorrego
Square." Courtesy of Adri-
ana Goisman, Contact Press
Images, Inc.

tango is not the same thing as the lyrics' description of events or their enactment. This observation underscores how displayed culture is essentially voyeuristic, since it is typically based on the open performance of individuals' private lives. In turn, this concomitantly underscores the relationship between private and public and how public domains exercise the right to contemplate the private, even if only in the way in which real individual lives are modeled by the fictional characters of cultural texts. Nevertheless, it may well be important to maintain a difference between the public enactment of cultural products and the features they model of public/private life made public.

The public spaces represented internally by the tango are, first and foremost, the stages of the life of the classes it sings about (immigrant laborers, with incidents of precarious social climbing, especially for women, into the middle class, often as courtesans): streets, dance halls, brothels, cabarets and bars, hospitals and asylums, boarding houses, police stations and detention centers. These are all forums where the identity of the individual is enacted, whether it be the identity of another that is sung about or, typically in the first-person lyrics of the tango, the drama of one's own sexual and amorous entanglements. The staging of the tango imagines the rest of society assembled in these spaces listening to or overhearing the personal story being told. This circumstance is most vividly seen in films where, when the thin thread of narrative stops for the star to sing, everyone else stands around and listens, as though there were nothing else in the world to do but to hang on every word of the song.

However, the audience, either when literally seen, as in the case of the film or a tango-driven dramatic work, or imagined, as in the case of the isolated singer, the audience is not a passive bystander. Rather, the function of the audience, beyond simply serving to justify the song being sung as an act of social communication, is to serve as a gauge for the legitimacy of what is being sung. While there may be occasions in which, when the song is sung in a work framed by characters other than the singer-narrator, some other character steps forward and comments on the content of the song, saying something like, "Che, hermano, compartimos tu pena,"[6] this explicit reaction is not necessary. The very act of singing, of engaging in an explicit articulation of one's personal drama, is to solicit support from those who are imagined to hear it, and if that articulation takes place in a public space, where the audience is likely to be partially or wholly made up of strangers, then the approval sought is in terms of the overall ideological structures of the society the audience represents.

What I am envisioning here, then, is the way in which tango lyrics, quite aside from specific references to urban public space, are constructed so as to have meaning in that space, to the extent that they seek to engage the understanding and the acquiescence of the audiences of those spaces for the legitimacy of what the singer is narrating. Specifically, since the overwhelming content of the tangos is love that has gone astray, the lyrics appeal to various facets of hegemonic heterosexuality, not only in the sense of the privilege of man-woman love, but also the particular quality of the relationship between man and woman, especially the subordination of the latter and the presumption that, as a daughter of Eve, she will likely end up betraying men. A basic understanding of that fact is necessary in understanding the way in which tangos naturalize betrayal as the default of romantic love (compare with "Percanta que me amuraste [mujer que me abandonaste],"[7] by Pablo Contursi and Samuel Castiosta). Such a naturalization leads to the prominent contradiction inherent in heterosexist romantic love, and that is the way it is presumed to be. It is the only legitimate form of human love, as recognized by religion, law, and accumulated social practice, while at the same time it is assumed that, at least in dominant forms of cultural production that include the tango, romantic love is going to end in failure. It is precisely that failure that gives the tango and other cultural forms something to talk about.

Of course, one might well argue that the tango is not about romantic love, but rather special cases of sexual attraction that veer close to the alleged sinisterness of sadomasochism. Indeed, it would not be completely captious to wonder if the tango is bound to see straight love as always leading to forms of sadomasochistic suffering, given the enormous suffering its lyrics are likely to transmit. The tango undoubtedly does not model the version of joyful man-woman union certain versions of the patriarchy endorses, particularly the public ones centered on church weddings and its accompanying manifestations. But I would insist that the tango does, nevertheless, deal with heterosexist love and that it is that type of love, so much so that romantic love is virtually a tautology, that has a privileged place in the Western cultural production, even when it usually ends up being narrated in terms of disappointment, betrayal, and frustration, as in the case of that other form of publicly enacted culture that is more of an integral part of bourgeois culture than is the immigrant, labor-class based tango: the soap opera.

In sum, the tango presupposes the public recognition of the necessity of heterosexist coupling and its subsequent betrayal, and it demands the public approval of the masculinity of the narrative voice and the legitimacy of his lament. How this is carried out in a typically urban tango may be seen in "Bailemos" (Reinaldo Yiso and Pascual Mammone), a text that makes overt reference to the tango as a danced enactment of an interpersonal relationship; significantly, that dance takes place in public, and there is an explicit appeal to societal reaction in the form of the observers. Moreover, it is clear that the masculine narrative voice is exercising explicit censorship on the already silenced voice of his female partner, with the implication that her discourse would exceed the bounds of public display: "No llores, no, muchacha, la gente está mirando / bailemos este tango, el tango del adiós" (Don't cry, don't, little girl, people are watching / let's dance this tango / the tango of farewell) (Albuquerque, 10). Of interest is the fact that the tango is both the enactment of their failed affair and, therefore, a sign of its closure, "el tango del adiós." To complete the dance of the tango is to complete once and for all the affair, and it is this double finality that is performed before the world at large: "el tango ya termina . . . salgamos a llorar." Crying is a different language of expression than either singing or dancing, and the disjunction between the two sets is marked by the latter being performed before the people, while presumably the force of "salgamos" is that crying will be done in private and, one assumes, individually.

So much of the tango involves pathetic fallacy, a lot of which is trite and kitschy, but which serves to establish a range of easily identifiable paradigms for the public nature of the tango. Homero Manzi's and Aníbal Troilo's "Barrio de tango" is only one among many texts that devotes itself to the assembling of such clusters of pathetic fallacy, beginning with the proposition that tango and neighborhood are interchangeable terms: the entire lived collective space exudes the tango.

> Un pedazo de barrio allá en Pompeya
> durmiéndose al costado del terraplén,
> un farol balanceado en la barrera
> y el misterio de adiós que siembra el tren.
> Un ladrido de perros a la luna

y el amor escondido en un portón,
los sapos redoblando en la laguna,
y, a lo lejos, la voz del bandoneón.

Barrio de tango, luna y misterio,
calles lejanas ¿cómo estarán?
Viejos amigos que hoy ni recuerdo
¿qué se habrán hecho, dónde andarán?

Barrio de tango, ¿qué fué de aquella
Juana, la rubia que tanto amé?
¿Sabrá que sufro pensando en ella
desde la tarde en que la dejé?

Barrio de tango, luna y misterio
desde el recuerdo te vuelvo a ver.

Un coro de silbidos allá en la esquina,
el codillo llenando el almacén
y el dramón de la pálida vecina
que ya nunca salió a mirar el tren.

Así evoco tus noches, barrio de tango,
con las chatas entrando al corralón.
Y la luna chapoteando sobre el fango,
y, a lo lejos, la voz del bandoneón.

Barrio de tango, luna y misterio,
desde el recuerdo te vuelvo a ver . . . (Albuquerque, 99)[8]

A mosaic of the narrator's subjectivity is confirmed via the identification of his voice with a specific neighborhood scene, which he evokes and is able to contemplate with his memory's eye. The text is dominated by a pathetic fallacy in which, successively, the recalled experiences of youth are anchored in the barrio, an emotional history has its origins in a member of the society of that locale, and an inventory of identifying features, the specific trappings of Buenos Aires neighborhoods at the turn of the century. The initial rhetorical move of the text is to situate the speaker as "seeing/hearing" the barrio from his memory and of confirming its concreteness through physical commonplaces, some of which are material (doorways, hanging lanterns, mud puddles) and some of which are im-pressionistic (the sound of a *bandoneón*, the mystery of moon-washed streets, the sad drama sensed in the pallidness of a woman). The physical commonplaces are in turn associated with individuals who provided the speaker with a sense of belonging to a community: "viejos amigos," Juana (such neighborhood girlfriends are always recalled in tangos as first loves), the crowd hanging out at the corner grocery store.

Such physical features and individuals provide the speaker with the sense of a community, not necessarily one he has lost, but one that the twists and turns of life have separated him from, and the nostalgia of his evocation would lead one to assume that he is the worse for it, which is of course the justification for his melancholic return to it in his mind. Such a topos of the lost Garden of Eden of the innocence of youth, correlated with the old neighborhood, is unquestionably one of the sentimental pulls of the tango, as much as it is a veritable narreme of the culture of Buenos Aires, the city of "one hundred neighborhoods."

But there is an interesting internal duplication in "Barrio de tango" that brings us back to the way in which the neighborhood, attested to in later age by the mind's eye, is itself a collective hypostatized witness to the life of its members. This is the case of the comment on what is assumed to be the tragic story of the "pálida vecina," but, more significantly, it is the case of the reference to "el amor escondido en un portón." Such love trysts, which presumably were the case of the narrator and "aquella / Juana," are a game with public display and the public commentary they evoke: the desire for privacy of the lovers hiding in the shadows of the specifically eroticized space of the doorway is counterbalanced by the need for such trysts to take place in public spaces like doorways because society provides a guarantee of relative (and always precarious) privacy, at least in the case of those with limited economic resources, only for men and women who are lawfully married. As members of the proletariat, they belong to those classes who most feel the repression of social convention.

As a consequence, there is no alternative but to make a public spectacle of love, which likely also means intercourse, since the tango also speaks frequently of women who are seduced, abandoned, and often left pregnant (perhaps, in fact, the case of the "pálida vecina"). One way of reading this reference in the poem is to refer to the narrator's own meetings with Juana:

in evoking the barrio he also sees in his mind's eye himself and Juana exchanging kisses and intimacies in a doorway. In this way, "Barrio de tango" brings us back to the way in which the personal stories of individuals always ended up correlated with the scrutinizing gaze of society, because, unlike other types of songs that narrative sentimental stories (for example, the Mexican *canción ranchera*,[9] which rarely has a geographically specific anchor), the tango is insistent in its involvement with Buenos Aires in general and with certain specific locales associated with the social classes of the tango (compare with Mafud; Castro; Vila; Collier).

The tango is filled with precise references to districts of Buenos Aires, to streets and intersections, to bars, cafés, and cabarets, and to other notable landmarks, all of which could provide a geographic inventory of Buenos Aires on the basis of tango lyrics. However, my interest here is not in providing such an inventory, but in demonstrating that the urban society of the tango, and most definitely the exact social classes of the tango (to which upscale audiences accede through the tango in the interesting dimension of "slumming" that they provide), must be understood as the legitimating force of what is being sung about in those lyrics. Certainly all cultural production, whether it speaks of direct societal correlations or not, depends on the legitimation provided by some version of the hegemonic ideology. By consequence, then, that cultural production anchored with sociogeographic specificity is only making explicit (with or without irony) its grounding in a specific ideological legitimation.

Therefore, when the tango speaks of the social formation of the narrator—that is, when the lyrics recall the process of his coming of age in a specific social group—it may do so by making reference to specific locales ("Un pedazo de barrio allá de Pompeya" in "Barrio de tango") or to specific institutions, as in the case of "Cafetín de Buenos Aires," by Enrique Santos Discépolo and Mariano Mores:

> De chiquilín, lo miraba de afuera
> como a esas cosas que nunca se alcanzan . . .
> la ñata contra el vidrio,
> en un azul de frío . . .
>   que sólo fué después viviendo
> igual al mío . . .

Como una escuela de todas las cosas,
ya de muchacho me diste entre asombros
el cigarrillo . . .
. . . la fe en mis sueños
y una esperanza de amor . . .

  ¿Cómo olvidarte en esta queja,
cafetín de Buenos Aires?
Si sos lo único en la vida
que se pareció a mi vieja . . .
En tu mezcla milagrosa
de sabihondos y suicidas
yo aprendí filosofía . . . dados . . . timba
y la poesía cruel
de no pensar más en mí . . .

  Me diste en oro un puñado de amigos
que son los mismos que alientan mis horas;
José, el de la quimera . . .
Marcial—que aun cree y espera—
Y el flaco Abel—que se nos fué—
pero aun me guía . . .
Sobre tus mesas que nunca preguntan
lloré una tarde el primer desengaño,
Nací a las penas . . .
bebí mis años . . .
y me entregué sin luchar. (Albuquerque, 8)[10]

There is one, probably unintentional, irony in this text: if the *cafetín* taught the speaker to "no pensar más en mí," then why is he engaging in the solipsistic nostalgia of the tango? Otherwise, the text is the straightforward enumeration of the details of social formation. Specifically, that social formation is the masculinity of the speaker, his transition from being a little boy to being a fully defined man who has the right to enter into a privileged masculine space such as the café. There can be no mistaking the involvement of the tango with a cult of masculinity, even if it is a masculinity that is constantly under siege, constantly threatened in the often futile efforts to maintain its integrity. That cult has often been criticized as perpetuating, through the intense romantic monumentalization of the tango in Argentine society, a myth of masculinity that defends sexism, homophobia, male rage against threats to male integrity (as in the case of being abandoned and betrayed by a woman, as is so often the case in the tango), and, when other than in moments of rage, an overarching glacial masculine aloofness from the everyday affairs of life (see López Badano concerning masculine violence in the tango). While the tango, like much of Western culture, may assume the naturalness of masculine identity and masculine privilege as something that is, has been, and will always be, "Cafetín de Buenos Aires" echoes, *avant la lettre*, current theoretical proposals (for example, Katz) regarding the complex process involved in inscribing a subjectivity as masculine and the enormous project involved in maintaining masculine identity through constant acts of assertion, confirmation, and defense.

From such a theoretical point of view, since masculinity is an assumed identity, it must be sustainedly exercised in order not to fall away, and no challenge to it can go unanswered, because to do so would be to open a fatal breech in its facade. Masculinity, even more than femininity (which is, of course, also a closely guarded facade), must be constantly affirmed in a masculinist society. Since power is in the hands of masculine subjects, who compete mightily for its benefits, an imperfection in one's inscription into the codes of masculinity weakens his right to compete and endangers his success in competing by moving him closer to those social constituencies (for example, "women" or feminized males) that are excluded from competition. This is all fairly standard contemporary feminism. Where it becomes interesting for the tango, above enabling one to understand the machismo of the tango, is in giving importance to tangos like "Cafetín de Buenos Aires" and how what they are really doing, aside from the nostalgic topos of the café as a paradigmatic neighborhood institution, is detailing how that institution is a factor and a site in the creation of masculinity.

The foregoing would explain the construction of the text around an axis of outside/inside. The little boy, not yet a fully constituted masculine subject, stands outside the café, in the cold, pressing his nose against the glass of the window; later, as a man, he is ensconced within the warm cocoon of its smoke- and coffee-vapor-filled interior. At the outset, the café represents a world the narrator thinks he will never attain, the world of men and the social symbolism of the patriarchy they exemplify. As a man, he is now ready, as in the final line of the tango, to give himself up to its world, which is clearly the world of male identity and masculine privilege. The *cafetín* is both a paradigm and a microcosm. As one of the most important places where men gather, it is also a place from which non-men are excluded: children, women (except for indecent women, who are allowed to partake of masculine privilege), and gays (about whom the tango has noticeably very little to say, except for vague references to men who are feminized not by virtue of their sexual preference, but by belonging to higher classes, the sleek and fancy dudes who steal women away from their neighborhood lovers, only to abandon them for fresher meat after dishonoring them—that is, leaving them pregnant with little choice but to become prostitutes). The all-male world of the café is also a homogeneous world, because entrance into it means turning oneself over without a struggle to its codes and practices, which means that the individual is constantly measured in terms of the degree to which he abides by those codes and practices—that is, the degree to which he fits in. To deviate from custom, to fail to abide by the rules, means being cast back out into the street, reduced to going back to standing out in the cold and pressing one's nose against the window. Few men would run the risk of such banishment, and the economy of the café depends on the virtually absolute compliance of its members (see Bossio concerning the history and culture of cafés in Buenos Aires).

The café is a microcosm because, although it is a public space within a public space—one accedes to the latter by birth, but to the former only through initiation and confirmation—it is the stage for a spectacle of masculinity that is repeated, although with perhaps less intensity because one no longer mingles only with homogeneous subjects, in all social settings. But the important point to be made is that, while cafés and societies at large are the stage for the enactment of the dramas of masculinity, stages always have audiences, and the members of the audience are there to assess critically what is performed on the stage and to legitimate it or to repudiate it. Performers certainly implore their audiences for legitimation, and in this case it is the legitimation of what one has learned to be as a man (his *"filosofía"*) and what he does with that knowledge, which means to always act like a man. The tables of the café may well never question him, but his fellow men do, if only with the glacial aloofness of their manner, for which the only emotion allowed, other than male rage, is the tears of deceit. To be jilted by a woman is potentially one of the most serious threats to masculine integrity. In such a formulation, tears trigger the revenge to which men are entitled, even if it's no more than the verbal aggression mentioned above with reference to "Volvió una noche" (She Came Back One Night).

In this way, the urban institution of the neighborhood café institutionalizes masculinity and provides first and foremost a locus for its inscription and its careful maintenance. Moreover, it provides a stage for the enactment of the dramas of masculinity and for the confirmation of the appropriateness of one's conduct as a man. Significantly, the tango is insistent in confirming the appropriateness of macho behavior, and, just as there are scant references to incomplete masculine subjects, there are equally scant references to the failure of the man to perform properly in the face of his peers. The much changed urban cafés of Buenos Aires—which continue to prosper although in recent years many have been taken over by individuals the culture of the tango would consider inadequate masculine subjects, including gays and lesbians—continue to be the sites for the staging and the witnessing of social drama and the quest for ideological legitimation. In this they continue to function both as major paradigms and microcosms of Porteño society.

I would like to close this part of the discussion by focusing on the appeal of the tango, particularly to a generation for which, in Argentina as well as the West, there is much debate over the codes of masculinity. In Argentina, one will recall, the debate has centered on the military and its exercise of government by force and the way in which the armed forces can be viewed as a grounding, authoritarian, patriarchal institution of Argentina that is also the repository of the most unequivocal interpretations of masculinity and its attendant ideologies of heterosexism, sexism, and homophobia (for an examination of cultural texts dealing with these aspects of military institutions, see Foster, *Violence in Argentine Literature*). The tango may not have a universal allure in Argentina; quite understandably, many sectors of musical culture in the country prefer rock, which played an important part in resistance to the military and in the process of redemocratization following the withdrawal of the military from governance in 1983 (see Charly García's magnificently outrageous rock version of the Argentine national anthem, the latter one of the primary icons of the armed forces; see Fernández Bitar; Marzullo and Muñoz). But enjoyment of the tango cuts across social classes, gender boundaries, and sexual identities, and it is cherished by many Argentines who are quite uninvolved in its uses as a tourist attraction. One can never generalize in any useful way about the involvement of complex social subjects with complex forms of cultural production, and it is likely that we still have only a primitive understanding of how individuals interact with their culture (for example, only very recently has gender subjectivity began to be taken into serious account). The conventional wisdom about the process of "identification" between spectator and spectacle certainly continues to have some validity. One finds in the tango either a heightened version of personal tragedies or something like an example of the erotic sufferings one has striven to avoid: resigned sentimental confirmation versus supercilious grim lesson.

But I would like to complement such conventional possibilities with a third alternative: the way in which the tango affords the opportunity to play sexual monitor. If my analysis is true, that the urban dimensions of the tango are less concrete evocations of the city's image than a sense of the city's dominant sociosexual ideologies, then the tango, in its insistent enactment of dramas of erotic love, figures the way in which the city is a witness to that love. And in the role of witness—which is assumed over and over again by each audience member in the performance of the tango, whether as a song, instrumental music, dance, or any possible combination of the three—the spectator is invited to enforce the dominant sociosexual ideology of the city. That ideology may be strictly circumscribed. It is most assuredly trenchantly heterosexist, and it is closely tied to particular social classes, some of which have either disappeared or been considerably assimilated into what is the demographic norm of Buenos Aires (that is, the old immigrant labor class, quintessentially Italian, that provided one major basis of the tango has become part of the large urban petite bourgeoisie and even the professional middle class). Furthermore, one might hypothesize that many audience members of the tango do not subscribe to the sociosexual ideology that underpins it, at least not in its defense of masculinist privilege. However, the opportunity to play the role of interpellated sexual monitor and to echo some vaguely prevalent and precarious maintained sexual norm is strong, and the urban modeling of the tango, in one of its powerful dimensions, provides just such an opportunity.

Mario Pauletti has claimed that the only music Borges ever listened to was the tango, although it is probable that he preferred the tango as instrumental music, since it is unlikely that he would have had much use for the sort of lyrics the commercial tango song came to offer. From the publication of his first book of poetry, *Fervor de Buenos Aires* (Fervor of Buenos Aires; 1923), the city of Buenos Aires is a constant presence in Borges's poetry (Goloboff; Salas; Albert Robatto, 61–110; see also Fuentes on his discovery of Buenos Aires through Borges's writing). While it is true that he quickly abandoned his attempt to depict the essence of the city through elaborately imagistic metaphors, Borges continued to use the city as the backdrop for an extensive inventory of his texts over the next seventy-five years. Those texts may speak of Buenos Aires for immediately biographical reasons ("Arrabal" [Outskirts], *Fervor de Buenos Aires;* "Elegía de los portones" [Elegy of the Doors], *Cuaderno San Martín* [San Martín Notebook]; "Buenos Aires," *Elogio de la sombra* [*In Praise of Blindness*]). A detail of daily life in Buenos Aires may evoke for Borges some crucial aspect of human experience ("El Zahir" [The Zahir], *El Aleph* [The Aleph]; "El truco" [truco is a poker-like card game], *Fervor de Buenos Aires*). A historical icon, like the *compadrito* (buddy), may signify for Borges some highly pertinent feature of social experience ("Hombre de la esquina rosada" [Man from the Pink Corner], *Historia universal de la infamia* [Universal History of Infamy]; "El sur" [Southside], *Ficciones* [English translation has the same title = fiction/imaginary writings]; "Juan Muraña," *El informe de Brodie* [Dr. Brodie's Report]). Some aspect of the culture of Buenos Aires may allude to questions concerning the nature of the cultural enterprise ("Barrio norte" [North Neighborhood], *Cuaderno San Martín;* "El tango" [The Tango], *El otro, el mismo* [The One, the Same]; "Buenos Aires," *Elogio de la sombra*). Or, some apparently inconsequential trace of urban life may be viewed *sub specie aeternitatis* as the trigger for one of the writer's particularly droll meditations on the vagaries of human life ("Buenos Aires," *El otro, el mismo;* "El sur," *Ficciones*).

Clearly, there would be little point in constructing an inventory of images of Buenos Aires in Borges. Borges, especially after his abandonment of concerns of groups such as those associated with reviews like *Martín Fierro* (1924–27), hardly had any interest in a folkloristic or local-color depiction of the city, and he always made it clear that the city was of neither God nor Man, but of his own personal mythology. If it is now possible to understand that Borges's writing was, in fact, imbricated with the sociohistorical reality of Argentina, this does not mean that one is likely to discover much in attempting to discern any material significance in his references to the city. Unlike the rather transparent metaphors of Eduardo

Mallea or the dirty realism of Enrique Medina, Borges's Buenos Aires is not quite about any specific urban habitat by that name.

How, then, can one undertake to examine the lexeme "Buenos Aires" and its subsets that appear in Borges's texts? It would be facile to say that Borges creates metaphors or allegories of Buenos Aires, since such a pronouncement would only refer to what all literature and, indeed, all languages do. Or, equally facile would be to insist, on a more specific level that would take the foregoing into account, that Borges's texts, in some sort of metapoetic way, are conscious of and, in fact, thematize their metaphoric/allegorical renditions of Buenos Aires. Of greater interest should be the way in which Borges metonymizes Buenos Aires: how he selects specifically salient features and then undertakes to conjugate those features with sets of associations. In this way, Borges is confirming his belief that texts evoke other texts, beginning with how lexemes evoke other lexemes (or, on an even more fundamental level, how sememes—basic units of meaning that underlie lexemes—evoke other sememes) and how the human comprehension of experiential reality takes place along a sliding scale of signifiers. This does not simply mean that Buenos Aires is a metonym for something else, that it is a handy signifier that facilitates other more abstract or more complex signifiers, whether in a "this to that" transition or in terms of a concatenation of signifiers whereby one moves from the immediate concreteness of Buenos Aires (particularly for Argentine readers) on through references to intermediate signifiers until the putatively abstract, complex cluster is attained.

Buenos Aires was, to be sure, highly problematical for Borges. There can be no doubting his immense affection for many icons of the city and his sensitivity toward what they signified in terms of cultural experience. If Borges was primarily interested in the processes by which human culture is forged and how it has meanings for individuals and societies—meanings in a universe in which the only meanings are the ones created by mankind—there is no reason to suppose that he held Argentine culture in less esteem than his supposed preferences for international culture. Indeed, Borges made numerous claims about how Argentine culture was part of the larger human culture and how Argentines were as much citizens of that larger culture as they were part of their local, most immediate culture (see Borges, "El escritor argentino y la tradición" [The Argentine Writer and Tradition], *Obra completa*, 267–74). The point is, surely, that it must be impossible to separate "Argentine" culture from global culture, or from the universal cultural principle. Certain cultural icons and clusters of icons may be specifically Argentine, but it is questionable that they constitute an "Argentine" culture in any systematic way. That is, there is no specifically Argentine cultural system in Borges's view, which is why some of his most interesting texts are those in which he defies structural definitions that separate one culture from another. It might occur to one to state that to write in Argentine Spanish about Kafka is just such a mixing, but such a proposition would fall into the Creolist trap of assuming that there is a systematic subset of the Spanish language identifiable as "Argentine" Spanish. In any case, one will recall that one of the greatest briefs against Borges was his refusal to acknowledge the existence of an Argentine culture; his refusal to subscribe to the notion that the greatness of Argentina must lie in the repudiation of "foreign" cultural influences and of any appearance of seeming to consider them superior to models for Argentine culture; and his refusal to accept the widespread belief that Argentine culture was, in fact, a superior culture. His agnosticism in this regard had to do as much with the cultural nationalism of the right (specifically, the followers of Juan Domingo Perón in the 1940s, and older nationalists) as it did with the left (especially those inspired by the Pan-Americanism of the Cuban revolution and by an opposition to what was viewed as U.S. cultural imperialism).

Borges certainly has much to view with dismay in Argentine culture (if one may be allowed to hold on to this term, even if Borges seems to place it continually under a sort of Derridean erasure). For example, one of the constants in his work has been machismo and the cult of violence (Dorfman), a topic that has received recent attention with respect to issues of gender and sexual identity in Borges's writing (Altamiranda; Brant 1996). Although he at times seems to have almost a morbid fascination for the myths of masculinity in their Argentine versions, it is quite apparent that on many occasions he is appalled by these myths and their recurring historical projections in Argentine social history. The same may be said about images relating to the modern city. While Borges may not have suffered from any nostalgia for the past—a common feature of cultural nationalism, particularly in its right-wing manifestations—he had no particular reason to be enamored of the present, either, particularly in the notably difficult and sinister forms modernity took beginning in the 1940s. I am not proposing that his literature be read only for traces of such issues, whether related in particular to Buenos Aires or not. Rather, I am suggesting that the most interesting way of understanding the images of Buenos Aires in Borges is in terms of the ideological resonances that accompany his evocations of the city, be it in terms of an general entity, certain barrios, or a historical figure.

Yet there is always a certain immateriality about Borges's treatments of Buenos Aires, not because of his falsely vaunted "philosophical" stance, but because of his concerted eschewal of local-color elements. It is for this reason that his texts may not be included in books on Buenos Aires where literary compositions illustrate photographic or other representations of the city, such as *Buenos Aires, mi ciudad* (Buenos Aires, My City [published in 1963 by Universidad de Buenos Aires]) and Miguel Rep's *Y Rep hizo los barrios* (And Rep Made the Neighborhoods). In the case of the former, nostalgic black-and-white photographs evoke the cityscape of the 1950s and 1960s, the end of seigniorial Buenos Aires, the Paris of the Southern Hemisphere. This end was brought about by the emergence of the popular classes under Peronismo and the neoliberal transformations imposed by the military dictatorship and pursued vigorously by current democratic administrations. Among sixty texts, Borges appears four times. In the case of *Y Rep hizo los barrios*, in which Rep provides a nonromantic image of the "One Hundred Neighborhoods of Buenos Aires" by the editorial cartoonist of the highly critical daily *Página 12*, Borges is not represented once among forty-eight texts. Rep's images capture the raw vitality of neoliberalist Argentina and the contradictions of the promiscuous mix to be found in the city, not just of the old and the new that can be found in any city not completely stagnated, but between the stately and the glitzy. In neither graphic project is there much room for Borges's writing, as much because there is not a shred of romanticism in any line Borges ever wrote as because an aging, infirm, and blind Borges was never able to live as fully as he could have wished in the Buenos Aires he evokes. As in the case of Beatriz Viterbo in "El aleph," after whose death life goes on, as evinced by the material changes in the landscape of the city, there continues to be a Buenos Aires after Borges ceased, even before his death, to be able to grasp the city.

Although references to the city in canonical texts like "El aleph" and the earlier "La muerte y la brújula" (where, in typical Borgean irony, the actual geometric layout of Buenos Aires does not match the coordinates given in the story, despite the common assumption that Buenos Aires is the city in question), Borges's most often anthologized reference to Buenos Aires is "Fundación mítica de Buenos Aires" (Mythical Foundation of Buenos Aires), the opening poem in the 1929 *Cuaderno San Martín* (Madrid). There is no question that the specific quadrant of the city Borges refers to in the poem is the block where the family house of his childhood stood, a block now inhabited by elegant apartment buildings in Palermo. The Palermo of Borges's youth, rather than being the prized upper-middle-class district (sort of Buenos Aires's upper East Side) it is today, was a suburb of modest dwellings that, during the period of his youth, was a principal point of settlement for thousands of Italian immigrants from southern Italy, as its name makes abundantly clear (even though the name Palermo appears to have antedated that immigration). In the due course of social history, the sons and grandsons of many of these immigrants, now prosperous businessmen, professionals, and high-level bureaucrats, inhabit the apartments that stand on ground where their ancestors may have dwelled in tenement houses or other types of modest lodgings. Interestingly, until his death, Borges occupied an apartment downtown a couple kilometers from one of the streets (Paraguay) in the quadrant his poem evokes.

The basic semiotic practice of the poem is to "suppose" what might have been the circumstances, not just of the material founding of Buenos Aires, which is expressed in terms of key preterits like *vinieron, arribaron, prendieron . . . empezó* (came, arrived, put down, began: basic and conclusive predicate in the series), but of the establishment of a set of acts that are primes for present-day social knowledge and behavior. Borges engages in a sort of retroprojection, imagining what might have been the circumstances in the remote foundation of Buenos Aires that explain some of the human landscape of contemporary life there.

"Fundación" is one of Borges's many texts that refer specifically to the *compadrito*, a term that, aside from its implications with respect to the political system in which *compadritos* were used as enforcers, messengers, and factotums, is generally understood to refer to a lower-class macho type whose attitude is intended to communicate his masculine privilege, including a disdainful attitude, often translated into violent aggression, toward that which falls outside the scope of what he understands to be properly masculine (see Savigliano, *Tango and the Political Economy of Passion*, 31, on Borges and the *compadrito*).

Compadrito is the diminutive of *compadre* (companion/buddy), a term that evokes the homosocialism of the society of these men, in the sense that the spheres of social control, from the highest levels of government down to neighborhood institutions, are based on a relationship of bonding and interdependence among men. Indeed, *compadre*, much more than *compañero*, the direct cognate of "companion," is based on the key term of the patriarchy, *padre*, and refers to those who share the same father. Here, however, the relationship is not one of consanguinity, but rather one of descending from the same symbolic Father in the sense of their subjectivity deriving from the same patriarchal ideology. Thus, in its more general sense, a *compadre* is someone with whom a man shares paternal responsibility toward his son (a godfather). It is this ideology that defines maleness, manhood, and masculinity. The social violence derived from exercising patriarchal authority and, more significantly, from internally regulating members of the homosocial realm fascinates Borges in "El hombre de la esquina rosada" (from *Historia universal de la infamia*). Indeed, the common thread in *Historia universal de la infamia* is machismo, and it is the perception of Borges's abiding interest in constructions of masculinity and images of manhood in Argentina that has begun to make him interesting to gender studies. Moreover, as gender is examined more closely in Borges, it will be necessary to distinguish between his homosocial cult of the *compadrito* and the self-pitying masculine subject in the commercial tango of the 1930s and 1940s who sings of his implied defeat as a man, because he is repeatedly deceived by Woman, rather than of the manly virtues Borges defends.

In "Fundación mítica" these images are not just historical harbingers; they are, as the title of the poem indicates, foundational myths, sources of social and cultural institutions. The following stanza anticipates "El hombre de la esquina rosada," both in theme and in the iconic importance of the color *rosado*, as will subsequently be confirmed as the distinctive color of the government house. (*Rosado* in Argentina is what in English might be called "old rose." It is not to be confused with the brighter, louder color *rosa*, which in English would be pink. This is an important distinction, given the contemporary sexual connotation of the latter):

Un almacén rosado como revés de naipe
brilló y en la trastienda conversaron un truco;
el almacén rosado floreció en un compadre,
ya patrón de la esquina, ya resentido y duro. (Borges, *Obra completa*, 81)[11]

If, as the closing couplet of the poem affirms, Buenos Aires is "tan eterna como el agua y el aire," the social primes identified by the poem, which provide the basic horizons of social experience and, more importantly, social meaning, are also as eternal as the elements. "Naturalization" means the process by which the cultural—that which has been created by human society as part of its social evolution—is made to appear natural—that which is outside of human history and therefore unavailable to the subjection of cultural critical analysis. Questioning the process of naturalization and deconstructing what is alleged to be natural is an important task of cultural studies, which only echo what critical and contestatorial writing (that is, cultural production in general) has always done. Borges posits the historical origins of the foundation by showing the mythic to have been historical rather than eternal. He does this by showing that the process of human industry was involved in the establishment of the city (using the aorist verbs referred to above—the processes of myth are not marked by temporality), and thereby demonstrates that "eternal" really means "abiding" in some sort of triumphant or categorical way.

Borges actualizes the foundational practice by referring to contemporary political events. Hipólito Yrigoyen, the first populist president of Argentina, was in office for his second term at the time Borges published the poem, although the following year (1930) he would be overthrown by the country's first military coup d'état:

El primer organito salvaba el horizonte
con su achacoso porte, su habanera y su gringo.
El corralón seguro ya opinaba YRIGOYEN,
algún piano mandaba tangos de Saborido. (Borges, *Obra completa*, 81)[12]

In this way, Borges establishes a concatenation of cultural instances whereby the sites of contemporary Buenos Aires culture, synecdochized by the *corralón* and populated by important cultural icons of the period (especially the quintessential tango), are the continuing actualizations of the founding primes.

Borges's personalization, which he accomplishes by reference to the actual city block where he was raised, of the founding and its contemporary instances is noteworthy because it confirms his critical stance toward the patriarchal traces in the historical and current instances he cites. It is important to remember that only in cases of a nightmarish delirium, as in "El sur," where the coma inspired by a household accident provides the stage for Borges the character to live out—and die as a consequence of—an incident of macho aggression, does Borges figure himself as a participant in the dramas of masculinity that he describes so effectively.

The foregoing characterization of "Fundación mítica de Buenos Aires" has sought to demonstrate that the importance of the images of Buenos Aires in Borges cannot be found in how they may or may not describe, realistically or fantastically, the concrete reality of the city, although there are, to be sure, traces of the specific features of the city in Borges's writing. Rather, the interest of his texts lies in how Borges sees through urban phenomena—a city block; the remains of past features, institutions, and activities; personal recollections and projections of what might have taken place there—to suggest an interpretation of a significant element of the city's social text, in this case, the masculine dominance that goes back to the historical fact that Argentina, like most of Latin America, was initially colonized by men alone and the masculine privilege that continues to prevail in the modern city.

Borges wrote numerous texts on the tango (Paoletti)—a logical extension of his interest in the *compadrito* and in the perhaps more explicit and evident nature of masculinity to be found among the popular classes. Arguably, this is not, in fact, the case: the codes of masculinity are just as transparently manifest in the bourgeoisie to which Borges belonged as in the upper bourgeoisie and oligarchy that have always controlled the reins of power in Argentina. Equally arguably, one might sustain that power is maintained because the codes of masculinity function so effectively among the upper classes. However, a concomitant argument might be that these classes undertake to conceal the efficiency of their functioning: critical culture exists to reveal the functioning that is concealed by those who have forms of cultural expression to effect the concealment; in the case of marginal sectors of society, cultural forms function more directly to identify the existence of the codes of masculinism, since these classes only sporadically have access to forums of concealment and it is more a matter of recording the social text that, less than concealed by the hegemonic classes, is alleged either not to exist or to have no importance.

Borges's interest in these components of urban culture extended to his own writing over six decades, as well as to his collaborations with Adolfo Bioy Casares, under the cloak of shared pseudonyms, and the anthologies he prepared with other writers, such as *El compadrito* (see the extensive references to Borges and the tango in Lara and Roncetti de Panti). His own bibliography of exclusive authorship includes, in addition to *Historia universal de la infamia*, *Para las seis cuerdas* (For the Six Strings), eleven poetic texts focusing on the *milonga* dance and its culture. Borges, in an uncharacteristic gesture toward essentialism, considered the *milonga* a more specifically Argentine form than the tango, as well as having its origins in the suburbs dominated by the *compadritos*. The tango, with its origins in riverfront brothels, is more directly urban than the *milonga*, and it contains the traces of multiple foreign influences. By the thirties it was completely commercialized. There are many other poems, essays, and stories scattered throughout Borges's oeuvre that provide an intersection of urban (or semi-urban) culture, the *compadrito* and his allies, and the codes of masculinity.

"El tango," from *El otro, el mismo* (1964) is from the same period as the aforementioned compositions on the *milonga*. Since one of Borges's so-called "philosophical" preoccupations is with time, as in the case of "Fundación mítica de Buenos Aires," he is also interested in the link between cultural phenomena of the past and their reflexes in the present:

> ¿Dónde estarán? pregunta la elegía
> De quienes ya no son, como si hubiera
> Una región en que el Ayer pudiera
> Ser el Hoy, el Aún y el Todavía. (Borges, *Obra completa*, 888)[13]

By contrast, the poetic voice makes it clear that there is no culture *sub speciae aeternitatis*: the tango, by way of refuting a cultural nationalism that would see in it an everlasting, and the most original, of Argentine cultural institutions, is not eternal. The use of pretentious capital letters with the temporal adverbs is an ironic subversion of any eternal permanence to be attached to that which stretches in an unbroken chain of permanence from Yesterday to Today, from Ever to Always.

Borges avails himself of the hoary medieval rhetorical figure of the *ubi sunt* to inquire where the tango, and more significantly, its human voices have all gone. This figure allows Borges to create an inventory of elements of the tango—or, at least, of those associated paradigmatically with the tango as its most consecrated form within Argentine cultural nationalism. He identifies the tango as

> Una mitología de puñales
> lentamente se anula en el olvido;
> Una canción de gesta se ha perdido
> En sórdidas noticias policiales. (888)

What is interesting about this characterization is that any allusion to the tango as a cultural product centered on heterosexual love and/or on erotic enactment is skimmed over in terms of how the tango stages acts of violence that replace the song (specifically the artistic) with a police report (a routine administrative document of the social text). Once again, Borges ends up focusing on the dynamics of the homosocial component of the masculine code. While it is not stated whether the questions of *puñales* are the consequence of jealousy between men or acts of revenge by a man against an unfaithful woman (women usually do not have enough agency in the tango to avenge wrongs done by unfaithful men). But this does not matter, since the homosocial imperative will always prevail: if it is not a duel between men over a woman, violence against a woman is always about another man and his threat to the masculinity of the avenger. The violence recorded on the police blotter is equally a matter between men, since even if, as far as the tango is concerned, the citizen who becomes a matter of attention for the police is a woman, it is likely to be because she has been involved in a violation of the code of masculinity. Violence in the tango is always about the affairs of men, from beginning to end, which is why a tango about women's lives in any feminist sense of the phrase would be inconceivable. Even a tango like "Malena baila el tango" (Malena Dances the Tango)," for example, concerns Malena as a participant in the male-dominated world of the tango.

Borges does not deny the contemporary existence of the tango. Rather, the tango has become a repository of the past. The participants in a specific Argentine social text, that of the acute heterosexist masculinity of the turn of the century, are today to be found as characters in a cultural text that continues to give them validity. The tango makes interpretational sense because of the dynamic it evokes. While it is no longer enacted by the *malevaje* (thuggery) of a hundred years ago, it still has sense in the contemporary social text:

Hoy, más allá del tiempo y de la aciaga
Muerte, esos muertos viven en el tango.

En la música están, en el cordaje
De la terca guitarra trabajosa,
Que trama en la milonga venturosa
La fiesta y la inocencia del coraje. (889)[14]

One will note that, as in the stanza just cited, Borges has the tendency to merge *milonga* and tango, despite his avowed preference for the former. Also note the assertion that the *milonga*/tango concerns "la fiesta y la inocencia del coraje." It is surprising to believe that, all of a sudden, the violence of the tango can be reduced to an innocent celebration. Perhaps the innocence derives from the fact that the specific versions of violence in the social text of the past evoked by the cultural text of the present no longer occurs (a rather debatable proposition, given the evidence of masculinist violence). More likely, Borges is referring to how the cultural text makes the social text seem innocent. Were we to witness one of the acts of violence it describes, we would be horrified, just as we would be appalled were we to learn about it from a news report. In both cases, the violence would be "real" in a way in which it is not when it appears in a cultural text. In this way, the cultural text "sanitizes" the masculinist violence of actual lived experience. While cultural texts may be effective challenges to the ideological sleights of hand that take place in the social text, they can come across as "innocent," as not really blood-spattered, because of the artistic transformation of the cultural text.

Thus, the tango translates the social text, which in a sense is what allows for the sustained contemplation of the circumstances of the latter that the artistic text demands of its reader/viewer. At the same time, by underscoring the way in which the violent becomes innocent, the poem brings the reader back to the way in which it is really a declaration of actual forms of violence, the evocation, despite however the tango may appear to be nostalgically unreal, of actual circumstances of life in the urban space:

Esa ráfaga, el tango, esa diablura,
Los atareados años desafía;
Hecho de polvo y tiempo, el hombre dura
Menos que la liviana melodía,

Que sólo es tiempo. El tango crea un turbio
Pasado irreal que de algún modo es cierto,
El recuerdo imposible de haber muerto
Peleando, en una esquina del suburbio. (889)[15]

Borges is drawing a fine line here. He is claiming that the tango is both a cultural phenomenon that turns social reality into an innocent celebration of manhood and the neighborhood scenarios of its display. But at the same time, he is claiming it is "de algún modo es cierto"—the social reality it conjures up is more than innocent panache. In this text and others, Borges focuses on the tango because of its extremely problematic role in Argentine culture. It is a mainstay of cultural nationalism (not to mention of the tourist trade) as much as an exemplification of the raw nature of Buenos Aires's urban life during the period of mass European immigration. It is a highly complex conjunction of music, poetry, and dance, while at the same time a not-particularly-subtle enactment of masculinist violence that in recent years has been a point of reference for feminist attacks on male rage and privilege.

Ironically, the tango refers generally to men from a social class with difficulty in acceding to political and symbolic power, which is why it was important to Peronista populism. By the same token, masculinity is closely monitored in the tango. As a way of aspiring to male power, especially symbolic power, the tango represents in a purified form the male dominance that must be strategically attenuated if not ideologically concealed in the sectors of bourgeois decency, which in fact wields political and symbolic power. Of course, by the time Borges wrote "El tango," the social reality that was the original base of the tango had disappeared. This is the rhetorical force of the *ubi sunt* (where are they) figures, and the symbolic power of the tango is no longer that of the lived social text as such. This is precisely the point of Borges's poem, to show how the tango, which has made the transition from social text to cultural production, still has meaning for the social text through the symbolic power it exercises.

chapter 4

Homoeroticism and Contested Space

En consecuencia, . . . podemos imaginar . . . los otros sitios que
nos convendrían [amén de los bares], como podrían ser sedes
sociales, bibliotecas, clubes, gimnasios, salas de cine y teatro;
en suma, todo aquello que una comunidad libre y vivaz puede
crear.[1]

—Alejandro Jockl, *Ahora, los gay*

Abstenerse de exaltar el triunfo del mal sobre el bien, la diso-
lución de la familia, la traición a la Patria, el vituperio a los
forjadores de la nacionalidad, la burla a los defectos físicos, el
desvío sexual o el erotismo.[2]

—(Reglamentación del Decreto-Ley 15460/57, conocido como
Ley de Radiodifusión [1965], quoted in Avellaneda 1.74)

In the agenda of the contemporary gay and lesbian rights movement in
Argentina, high on the list is the question of visibility: the right for the
manifestations of homoerotic behavior to enjoy at least the same level of
public display as the signs of so-called straight sex (for a valuable detailed
survey of the Argentine lesbian and gay movement, see Brown). Such a
struggle for visibility, beyond its crucial place in a defense of the rights of
sexual preference, is an attention to the principle articulated by Jones in
his article on contested spaces in Latin America: "[The representation of
space] concerns a 'spatialised politics of identity' in which space must be
regarded as essentially hybrid command of which is always provisional and
contested" (2).

The goal of visibility is a complex one, since it involves the definition of
what might, in a Latin American society, be considered the legitimate
public display of any form of sexuality; what constitutes homoeroticism;

and, crucially, what constitutes public display (see Núñez, "La represión sexual," concerning the history of sexuality in Argentina). One cannot, of course, generalize about Latin America in such matters; nor is it even possible to generalize about a specific country, since one must expect to find major differences between the capital and other areas of the country (see "El día que me quieras" concerning recent sociology research on the acceptance of gay rights in Argentina). Even in countries like Brazil and Mexico, where there is more than one major urban area, differences can be great, especially since the homogenization among demographic concentrations in the United States has yet to be the norm in Latin America. The difference in Mexico between Guadalajara and Monterrey is as great as that in Brazil between Rio de Janeiro and São Paulo, to speak only of contrasting cities that are not national capitals.

The public/private axis has long been central to the discussion of sexuality in Latin America, and it has played a prominent role in the discussion of homoeroticism, especially when it comes to contrasting U.S. definitions of same-sex behavior with the "Mediterranean" code (Almaguer; Lumsden; Núñez Noriega; Murray). In this discussion, I will set aside the question of who is identified as a "homosexual," since it is not directly pertinent to the matter of contested spaces. But suffice it to remember that in Mediterranean societies, only the so-called recipient member of male-male sex is marked as sexually deviant. Homosexuality, or its semantic equivalent, is not customarily attributed to women (since the penis is always the operant signifier), nor is it attributed to male inserters, since, irrespective of the body of insertion, inserters are fulfilling the defining function of men, which is the active utilization of the penis, itself a form of display, the effects of which may be public (for example, pregnancy) or semipublic (for example, rumor that one man has been the object of another man's penetration).

Where the public/private axis is pertinent to the discussion here is in the matter of what is permitted in public display, or what is considered public display, and what is not; concomitantly, it includes what can be considered to exist, because it may be displayed in public, and what does not, in effect, exist, because it may not be the object of public scrutiny in Latin American societies. Sexual acts between a legally constituted heterosexual unit traditionally have not been part of public scrutiny. Although the matter of sodomy (an act whose definition has sometimes meant any-

Members of the Comunidad Homosexual Argentina and the Campaign against AIDS congregate at the Plaza de Mayo in front of the Casa Rosada (government house) in 1992. Photo courtesy of Mónica Arroyo.

thing not conducive to pregnancy) may be of institutional concern (to the family, the police, the Church, and medicine), it is best to begin with the assumption that the sanctity of the marriage chamber overrides any competing public concern over what goes on in that private space (probably the only other space more private than the legal boudoir is the confessional). Historically, the manifestations of heterosexual love have been extremely circumscribed because of the ways in which they are considered to be synecdoches of bedroom activities, and one might venture to say that, in what has been considered to be conventional bourgeois society, erotic metonymies are permissible (the giving of flowers, the dropping of a handkerchief, the language of the fan), but not erotic synecdoches (touching, kissing, caressing, all but the most formalized forms of dancing). Cultural production has often come under the attention of moral censorship less because it makes direct reference to sexual acts (few would dare, until relatively recently, to engage in the public, as opposed to clandestine, production of explicit sex), than because it gives a heightened rhetorical representation to suggestive synecdoches or to creative metonymies, which is often the case with slick commercial advertising, as, for example, in the recent furor over Calvin Klein underwear spreads.

My point here, rather than any survey of what may be considered to be the public display of sexuality, is the need to problematize what may be considered to be public display. To be sure, no one will assume that any and all forms of sexuality may be displayed in public, and phenomena like kiss-ins (with a broad and creative definition of kissing), nude-ins, and sex-ins (with perhaps circumscriptions on the literal meaning of the operant verb) serve, in name if not in fact, to question and challenge what is held to be the legitimate restriction on public sex. More important is the need to understand that even presumedly "modern" Latin American societies may have radically different ideas than those of the United States as to what is considered to be legitimate public sexuality, as young tourists often find to their chagrin; conversely, other societies, "modern" or otherwise, may seem to be more liberal or indulgent (aspects of corporal display in Brazil, for example).

Recent neofascist military dictatorships in Argentina, along with their persecution of anything deemed to be a manifestation of homosexuality, also sought to generally control public displays of the body and public displays of affection, on the premise that any form of sexuality other than that strictly controlled by the institution of marriage constituted a dimension of the very weakness of character that military authoritarianism existed to combat in the first place. Young people hanging out and engaged in the sort of formless and licentious sexuality encouraged by advertising and cultural production in general (especially foreign imports) were taken to be major signs of the collapse of the moral fabric of Argentine society that allowed for the fatal invasion of corrupt foreign ideologies. "Do you know where your children are and what they are doing?" was an official call to parents to make sure their children were well withdrawn from the public arena and safely ensconced under the vigilance of parental (= state) authority (Kovadloff; I analyze this essay in *Violence in Argentine Literature,* 51–55). Since it was alleged that a relatively unsupervised public arena encouraged indecent behavior, the demand for withdrawing children from public spaces was in effect an attempt to combat the sort of youth-culture "puppy love" that was believed to lead to consequences inappropriate for a strictly enforced heterosexist ideology. One such untoward consequence, surely, was the possibility of the homosexual seduction, which was usually understood characteristically to happen when a young person fell into the unscrupulous hands of an older, sexually experienced person.

It might be worth mentioning here two important components of Argentine sociocultural history. Thanks to the long conflict between the capital and the rest of the country, between *civilización* (civilization) and *barbarie* (barbarism), the culture of the former has often been associated with effeminate men. But from the point of view of the "civilized," the noncity is not just the "outback," but rather, in true binary fashion, whatever is opposed to urban privilege and its particular cultural parameters, which may include elements within the city that are opposed to its privilege. This point can be profitably developed with reference to Peronists and anti-Peronists, the latter being associated with the privilege of the city. There has yet to be an adequate examination of the construction of masculinity in Domingo Faustino Sarmiento's *Facundo* (1848). When it is examined, one will necessarily have to deal with the hypermasculinity of Facundo Quiroga, the narrative voice of Sarmiento and his identification with metropolitan privilege (including the continual defamations he has experienced in Argentine history), and the bridge position of the authoritarian dictator Juan Manuel de Rosas, whose authority derived from his class privilege but whose political power depended on resonances in the nonprivileged masses. Argentine machismo is typically associated with the mythified countryside: witness the figure of the Gaucho, the suburban *compadrito* (tough), the Peronista/unionized laborer, many of whom are either urban marginals or rural immigrants. For these groups, individuals who enjoy metropolitan privilege are viewed as dandies, which is often a euphemism for effeminate.

The other topic has to do with the tradition of single-sex education in Argentina, in both parochial and private schools. Many sectors of public education exhibit de facto segregation of the sexes as the consequence of programs of study. The circumstance of forced homosocialism intersects the period of the formation of sexual identity and the beginnings of sexual experimentation. Schools are universally seen as continuing the formation of the social subject, which parents have done for an initial period in the name of the state (as opposed to the rather naive belief that schools continue the authority of the parents, who can never effectively oppose the state, except in minor symbolic ways). Homosociality does not equate with homosexuality; indeed, homosociality is a requisite component of compulsory heterosexuality, since it is a consequence of the hierarchy of sexual roles and the need to conform male-male bondings in the execution of the patriarchy (Segdwick). However, homosocial space provides, as the veritably mythic all-male English boarding school informs us, many opportunities for homoerotic conduct. Issues of the homosociality of both sexes in institutional contexts in Argentina and the presence of homoerotic opportunities remains an unexplored topic, although it has been examined in fictional works like Enrique Medina's *Las tumbas* (The Tombs), where the homosocial space is an all-male reformatory (see Foster, *Violence in Argentine Literature*, 75–97), or Manuel Puig's 1976 *El beso de la mujer araña* (The Kiss of the Spider Woman), which centers on two male prison inmates (see Foster, *Contemporary Argentine Cinema*, 123–35, on the use of homosexuality in the film version).

The foregoing leads us to the question of what may have been understood to be the signs of homosexuality. The principle of a private/public axis may give the false impression of a clean dichotomy between what one did in private and what one did in public: the latter could be controlled, often in a draconian fashion, while as long as the former was maintained with strict discretion, it would not fall under the purview of public scrutiny. What is frequently cited here are constitutional guarantees of the privacy of the body.[3] But even when it would be foolish to assume that de facto authoritarian regimes would concern themselves much with a constitutional premise, since their very existence would mean a global suspension of the constitution, it would be as equally naive to assume that the division between public and private could be effectively maintained. To be sure, certain accumulated traditions and code law specified what was public and what was private. However, the transgression of this level of separation is not what is at issue here, except to insist that any military government that felt it had the right to break into any private residence during the middle of the night would not likely respect the public/private distribution of sexual behavior, particularly when sexual conduct was a central part of the plan of social reformation that the military government sought to impose.

Rather, what merits close scrutiny are the slippages between the realm of the private and the realm of the public, with an emphasis on how any forms of public behavior are susceptible to being read as signs of the private, whether the domain of one's inner private being or what one would

The puppets represent President Carlos Menem and Argentine Primate Monsignor Quarracino: "Menem and Quarracino: Una unión contra natura" (Menem and Quarracino: A Union against Nature). The motive of the protest was Quarracino's comment on a television program in 1994 that homosexuals should all be put together in one place, to live among themselves without bothering anyone else.

consider to be the physically private. The sort of slippage I have in mind here is most vividly illustrated in the long tradition of the intense homophobic gaze, whereby individuals, typically men but often women, are scrutinized for any trace of deviancy that could be taken as symptomatic of sexual degeneracy (see Blumenfeld on all the ramifications of homophobia). Elements of dress (clothes that are too colorful, too tightly fitting, or too "open" in strategic zones), elements of language (accents, registers, vocabulary that does not maintain the dichotomic binary of male/female or the crossover boundary from one to the other), elements of bodily appearance (hair that is too long or unconventionally cut; the use of fragrances or other cosmetics; inappropriate distributions of bodily masses, such as hips that are too wide or fleshy breasts), and elements of body language (a general looseness of bodily articulation and paradigmatically the limp wrist and unfirm handshake, unassertive bodily movement, non-rigid posture when either standing or sitting) are all subject to public interpretive readings that allow for such minimal traces of alleged conclusive coincidence to signify the most egregious forms of sexual irregularity in private (see Litvin's book of gay jokes, which allows for a reading of what the ideologemes of gay culture in Argentina are).

For example, recent military dictatorships in Argentina virtually fetishized long hair, turning it into an overdetermined sign of homosexuality. Such a fetish was incapable of excusing long hair even for religious reasons, resulting in a religious persecution of Buenos Aires's large Orthodox Jewish community. Much less could it have any respect for a Che Guevara–style "hippie mode" that was usually as adamantly heterosexist as the military. Of course, the military understood that long hair signaled a general rebellious stance and that it was an international icon of political adversity. Thus, often the attribution of homosexuality to those who displayed long hair was only a secondary and rather grimly arbitrary denunciation of their social subjectivity. However, since those identified as homosexuals, whether on the basis of such an overinterpretation or because of a reading of some other somatic sign, often received extra-harsh interrogation, including more savage forms of torture, such identifications were hardly of little consequence. In this regard, one would wish to assert that the consequences of homophobic interpretations are rarely of little consequence, and gay-bashing takes many forms short of actual bloodletting. In this case, however, they were unquestionably of substantially greater consequence: the humiliation of a public scorning of offending youths was only the mildest form such violence took.

But there are other ways in which it is difficult to distinguish between the public and the private. Since sexual experiences are among the most private of human affairs, and since our social codes are obsessed with matters of sexual conformity, it is quite impossible to see how any meaningful distinction can be made between the public and the private. Even in the case of the individuals who most conform to the criteria of compulsory heterosexuality, the respect, social worth, and praise they are due is the consequence of the ways in which, even if only subconsciously, they are viewed as fulfilling sociosexual roles in an exemplary fashion. For someone to be "nada menos que todo un hombre," "nada menos que toda una mujer" reflects the completeness of their role performance, and it is quite clear that sociosexual role compliance refers, by extension, to all manifestations of social integrity.

The question of visibility, therefore, for gays and lesbians in Argentina cannot be viewed as simply creating a public discussion of the sexuality, both straight and queer, that custom and law have long treated as beyond the pale of the public forum; nor can it be the specific creation of a public debate of queer culture, since Argentine society, officially and casually, has always dealt in some way or another with sexual deviance, to the extent, as I have insisted, that an array of presumed traces of homosexual conduct has been used to measure and control social behavior. One will recall that the founding text of Argentine fiction, Esteban Echeverría's long short story, *El matadero* (written circa 1839–40 but not published until 1874) ends with the attempted homosexual rape of a political opponent, a powerful example of the way in which the victim is feminized and homosexualized and rape is assumed to be a proper form of social control (see Donat and D'Emilio concerning the historicization of rape as a form of social control in the United States). In this sense, Argentina has always had a public discourse on deviant sexuality, even if, clearly, that discourse has had little to do with the discourse gay liberation groups intend to encourage (although no study exists concerning the history of sexuality in Argentina, Acevedo illustrates many of his general comments with reference to Argentina; the military edicts reproduced in Avellaneda provide an oblique history of authoritarian views in Argentina regarding sexuality in general and deviant sexuality as it is understood by such views).

What might be the level of discussion sought by the gay liberation movement, as opposed to the long-standing parameters regarding homosexuality? (Jockl constitutes something like an inventory of issues to be addressed in Argentina).[4] I think one would have to put as first and foremost the recognition of lesbian sexuality. In this regard, it is important to underscore the alliances that have begun to be forged between gay male groups and lesbians (see the discussion in chapter on feminine space in Fuskova and Marek's, *Amor de mujeres: El lesbianismo en la Argentina, hoy* [Love of Women: Lesbianism in Argentina Today]; see also Fuskóva-Kornreich and Argov). Although women have always been put down by attributing any sign of assertiveness to often vaguely defined sexual irregularities, and certainly the first manifestations of feminism in Argentina would only have augmented such attributions, Latin American sexual ideologies have only with difficulty allowed for the existence of the lesbian and any idea of what lesbian sexuality might be. "What do they do together" is almost iconic in its expression of ignorance with respect to lesbian specificity. Thus, the need to bring lesbianism into the public discourse, while at the same time recognizing the historical difference of women and the fact that lesbianism is not simply a female-marked homosexuality, with the latter defined from the perspective of male privilege, constitutes a compelling imperative in view of just how many different issues it brings with it (Jockl speaks of the collaboration with women, 85–88; see Fuskova and Marek on lesbian issues in Argentina).

Next in importance to the gay liberation movement is the need to repudiate, if not the word "homosexual" itself,[5] at least the medical and legal constructions of nonstraight sex. In this sense, the gay liberation movement, with its emphasis on lesbian and gay pride and on the acquisition of legal rights (and, concomitantly, the suspension of formal bases for discrimination), reveals its international connections (see the discussion of Buenos Aires in Miller, 182–217; see Jáuregui on gay pride marches in Buenos Aires; note that Manuel Puig's published articles in Buenos Aires in the popular magazine *Siete días ilustrados* in 1969–70 report on the gay community there ["Bye-Bye Babilonia," in *Estertores de una década*, 61–163]). And, finally, in addition to the ways in which, like the international gay movement, the Argentine movement has fought for the right to bars, parades, and cultural institutions, I would return to the specific question of visibility by underscoring the need for a cultural production (however "culture" is precisely to be understood) that brings people with queer affiliations into the mainstream of public discourse in ways other than as an insistent point of reference for social dissolution and political subversion (or, one might add, as the cross-dressed comic stereotype) (see Núñez, "El circuito gay," "El ghetto gay"; see Sebreli on the history of homosexuality in Buenos Aires; concerning the new visibility, see the recent newspaper report on a sociological survey, "El temor a la diferencia." It is important to note that not only does this report begin on the first page of the newspaper, but that the bottom half of the page is occupied by the photo of two men kissing).

Cultural visibility, in view of the need both to counter a long-standing but highly charged "homosexual" discourse and the imperative to naturalize a more theoretically and politically driven definition of lesbian and gay

Various photographs of the 1993 gay pride march in Buenos Aires, from Casa Rosada to the Congress building. In the top right figure, the late Carlos Jáuregui, one of the major spokespersons in Buenos Aires in the 1990s for gay and lesbian rights, appears at the far right.

life, necessarily assumes two asymmetrical dimensions. The first is the need to enact homoerotic desire—if not "erotic reality," at least its metonymies and synecdoches—in the public realm; the second is for cultural texts to refer to that erotic reality, and to show it being enacted in the public realm. For example, virtually all forms of institutionalized culture (what is commonly called consciously produced Culture—high or otherwise—as opposed to small "c" anthropological culture) are public texts. Even works of literature like poetry and the novel, which are customarily read in private, are public in the sense that they are sold publicly (typically with covers that make a public statement about the contents), and they are likely to be advertised and commented on publicly (in the latter case, either in the context of published professional criticism or in general open conversation). Alongside this sort of oblique publicness, theater and film involve a much more directly public display of culture, since they are viewed in ways that involve multiple spectators in spaces to which individuals have free access; television becomes a public medium when it is viewed in bars, waiting rooms, and the like, although one could insist that the nonprivate viewing of television in homes (in Argentina, middle-class families and below are likely to have the television set in the dining room or eating area) is tantamount to making it a public form of culture, at least in the sense of "public" being equated with "communal."

All of the foregoing forms of culture may deal with homoerotic desire as a private issue: something that takes place between two or more individuals in any sort of space that can be claimed to be private or semiprivate or circumstantially private. But it is also possible for a cultural text to represent homoerotic desire as taking place in a public space, even when such a space cannot reasonably be claimed to exist as an actual social reality—such an image is wishful thinking or utopian modeling. In the latter case, the issue of public visibility becomes reduplicated: public display is thematized in the text, and that text is exhibited publicly. It would be useful to inventory TV programs, movies, and films in Argentina that show homoerotic desire, and it would be useful to underscore those in which homoerotic desire is thematized as taking place—and again I would insist, if only in terms of metonymies and synecdoches—in public spheres. However, what I would like to do here is examine some texts in which both dimensions are present, but where a problematics of visibility additionally informs the text at hand. By problematics I understand a perception of the difficulties of public display: American commercial texts often seem to assure that by optimistically showing something as possible, the audience will take it as already existing as a social reality. I would venture to propose that Latin American texts, on the other hand, are much more cautious in what they suppose to be possible in terms of constructible social realities. Moreover, I would expect to find some sort of reflection about the distinction between private and public, in order to question to what degree the private can ever exist in any meaningful way and to what degree whatever one understands to be private is also necessarily public and, therefore, open to the assessment and control of scopic vigilance.

One final point: while cultural products that represent the incursion into public spaces of gay and lesbian culture as it is defined by those who subscribe to it (since long-standing representations of homosexuality have typically been the business of those in homophobic opposition to it), it would be reasonable to expect that primary interest in such representations would lie with those spaces that integrate homoerotic culture into the global spheres of society. Representations, to be sure, of private or semiprivate spaces matter—spaces such as bars; meeting places of activist associations; homes of "families that we choose" (to use Weston's title); scenes of a homoerotic-marked cultural production, such as the set of a gay soap opera; or specialized forums, such as conferences and other academic-type events. But these spaces promote the separation of gay culture from society at large, whether one seeks such a separation for ideological reasons ("We have no hope of being accepted out there, so we will create a privileged space in here") or whether one acquiesces in the imposition of segregation ("They would prefer to be with their own"; "They can exist as long as I don't have to see them").[6]

In the attempt to overcome such sought or accepted segregation, lesbian and gay cultural production may choose to stress the proposition that "We are everywhere," which results in emphasizing the most public of spaces, those in which the widest possible sectors of society might be expected to be found. These include political manifestations, schools, offices, the bosom of paradigmatic families, and the streets (the Argentine sociologist Perlongher authored a widely cited examination of homoerotic street culture in São Paulo). Concomitantly, the characters who are shown to be gay-marked will be "normal hearts," to echo the title of Larry Kramer's 1985 canonical play, *The Normal Heart*, rather than individuals who fulfill homophobic stereotypes, a choice that does not necessary prejudice stereotypes, which, as roles chosen to be played by specific social agents, deserve respectful analysis; rather the choice is meant to undermine the homophobic principle of focusing obsessively on stereotypes.

I have analyzed elsewhere (Foster, *Contemporary Argentine Cinema*, 135–49) Américo Ortiz de Zárate's 1986 film *Otra historia de amor* (Another Love Story), which centers on the love affair between two men who work together in an office, one of whom is married. The pathetic consequences for his marriage, when a workplace jealousy leads to his wife being tipped off about the relationship, brings the issue of homoerotic relationships to the center of the social microcosm that is the family. The conduct of the affair within the confines of that other microcosm, the workplace, and the scouring of the streets of Buenos Aires, where such a relationship can only with extreme difficulty be openly manifested. Spaces in which to meet, and the way in which the two loves unite in a long and enthusiastic embrace in the parking lot of Ezeiza International Airport (the major port of entry and departure from the Argentine social text), are a sign that the differences between them that almost lead to one of them accepting a job abroad are paradigmatic examples of the way in which Ortiz de Zárate carries the question of same-sex love into public spaces never previously used for such love in Argentine culture. Although there are scenes filmed in private spaces, the impossibility of actually filming a couple fully making love stamps them with a certain romantic triteness (for example, a bathroom scene in which suddenly the two bodies are filmed through a bottle of thick shampoo), quite in contrast to the scenes of office flirtation or the closing embrace, scenes in which urban Porteño life provides the concrete circumstances of their relationship.

The other gay movie made in Argentina during the period immediately following the return to institutional democracy,[7] Enrique Dawi's 1985 *Adiós, Roberto* (Goodbye, Roberto), is even more insistent in using public space for various levels, real and fantasized, of gay identification. Dawi's film is the first explicit Argentine gay film, and, despite what one would expect in the way of nervous reviews (for example, Jorge Abel Martín in *Tiempo argentino*, as extracted in Manrupe and Portela, 7), it has yet to be matched in terms of its treatment of the psychological dimensions of internalized homophobia and self-loathing. The plot is a very simple one: a man (Marcelo) separates from his wife and small child because of the tensions imposed by his realization that he is gay. Since his resources are limited, a cousin suggests that he move in with a friend of his (Roberto) who lives alone; the latter man turns out also to be gay, and the main interest of the film is the game of seduction that takes place between the two of them and whether they will end up as lovers.

The ending of *Adiós, Roberto* is open, although the title refers to Marcelo's attempt to leave Roberto: Dawi evidently means to eschew a soap-opera happy ending such as Ortiz de Zárate opts for. Such happy endings are certainly positive factors in homoerotic cultural production, because they constitute something like a culminating transgression of the heterosexist affirmation that same-sex love will always end tragically, although, especially if handled in the "but, then, after all," fashion of soap operas, without substantial analysis of circumstance and motivation, they may give the false impression that such transgression is a simple matter and easily achieved. What is important about Dawi's ending is how it confirms that the gay identity of the recently separated husband is still under construction and that, through his faltering experiences, the most important thing is for the audience to contemplate the enormously complex process involved for an individual in the construction of a fully self-accepting homoerotic subjectivity.

The film is of interest for its representation of the relationship between the two men, one an avowed gay and the other still in the process of accepting his sexuality and experiencing frequent bouts of denial, including a crucial scene in which drunkenness will allow the latter to begin to undress the former in an amusing inversion of what one would have expected the path of seduction to take. The film is also of interest because it assumes the legitimacy of two men living together and sleeping together (the opening scene), even if, like *Otra historia de amor*, it can never directly represent a full playing out of homoerotic desire.[8] But most interesting is the representations of Marcelo's internalized homophobia and the way in which these representations are handled in paradigmatic public spaces within the city of Buenos Aires.

There are eleven instances in the film in which Marcelo's attempts to come to terms with his gayness are challenged; in nine cases, the challenge is made by specters from his own subconscious. These specters are the individuals charged with the formation of his subjectivity, and, since it is true that no one is raised gay, they confirm emphatically the priority and privilege, the compulsion, of a heterosexist subjectivity. These individuals are, in a first instance, his parents and, in a second instance, parallel agents of his parents, his priest and his wife. In a third category fall those individuals who, throughout a person's life, are charged with assessing his sexuality and with condemning the ways in which it falls short: friends, fellow workers, circumstantial erotic liaisons (in this case, a prostitute), medical professionals (in this case, a psychiatrist to whom Marcelo turns for help), and, especially significant for the question of public display, persons in general in the street. Dawi brings the scrutiny of all of these authoritarian sexual monitors to bear on Marcelo, and when one realizes that such is in fact not the special case of Marcelo, but rather that all individuals are subject to this same sort of sustained monitoring, the film takes on the added eloquence of the way in which it is able to make explicit what most of us experience unconsciously in the daily social routine of our lives: the discourses that are openly spoken to Marcelo as condemnations of his straying from the path of compulsory heterosexuality are ones that form part of the codes we are all supposed to have internalized to the point of not even knowing they are there.

What is remarkable about Dawi's film is the decision not just to make these codes explicit by embodying them in individuals who appear to harass Marcelo for the turn his life has taken, but that those scenes take place essentially in the public spaces in which Marcelo leads his life. In the main, these individuals appear to Marcelo and attack him verbally and physically without others around him having any idea of the aggression he is experiencing. For example, early in the film Marcelo's stern, authoritarian father appears to him. As he punishes him corporally with intense brutality, he demands to know where he and Marcelo's mother have gone wrong in raising him. The father states, with impeccable logic, that were he still alive, he would die with shame at how his son has turned out. Dawi is playing off expressions like "If your father were still alive, what would he say?" "Just wait until your father finds out about this," "That boy needs a good whipping to set him straight," and the like. The fact that Marcelo's fellow workers are unaware of the violence he is being subjected to right under their noses serves to underscore how the greatest violence prompted by homophobia is that of internalized hatred, the self-loathing occasioned by the discrepancy between the social codes that have been internalized by the individual, and the revised subjectivity he is constructing. At the same time, to internalize this conflict, rather than, say, having those around him be witnesses aware of the attack he suffers, would seem to suggest that, despite the sort of rumors that destroy the marriage of one of the characters in *Otra historia de amor*, not everyone around us is engaged in the project of sexual vigilance.

The other examples of the public spatialization of Marcelo's sexual drama include a neighborhood café, where he imagines that an old friend shows up to excoriate him for having abandoned his roots, which explains how he could end up sleeping with a fairy; his friend will reappear in a subsequent scene. At the other end of the affective scale from his childhood friend is the neighborhood bully, who, after Marcelo has read a newspaper report about the killing of a homosexual, drags him off to an unmarked car (a clear reference to the special forces who openly pursued alleged subversives during the military dictatorship) and tells him that he is going to take care of Marcelo's problem "en nombre de la moral y las buenas costumbres." While he is sitting in an amusement park, Marcelo's mother shows up to sob uncontrollably at his side. And in a culminating scene, Marcelo, who has left Roberto and is staying in a hotel, is visited by the combined forces of his father, his mother, the priest, a former girlfriend, his wife, and a prostitute, who in an earlier delirium has informed him that he is her first client "[que] se ha pasado para el otro lado" (who has gone over to the other side). In the face of what has now become a charging army, Roberto flees the hotel and, in the most important display of public sexuality in the film (since indecency is routinely equated with the public display of sexuality), Marcelo flees down the street, dressed only in his briefs. I do not wish to exaggerate the erotic potential of this scene, except to note that it would be impossible to deny any erotic implications of Marcelo appearing in public undressed to this degree (and this irrespective of any particular attractiveness of the body of the actor playing Marcelo, Carlos Andrés Calvo). Marcelo is, of course, picked up by the police, and as he attempts to call Roberto to come bail him out, he experiences the only positive vision of the film: a crowd of mothers carrying placards urge him to return to Roberto with the slogan "Volvé Roberto" (Come Back, Roberto).

This is the second major political allusion of the film to the neofascist military dictatorships, for one will recognize immediately a reference to the Madres de Plaza de Mayo, who have marched since the late 1970s in demand for information about their disappeared children, many of whom were identified by their military captors as queer (on the basis of the semantic reciprocity of sexually queer and politically subversive) and treated accordingly. Many of these children will necessarily have actually been queer,[9] if for no other reason than by virtue of statistical probabilities. The defense of Roberto by these mothers is by extension an opening, in the context of political redemocratization and institutional change, toward the acceptance of gay children by their parents. Finally, the Madres de Plaza de Mayo effected an important political paradigm shift in Argentina when they became the only organized public protest of tyranny to successfully challenge authoritarian repression. Because of the homophobia of military authoritarianism, by associating Marcelo's ability to see, via this vision, an escape from the homophobic social codes chorused against him by the specters who assemble in his hotel room, Dawi sets up a series of correspondences between the private (his personal drama) and the public (his defense by a crowd of marching mothers) that is especially rich in symbolic meanings.

Adiós, Roberto is valuable for a discussion of the question of a legitimating visibility for homoerotic desire in the urban space of Buenos Aires because it so cleverly spatializes the issues of Marcelo's sexual redefinition, both in terms of being, as a film, a form of public culture and by thematizing the details of his redefinition in a series of interrelated public and private spaces. As the lesbian and gay liberation movement continues to mature in Argentina, bringing with it expanded opportunities for the visibility of homoerotic desire, it will be interesting to see where a production of gay-marked filmmaking will go and what the overall range of the cultural production will be. The fact that the two films mentioned here are both from within three years following the return to constitutional democracy indicates the immediate importance the representation of same-sex desire had for these two directors, as well as the need to offer a specific gay-marked production to Argentine audiences. If one might be a bit surprised that nothing like these two films has been produced in the intervening decade, the fact is that Argentine audiences now have access to a large array of gay and lesbian films from the United States and Europe, which are being shown in movie houses, often as a part of special showings (Derek Jarman's *Edward II* [1991] was included in a 1994 cycle of recent British cinema), or are available through video rental. Exposure to this material, as well as to foreign literature available through translation, will contribute to the continued development of queer visibilities in Buenos Aires.[10]

chapter 5

Buenos Aires: Feminine Space

Mujer en Buenos Aires, pavada de proyecto.[1]
—Martha Mercader, *Solamente ella*

One of the truly distinctive features of Buenos Aires is the considerable degree of freedom women have in identifying for themselves the right to occupy the city in all its urban variety. Of course, women are evident in all cities, and except for the most repressive societies toward women as a social group, in the modern world women move with evident ease through most urban spaces. However, for most of Latin America, a combination of traditional feminine modesty (Mexican *marianismo*[2]) and issues relating to personal security combine to maintain a gender differential with respect to cohabitation in every reach of urban life. We can, of course, leave out of consideration here those spaces that, by mutual agreement or the strong force of as-yet insufficiently questioned convention, are gender specific, such as rest rooms or religious cloisters. Until 1994, the Argentine armed forces were strictly masculine preserves. And, certainly, from a U.S. or western European perspective, many professions remain gender specific, although there is ample evidence that a dozen years of institutional democracy and the sway of anything-goes neoliberalism have combined to bring changes: the chauffeuring of public transportation is no longer strictly masculine, nor is waiting on tables in upscale restaurants, and grade-school teaching is no longer only in the hands of women. Argentina has a long and distinguished tradition of women in the prestige professions, including the presidency of the nation, and therefore the changes taking place affect historically more conservative petite-bourgeoisie and labor-class occupations (unfortunately, for Argentina and Latin America there is no such study as Spain's on gendered spaces in U.S. and western European society).

To be sure, one is not only referring to the workplace, but to the sites of the city as a whole. In terms of the historical roles for women in Latin America, roles which are still evident in many parts of the continent and not just in small towns, public space is for most of the day unavailable to women alone or in groups. The time between sundown and sunset is reserved for lower-class women, whose work demands know no fixed timetable, and for prostitutes. Even today in Guadalajara, Mexico's second largest city, where public transportation ceases around 9:00 P.M., one cannot expect to see women of a certain social standing on the street alone or in public spaces, unless accompanied by a man. There is no need to exaggerate the evidence. The simple fact is that a woman alone in urban spaces and a woman of privileged social standing are not significantly overlapping demographic categories.

Yet, Buenos Aires, and perhaps a handful of other cities, is a significant exception. Even in the case of other Latin American societies where women do have a large measure of social autonomy—São Paulo, Rio de Janeiro, Santiago de Chile—questions of personal security that may affect many men serve to limit access for women altogether. Downtown São Paulo is dangerous for most people at night, and for someone who knows Buenos Aires, the contrast between the hustle and bustle of daylight and the vacancy of many spaces at night is impressive. Virtually no research exists on the round-the-clock utilization of urban space by the populace, much less from a gender-discriminated point of view. But one can begin with the heuristic observation that the metropolis is inhabited differently from one country to the next, and even within countries, in Latin America to understand that research in this area ought to reveal interesting, highly complex, and variegated patterns.

There are at least eight ways in which women enjoy greater public presence in Buenos Aires—and, to a lesser extent, in other Argentine cities (for sociological information on women in Buenos Aires, see the studies by Elizabeth Jelin; García de Fanelli et al.). Women in other Latin American cities may share many of these features, although usually to a lesser extent individually and categorically:

1. While women in Argentina continue to occupy a wide range of working-class positions in factories, hotels, domestic service, and the like, women have an unusually large presence in the professions. Until recent

decades, their participation was notably greater than that of women in the same and similar professions in the United States. Not only does this mean the presence of women in the specific contexts of those professions, such as the courts, the classroom, examining rooms and surgeries, and agencies, but also their presence in the infrastructures and services of such professions, such as bars, cafés, and restaurants; public transportation for the affluent, including planes; and, in general, on the streets in professional dress, coming and going between the sites of their professional occupations. For example, in the U.S. academy prior to the 1970s, male professors shared hallways with female staff (and the former had sole possession of the classroom, while nonfaculty offices were women's domains). In Argentina, since at least a generation before, male and female faculty have shared space with male and female support staff. Class (professors vs. clericals) and sex discrimination coincided in the United States, while class discrimination intersected sex discrimination in Argentina (still today in the United States, even if faculties have become integrated in gender terms, staff spaces continue to be overwhelmingly female). Finally, it should be noted that because of most social classes' general (although not completely optimal) access to a university education in Argentina, professional women are not restricted, as in other countries, to a privileged upper-middle class. Many are first- and second-generation immigrants and children of the working class in general. Salaries, however, continue to be low for academics in Argentina. Career access may be relatively high, but the likelihood of economic self-sufficiency remains low.

2. Women move not only in a range of spaces that virtually matches the extension of the city, but also at all times of the day and night. Buenos Aires is a vibrant city twenty-four hours a day. While subways cease running around 11:00 P.M., bus service is available on a twenty-four-hour basis, and taxis maybe be hailed in the street at any time almost anywhere in the city; on-call vehicles are readily available, and they are fairly inexpensive for someone earning a professional salary. Women are customarily seen traveling alone in public vehicles and on the street. In this sense, a greater participation in public life brings with it a greater participation as a single agent in public spaces.

3. The ostentatious display of prosperity, such as clothing or jewelry, in unsecured public is usually impossible or severely restricted in cities with high crime rates. While there is street crime in Buenos Aires, it has no-

where the same rate of frequency as in, say, New York or São Paulo. The consequence is that when incidents do occur, there is a tendency to treat them in news sources and casual conversation as signs of a veritable crime wave. However, it is also true that increasing property crimes in the past decade in Buenos Aires is changing this perception. The concept of *flaneur*—the gentleman of leisure who is able to stroll the streets of the city and partake vicariously in its delights—must certainly be extended to Porteño women (see Pile, 228–37).

4. Women represent a high incidence of small and large business ownership in Argentina. Reputedly the richest woman in Latin America is Amalia Lacroze Fortabat; her wealth is based on cement holdings, and she claims to have tripled in a decade the value of the company she inherited from her husband. A woman, Ernestina Herrera de Noble, owns the largest circulation daily in Latin America, *Clarín*. The phenomenon of the boutique owned by an upper-middle-class woman seeking an outlet for her time and energies is almost an Argentine cultural institution.

5. Women customarily retain their maiden names for professional purposes, a fact that underscores their individual social agency.

6. There is a remarkable incidence of women in the cultural industry in Argentina. Of course, women are prominent in areas of cultural production that historically have provided employment for them, such as acting, singing, and writing on "women's themes." However, in addition to women who write professionally as academics, the bibliography of women's literature in Argentina is exceptionally large.[3] Moreover, women are involved in filmmaking, television, and theater beyond the conventional role of actresses. The vast journalistic enterprise in Argentina—newspapers, magazines, and television—has long provided equal opportunity for women, and Argentina has a long tradition of magazines marketed for women.[4] Many Argentine women authors, principally novelists, have achieved an international reputation,[5] and Griselda Gambaro is arguably the most important woman dramatist working today in Latin America.

7. The Argentine woman is legendary for her strength of character. While the perception of this strength may be expressed in negative terms, such that the Argentine woman is reputed to be too strong and aggressive, unfeminine, defiant, and confrontational, popular knowledge in Latin America accords her a unique status. Not even the alleged sexual freedom of Brazilian women or the socialist rights of Cuban women come close to

matching the mystique of the assertive Argentine woman. This is, of course, a stereotype, and often a vicious one, but this sort of character reputation does have significant value in the perhaps oblique way in which it identifies a level of individual social agency Argentine women possess that is notably weaker elsewhere in Latin America.

8. The features enumerated to this point have the cumulative effect of providing Argentine women with a range of public forums not enjoyed elsewhere on the continent. The example of the Madres de Plaza de Mayo, who challenged the silence surrounding the disappeared, which was imposed by the military dictatorship, and who fostered an array of similar women's protest movements throughout Latin America, is especially noteworthy in this regard. Few will be impressed by the fact that Argentina has had a woman president, because of the circumstances of her political ascendancy and the dissolution of her government by military coup, which she seemed almost to encourage. Nevertheless, the political presence of women has been vigorous since the early part of the century—a clear extension of the overall professionalization of women in the country (concerning feminism in Argentina, see Calvera; Roulet; Camusso; Carlson).

Feminist geography has made much of how the city is necessarily gendered. Most societies invest gender issues with such enormously overdetermined meanings that it is impossible to believe that the city and its different spaces would not participate profoundly in structures of omnipresent gender overdetermination in public as well as private life (Spain; Massey 1994). A feminist analysis of urban space necessarily goes beyond a codification of what spaces are used by men and women and how they are used, and how different spaces and different uses correspond to variables of social class. Of greater interest, at least as far as a specifically cultural analysis goes, is how gender varies in the interpretation of the ideological meaning of different spaces. For example, is it true that churches are essentially women's spaces (with men who frequent them concomitantly feminized to one degree or another)? Most of them have a prominent public positioning in Latin America (on main streets, on main plazas, near other official buildings), and many have their interiors open to view from the street or plaza. In fact, some churches may be continuous with the street or plaza in ways that would be repugnant to sober American Protestantism. Is it true that gay men view concentrations of other men in public places (certain streets and street corners, buses and subway trains, cafés, bookstores, perhaps even sporting events) as opportunities for cruising new contacts? By the same token, straight men view the same concentrations as theatrical opportunities to engage in a confirmatory display of their masculinity through how they interact with other men or how they act toward women in the company of other men. Both men and women engage in the public judgment of a man's masculinity through a vast inventory of fixed minidramas that have yet to be fully inventoried and taken apart for purposes of analyzing their operational components.

I would like to examine a range of cultural production in order to see some of the ways in which consciously artistic texts display, in both a figurative and literal, theatrical sense interpretations by Argentine, specifically Buenos Aires, women, the artists themselves as much as their characters, of their participation in urban spaces. In order to go beyond the problematical underdifferentiated category of "woman," I will be specifically interested in those cultural products that refer in whole or part to lesbians. By doing so, I do not mean to juxtapose an underdifferentiated category of "lesbian" to an underdifferentiated category of "woman." Rather, I will use "lesbian" in the radical sense of nonstraight, a queer conceptual strategy that is meant to perturb the problematic generalization of "woman" as it is used in irreflective social parlance.

One will, however, wish to speak of lesbians as such, in the narrowly construed sense of those women (or "women," should one wish to subscribe to Wittig's famous formulation that "lesbians are not women" [8o]) who either self-identify as lesbians or who meet some sort of principled profile of what might constitute a social group made up of lesbians (obviously, this does not mean equating feminism with lesbianism, although one would assume that lesbianism is, by definition of its opposition to a masculinist patriarchy, potentially a strong ally of feminism). This is not the place to survey feminism in Argentina (see material on Argentina in *Women, Culture, and Politics*); although suffice it to say that the existence of feminist collectives like La Casa de las Lunas, *Feminaria*, the feminist journal edited by Lea Fletcher since 1988, the feminist studies program out of the psychology department at the Universidad de Buenos Aires, plus a host of lesbian activist organizations, are indexes of formalized concerns in that country and, especially, its national capital. Rather, what I wish to do here is refer to a representative range of cultural products that must figure

A press member interviewing Claudina Marek and Ilse Fuskova, the authors of *Amor de mujeres: El lesbianismo en la Argentina, hoy.*

prominently in whatever would be a history of feminism in Argentina and the record of women's, feminist, and lesbian culture in Buenos Aires, especially as it relates to the urban situation of women.

To the best of my knowledge, the only scholarly study on lesbianism in a Latin American society is Luíz Mott's *O lesbianismo no Brasil* (Lesbianism in Brazil). But Fuskova and Marek's documentary, *Amor de mujeres: El lesbianismo en la Argentina, hoy* (Love of Women: Lesbianism in Argentina Today) is the first book-length work relating to Argentina and the first work in which women recount their own experiences. The full author statement reads: Ilse Fuskova en diálogo con Silvia Schmid. Claudina Marek. This is important because the book is composed of a long dialogue between Fuskova and Schmid, while approximately the last fourth is Marek's independent text.

Fuskova and Marek are partners, and the selection of photographs includes material relating to the officialization of their union in the Iglesia de la Comunidad Metropolitana in June 1992. As a couple they have participated in numerous lesbian events and programs in Argentina, in the United States, and in various countries in Europe, and their book is unquestionably the best statement of "out and proud" that has come from Argentina. Argentina has seen considerable struggle and frustrating set-backs surrounding the attempt to get a lesbian and gay movement going since the return to constitutional democracy in the mid-1980s (see Brown's excellent survey). One of the urgent goals of such a movement is to engage a public debate over visibility for nonheterosexual preference in the country. The proposal to make the presence known of lesbians and gays in the urban space of Buenos Aires and other cities has been a crucial strategy for the legitimation of same-sex desire by naturalizing it through an open discourse. Certainly, from a feminist perspective—and it is important to underscore how many Argentine feminists do not support lesbian activism—visibility as women does not just mean a physical presence. Women are clearly physically evident in urban society. The point, however, as in the case of the Madres de Plaza de Mayo, is to find ways in which women are in evidence in actions and activities that do not correspond with, and indeed significantly disrupt, traditional gender role assignments (see Calvera, 101–7, on the Madres as part of a feminist tradition). Feminist activism accomplishes this to a large degree, but lesbian activism involves a geometrically greater defiance of conventional presence.

It is clear from the material included in this book that Fuskova and Marek are committed to the international movement of homoerotic liberation. They have little interest in analyzing the patterns of resistance to such a movement, either as part of the patterns of homophobia in Argentina, which have multiple origins, or as a way of understanding homoeroticism in ways that may not fit comfortably into the context of the international movement (that is, the way in which homoeroticism in Latin America may resist a correlation with identity politics). Clearly, the authors and the movement they represent derive from the internationalist climate in contemporary Argentina (one that intersects in problematic ways with a nationalist/anti-American and anti-European climate). For now, this may be the only effective way to promote a gay and lesbian agenda, particularly as concerns the forums for visibility provided by the current neoliberal economic process: an expanding television market; the massive importation of foreign films, many of which involve revisions of patriarchal ideologies; popular press magazines, which have enormous currency in Argentina; and fiction (regrettably, recent national theater has yet to offer any important examples, aside from a series of local versions of American gay theater [Foster, "Teatro norteamericano"]).

Fuskova's and Marek's separate documents provide a characterization of a lesbian coming-of-age in Argentine society. In addition to discussing their immigrant backgrounds (German and Czech, respectively), they also focus on their respective marriages and motherhoods. It is an important detail that they both enjoy good relations with their children and former husbands. The Fuskova and Schmid dialogue is very solidly structured, and it is apparent that they agreed beforehand on the essential topics to be covered. In addition to exploring the crucial points of lesbian identity and its construction as a refutation of the patriarchy, they explore, more importantly, lesbianism in the context of Latin America and Argentina. No attempt is made to attenuate the ways in which lesbianism is a forthright challenge to the patriarchy—no euphemisms, no compromise with the squeamishness and the defensive smugness of so much of the media in Argentina. The fact that the book was published by Planeta, one of the major publishing houses in Argentina at this time, and part of an international consortium, lends the book all of the legitimacy and mainstreaming that comes from being widely distributed and prominently displayed.

Amor de mujeres is not simply a declaration of principles, a testimonial of individuals involved in a social and political movement. Fuskova is a published poet. *Luna de vereda* was published in 1986 with Nelda Guixé and *Bailadora de sueños* in 1988 with Sabina Bertz, and various selections are reproduced in the book. Fuskova and Marek have used the book to enhance the public visibility of lesbianism. Not only do they themselves have considerable notoriety in their neighborhood, but their book, which after its publication was displayed in Buenos Aires's many bookstores, increased their television exposure, which is the greatest open forum now available for urban culture in Buenos Aires. This experience has not always been positive for them, and the assertive insertion of homoerotic desire into the public arena in Buenos Aires has clashed with a still dominantly patriarchal society.

Twenty years ago, I wrote about Absatz as part of a group of Argentine women authors—most of whom were publishing for the first time—who ran afoul of censorship as exercised by the authoritarian military government of the day (Foster, "Demythification of Buenos Aires"). All of these women have gone on to write major works, although Absatz has not, perhaps, had the same sustained accomplishments of some of the others. However, with *¿Dónde estás, amor de mi vida, que no te puedo encontrar?* (Where Are You, My Love? I Can't Find You), she has produced quite an interesting novel. The central idea is a call-in radio show dedicated to the lonely and loveless/lovelorn of the Buenos Aires night that often seems longer and more interesting than the day. Radio, both AM and FM, continues in Argentina to be one of the city's most vital cultural products. And, because the city has an abundant nightlife, there is extensive programming devoted to nocturnal listeners, programs with both a musical and a talk-show format. Radio devoted to cultural and political discussion is very much in evidence, especially in the morning hours, and, of course, there is a large measure of American music and American-style programming. Radio is an integral part of urban life, and issues related to urban life, both indirectly (songs whose lyrics discuss life in and of the city) and directly (conversations about the details of urban life), are constantly available to the listener.

Octavio runs the show, and Liliana (more often, in Argentine style, identified by her last name, Milman), who is a professional psychologist, provides interpretive support. Individuals call in with their frustrations and problems in finding a companion, and Octavio and Liliana do their best to advise them, to assuage their solitude, and to help them, in their acts of oral expression/therapy, to find the affective/emotional/sexual companionship they have, on their own, been able to declare as needing. The novel is as much about Octavio as it is about Liliana. Liliana's Jewish mother, who loses her apartment as the result of a bureaucratic mistake that declares her dead and cuts off her retirement pension, goes to live with her. Their two stories become intertwined, which ultimately tips the novel toward the women's stories and their experiences as women on their own in the city:

> A cierta hora de la noche Liliana dejó de pelear. No podía leer, no podía dormir, no podía tolerar lo que sentía. Se quedó echada en la cama, mirando la oscuridad detrás de su ventana. A cierta hora la sensatez la abandonó y se dejó ir por donde la oscuridad la llevara. Su mente circuló entonces por caminos extraños, rara filosofía y pensamientos estúpidos. En algún momento comenzó a clarear—a pesar de todo—entonces se vistió. Se lavó los dientes evitando el espejo, no

quería ver. Sin pensarlo demasiado sacó un abrigo y salió a la calle. Se detuvo en la puerta, herida por la luz y el aire helado. Se puso anteojos oscuros y bajó a la vereda. Le pareció que había pasado meses metida en su casa, y sólo había sido una noche de insomnio. Una noche eterna. La calle estaba desierta. El olor del aire todavía intacto. En el silencio de la madrugada los árboles comenzaban a reverdecer a pesar del frío, con extraordinaria puntualidad. Silencio. Un auto azul cruzó a lo lejos, por Callao, un chico y una chica vestidos de negro pasaron en silencio con las cabezas rapadas.

Sábado muy temprano. ¿Qué hacía ella en la calle? Sobrevivía, nada más. Cruzó la plaza en diagonal: los jacarandaes florecían descaradamente, a pesar del frío. Entró en la confitería que encontró abierta y pidió café. (256–57)[6]

The subtitle of *¿Dónde estás?* is *Sobre una idea de Juan José Jusid* (Based on an Idea by Juan José Jusid). Jusid is a well-known film director, but in this case his function is as the director of a television series of the same title and nature for which Absatz has written the scripts. In a typical Argentine postmodern, neoliberalist fashion in which genres are mixed back and forth, Absatz's novel is based on her scripts for the television show about a radio show, and the pacing of the narrative segments reveals very clearly their origin in the blocks that are defined by the sponsor-induced way of "reading" television narratives.

The salient characteristic of the various intertwined plotlines of Absatz's novel is the imperative for individuals to articulate and then to act upon their own personal sentimental/amorous/erotic agenda, thereby transcending the multiple layers of repressive silence that can be traced back to the dominant hegemonic structure of authoritarian-imposed silence in Argentine culture. In a certain sense, this is an Argentine version of "take back the night," in which the night is the realm of individual sexual expression freed from the overwhelming codes of decency, discretion, reserve, silence, and even self-castration imposed by the public discourse of eroticism in Argentina (the cover of the novel represents the Buenos Aires nighttime skyline).

Except for the stories of agents of the self-serving hegemony, all of the characters in Absatz's novel enjoy a happy ending to their quest. However, the happy ending in this case has nothing to do with the ideological nonsense of Hollywood stories, but rather with the intelligent working out of individual narratives that provides for the successful evasion of the strategies of silence. The dual context of the night and radio allows for a level of personal expression that would not, under the daylight aegis of self-protection, allow for the full play of desire. Put simply, Absatz's characters are able to express their desire in a way that is contrary to the prevalent erotic discourses of Argentine sociocultural history.

However, there is a significant gap in Absatz's record of contemporary Buenos Aires, one that bears directly on the concerns of this chapter. I do not know if it is her own decorum, the sense of propriety of the program's sponsors from which her text derives, or the "auteurial" impositions of Jusid; but, homoerotic desire, of either women or men, is nowhere recorded in this narrative, except for a very passing reference to one of Liliana's private patients who bores her because of his inability to confront his own homoerotic desire. This gap is truly notable, given the degree to which, by contrast with virtually all the rest of Latin America, Buenos Aires manifests a form of public discourse about homoeroticism that is changing the erotic landscape, if for no other reason than as part of vigorous public repudiations of social authoritarianism, whether understood as only part of past military dictatorships or as an abiding national "problem." No matter how one interprets the history of this discourse vis-à-vis masculinist authoritarianism, in Buenos Aires at least, there can be little doubt that gay and lesbian—and even something that can be called oppositionally queer—culture enjoys a measure of prominence within the public discourse of Argentine society. Indeed, the very proposition of an on-the-air discussion of individual sentimental and erotic needs (straight ones, of course), does, to a certain limited degree, break with the patriarchal criterion of modesty and decorum. For several of those who call in, to discover themselves speaking openly on the air what previously they had never shared with anyone in private, is initially very embarrassing. Embarrassment—and its counterpart, shame—whether spontaneous or provoked by another, is surely a control mechanism of a dominant sexual ideology.

Yet *¿Dónde estás?* is steadfastly heterosexist: men seek women and women seek men; men are successful with women and women are successful with men. But that is the extent of it. What about the benchmark 10 percent of Buenos Aires society—almost a million individuals—whose construction of desire may be homoerotic? Can they call Octavio and Liliana?

Can they find each other? Can they subsequently call back in to thank the program's sponsors for their brilliant social contribution? Until the question *¿Dónde estás, amor de mi vida?* refers to these individuals, a revision of the authoritarian, repressive, sexist, and heterosexist social text will remain painfully incomplete.

Without a doubt, the most notorious figure in Argentine sociocultural history is Eva Duarte de Perón (1919–1952), popularly known as Evita. The details of Evita's life are the stuff of legend and of an immense popular-culture production. Many of these details are of common knowledge, especially the rags-to-riches, impoverished provincial girl trying to make it as an actress in the big city who becomes the activist wife of a populist president (in which role she lobbied successfully for the female vote in 1947), and whose trajectory of life was abruptly cut off by cancer. Evita's life has been debated in Argentina and internationally with the release in late 1996 of Alan Parker's film, based on the Rice-Webber rock opera hit of the 1980s. Eva Perón's deviation from traditional female roles in Argentina was publicly visible. She was determined from the start not to be a conventional first lady, and she was fully aware that, even if she wanted to, she could not, due to the massive rejection of her by the oligarchy from which Argentine presidents and their wives were historically drawn (Argentina's earlier populist president, Hipólito Yrigoyen, 1916–22, 1928–30, was unmarried, and, therefore, there was never any question of an unsuitable first lady). Perón put her unconventionality and her open defiance of administrative, bureaucratic, and diplomatic custom on public display, thereby making her the first modern Argentine woman to invest Buenos Aires and, indeed, the entire country, with a strong feminine presence.

Most Argentine women with their own social agency do not use their husband's name. But, because Eva was a bastard, she may have renounced the Duarte of her absent father for the Perón of the one male authority figure she finally identified with, no matter how much the extent of that identity may be debated. Nonetheless, Eva Perón always claimed she was only doing her husband's bidding. From this point of view, it would be reasonable for her to have suppressed her own name. However, both Peronista hagiography and Latin American feminism tend now to underscore Evita's own social agency. In fact, identifying her as Evita underscores her individuality separate from her husband's persona. Thus, one cannot escape the simple fact that, while Perón has pretty much become a historical fossil of Argentine political history (Carlos Menem, the current Argentine president, has little need to evoke his name), there continues to be an abundant cultural production relating to Eva Perón.

Evita's invasion of public spaces and her aggressive visibility had to do both with her attempts to affirm her rightful place as the nation's first lady (for example, her famous appearances at the Teatro Colón opera house, her cross-country train trips, her radio broadcasts, and even her inaugural use of television), as well as to ensure that her personal imprint was stamped on every one of the specific projects associated with her name. A very real effect of Evita's visibility was an overarching communication between regions and sectors of the country that had not, until her frenetic activity, had much interaction. Hence, the enormous press coverage she made sure attended her every move in the Fundación Eva Perón, where she set out to deal with the demands of the poor and the marginal. The historical record may be less than adequate in regard to the direct instigation by Eva Duarte of the famous march in Buenos Aires on October 17, 1945, which demanded the release of Gen. Juan Domingo Perón, imprisoned by fellow officers in an attempt to break the political power he had accrued for himself in the turbulent early 1940s. When Perón was released, he married Evita and went on to run successfully for election as president. The now-ensconced Peronista establishment was free to write history however it chose. Whether Evita was primarily responsible for the October 17 march or not is, from the perspective of cultural symbolism, irrelevant, since both the popular imagination and most of the cultural production of Evita has made much of her role in freeing Perón. For the purpose of this discussion, the march, either as history or as symbol, marks an enormous public urban presence of a woman who, during her life and after her death, dominated her urban space and invited other women to do so as well, as women were drawn literally and symbolically toward Buenos Aires under the aegis of Peronista political and social programs. Indeed, when one examines the newspapers and magazines of the period, Evita seems to be virtually omnipresent, everywhere at once in every nook and cranny of Buenos Aires. The first television transmissions in Argentina on October 17, 1951, were images of the president's wife as part of a Peronista political act (Sirven). Eva as a socially symbolic figure must also be understood in "geosemantic" terms. She sought, even when it was not part of a conscious project, to provide a unity through her physical presence to a country founded on conceptual divisions such as the "civilization" versus "barbarism" that Sarmiento left as an abiding ideological legacy to Argentina in his mid-nineteenth-century interpretive writings.

Three recent narratives deal with the figure of Evita; two of them, a novel by Abel Posse and a biography by Alicia Dujovne Ortiz, include abundant material on Evita's public presence, along with the usual iconic photographs in which her image usually has the city or some institution of the city as a backdrop. Tomás Martínez's novel is less on Evita as a human being than it is on the fate of her embalmed body after the death of Perón. This body, which was the centerpiece for a vast public funeral and was then on public display at the headquarters of the CGT (Confederación General de Trabajo) in Buenos Aires until the overthrow of Perón in 1955, literally crisscrossed the city in an attempt by the military government to keep it from being snatched by Peronista sympathizers. The body was finally hidden in a Milan cemetery before it was returned to the exiled Perón in Madrid and then brought back to Argentina and buried in the oligarchic city of the dead, La Recoleta. This mausoleum has become a site of public veneration in the heart of one of the city's most upper-class areas. Undeniably, Eva Perón was during her life, and has become in death, the most prominent woman associated with the city of Buenos Aires.[7]

Abel Posse's *La pasión según Eva* (The Passion According to Eva) is an account of Evita's last year of life as culled from documentary sources. Posse, not surprisingly, although rather disappointingly, provides an essentially flattering portrait of Evita, one that does little to either go to the core of her subjectivity or to place her in any nonsuperficial way in sociohistorical coordinates. The book is interesting, but no significant new insights are provided beyond those of Posse's cited documentary sources. Although there are sections that would seem to cast Evita in a harsh light, they in reality only enhance the fundamentally soap-opera quality of Posse's narrative.

One assumes that Posse's book is made possible—indeed, perhaps even necessary—by the new face of Peronismo in Argentina. Carlos Menem has been widely recognized, and widely denounced, for having updated Peronismo, most specifically by eliminating the imperative social conflict (often interpreted as social resentment), trade-union domination, and welfare bureaucracy. For many, this means that there is nothing Peronista (or Justicialista) left in Peronismo, except perhaps for the lower-middle-class and immigrant social origins of its principal exponents, and that it constitutes nothing more than an appropriation of liberalism.

What all of this has meant is a radical revision of the icons of Peronismo. It is probably unnecessary to determine if this radical revision was needed to enable Menem's unique definition of Peronismo or whether that uniqueness has rendered many of the icons meaningless or incoherent. One such icon is that of Evita. Surely Evita remains as one of the most potent icons of Peronismo, and there are examples everywhere of the government's support of her abiding importance for the majority of Argentines. Nevertheless, when one recalls the potent uses of her symbolism in the context of the relegitimation of Peronismo in the early 1970s and the return of Perón in 1973, current images of Evita are pale indeed.

Pasión covers all of the standard narrative territory of the Evita legend, including her domination of public space and discourse. It quickly becomes clear that Posse, who never portrays Perón as anything but an oafish buffoon, is striving to reestablish the centrality of Evita in an Argentina beset by more social problems in its current democratic guise than during the military tyranny. By returning to the crucial disjunction, current in the halcyon days of left-wing guerrilla movements, between Perón and Evita, between fascism and social activism, between authoritarianism and humanitarianism, Posse clearly means for his novel to be a major voice, at a time when contemporary Argentine fiction is fashionably "postmodernist," in reconfirming an activist, engaged status for national cultural production. Yet it is questionable whether this saccharine novel, which is of undeniable archeological interest, will exercise a definitive influence. One recalls that the Paraguayan novelist Augusto Roa Bastos was able, with his 1974 *Yo el supremo* (*I the Supreme*), to construct an interpretation of a national icon that was neither mythificational nor defamatory, and one wishes that Posse had been able to accomplish a similar feat with *Pasión*.

The year 1995 was the fiftieth anniversary of the Peronista movement, which is usually dated from the October 17, 1945, march. Already, several books have been published to mark this anniversary, and there was a large exposition of Juan Domingo and Eva memorabilia, Los Cincuenta Años del Peronismo (Fifty Years of Peronism), in October 1995 in a specially prepared space at the Centro Cultural San Martín in downtown Buenos Aires. One could hardly expect much more from yet one more book, no matter how many iconic photographs it includes and how many documentary sources were, according to the bibliography, consulted.

Yet Alicia Dujovne Ortiz's *Eva Perón: La biografía* richly deserves the praise of the Paraguayan novelist Augusto Roa Bastos as "the definitive book." Dujovne Ortiz, who originally published her book in French (*Eva Perón: La madonne des sans-chemise* [Eva Perón: The Shirtless Madonna]), is the daughter of a famous leftist Jewish intellectual (León Dujovne) and the niece of the important social essayist Raúl Scalabrini Ortiz, whose *El hombre que está solo y espera* (The Man Who Stands Alone and Waits) posits another important Argentine urban figure and invests with symbolic importance the downtown street corner of Corrientes and Esmeralda (Foster, *Social Realism*, 50–59). *Eva Perón* is in many ways a straightforward documentary biography. However, it is unique in several regards. Dujovne Ortiz comes to the conclusion that, had Evita lived, she would have ended up affiliating herself with the left, which explains why someone of the author's background could be interested in writing about Perón in the first place. Dujovne also makes it clear that, fifty years after the inaugural moves of Peronismo, moves that took place on a Buenos Aires converted into a massive stage for a definitive populist drama, and over forty years since the death of Evita, one can no longer invest in the myths either of Eva Duarte as a whore or of Evita Perón as a saint. The novelist, rather, is interested in examining Eva Perón as a woman. Toward this end, she rehearses, and reinterprets, much of the canonical knowledge about Evita, but her emphasis is always on holding in view the agenda of a woman's history.

There are many passages in the book that recount Eva's invasion of the masculine spaces of the city, and her story is particularly fascinating in the juxtaposition between the ways in which she suffered in Buenos Aires as a barely talented starlet from the sticks and how she triumphed in many of the same venues in her performance as La Sra. de Perón. Evita's visibility in the public spaces and in her often stormy expropriation of male privilege in the halls of government and allied spheres is the main point of her story, as is made evident over and over again by the photographs that accompany the books about her. There is almost a chaotic enumeration surrounding the inventory of her activities, which indiscriminately mix appearances that are customarily associated with the wife of the president (schools, hospitals) and those that usually exclude feminist intervention (factories, labor unions, sports clubs, not to mention the forums for political speechmaking):

> Le ahorraremos al lector las idas y venidas de Evita como ferviente visitadora de fábricas, escuelas, hospitales, sindicatos, clubes deportivos y culturales. Tenía una energía sobrehumana. Digamos solamente que podríamos llenar estas páginas con la sola descripción de dichas actividades. Autores como Marysa Navarro [author of the most important feminist interpretation of Evita], Fermín Chávez y tantos otros se han tomado el trabajo de seguirla día por día. Hemos preferido dejar esa asombrosa cantidad de inauguraciones, presentaciones, manifestaciones y viajes como telón de fondo, para concentrarnos en la visión de una mujer que crece, se desarrolla, se afirma . . . y pronuncia discursos. (155–56)[8]

Taking her cue from the American anthropologist Julie Taylor's widely influential work on Eva Perón under the aegis of the socially symbolic, Dujovne Ortiz is interested in providing as balanced and detailed a consideration of the complexities of her character as is possible. Although she does seem at times to fall under the sway of the soap-opera motifs that have always provided the master narratives of Evita's life (for example, "No llores por mí Argentina" [Don't cry for me, Argentina]), Dujovne Ortiz is primarily concerned with what one can call the "Rashomon effect": the belief that historical truth is elusive if not nonexistent, and that the real task of the narrator is to provide a mosaic of possible meanings that constitute the effect of an ever-shifting reality. The result is a book of highly original observation and at times brilliant insight, particularly when the author avails herself of a securely assimilated range of feminist ideological principles that other writers have been unable to manifest. This is particularly apparent in two dominant subthemes: (1) the analysis of the construction of Evita's persona through dress, a dress that was meant for public display in both state and Fundación events; and (2) the analysis of a woman's body always in delicate health, a body on which her final cancer was always prefigured by that condition. The latter demands a nonpublic display of Evita, since hiding her health from the public was deemed necessary to preserve her power with the populace and to ensure her continued dominance of urban space; hiding Evita's health from herself later became necessary, it was thought, because she would be unable to handle the withdrawal from public display her imminent death constituted.

The last great icon of Evita is of her riding in the motorcade with her husband for the swearing-in ceremony for his second term. She received the accolades of the masses as she stood at Juan Domingo Perón's side, dressed, as usual, in the best clothes money could buy. However, few knew that Evita was only able to withstand the pain of the ride because she was strapped to a contraption that supported a body unable to stand on its own. This was in June 1952, and Evita died the next month; the motorcade was her last appearance in the streets of the city she had mastered so well. In the context of the masculinist principles of control, exemplified by Perón as the Macho Triumphant, the biographer's analysis of Evita's corporeal presence is particularly eloquent and effective:[9]

> Perón debía recorrer el trayecto entre la Residencia y el Congreso en un automóvil descubierto. Eva apenas podía levantarse. Pero para ese último papel, no quiso aparecer sentada junto a un Perón de pie. Entonces le aumentaron la dosis de morfina y le fabricaron un soporte de yeso donde logró permanecer parada. El amplio abrigo de piel ocultaba el cinturón con que la habían atado al vidrio de adelante. La gente decía que también le habían enyesado la manga derecha porque, débil como estaba, a todo lo largo del trayecto fue saludando al pueblo sin bajar el brazo. (279)[10]

Martínez's *Santa Evita: Novela* was published a week before the forty-third anniversary of Eva Perón's death; with it, Martínez complements his 1985 *La novela de Perón* (The Novel of Perón) and Posse's *La pasión según Eva.* Where the latter is a historical novel of some interest, but basically an example of official hagiography, *Santa Evita* is a liquidation of the master narrative of a historical figure who became a dominant cultural icon of an entire nation. Martínez writes from the proposition that Perón, in contracting the embalming of Evita's body (a still uncommon practice in Catholic Argentina) in order to use it as a political symbol, had no idea that he was burdening himself and Argentina with an albatross of monumental proportions. At the end of the novel, an Argentine president is quoted as supposedly having said, "Un presidente de la república me dijo: 'Ese cadáver somos todos nosotros. Es el país'" (387).[11]

Until its eventual burial in a specially equipped crypt in Buenos Aires twenty years later, Evita's body became an obsession, both for those who wished to recover it and use it to reinforce a Peronismo identified with Eva

Perón and for successive military regimes that were as much appalled by the legacy of the woman as they were by the fear that her body would be recovered and so used. As a result, the military was forced to retain possession of the body and to put in motion a series of stratagems to retain its control, keeping anyone else from knowing its whereabouts, and to preserve it intact. The latter concern was as much a fascination on the part of some of its custodians as it was a determination, driven by conservative Catholic commitments, to respect the dead (which apparently is why the body was never simply cremated). There was also the possibility of massive social unrest if it was ever discovered that Evita's body had been defiled.

The story of the consequences of these circumstances is truly gruesome. Martínez assembles a cast of freakish individuals in a carnival show of disappearing caskets that is only believable because the reader accepts the proposition that historical reality is stranger than the strangest fiction. Although the beginning of *Santa Evita* reads like the script for one of the bad soap operas the young actress worked in, it is not about the curious story of the provincial Cinderella becoming the richest and most powerful political woman of Latin American history and the dominatrix of Buenos Aires. Rather, the interest of the novel, through the fetishization of the feminine body (sick, wounded, punished), hinges on how the story of her body is the story of Argentina, its history of authoritarian rule, fierce class conflict, profoundly fissured cultural alliances, and a quality of morbid melancholy of which the Evita legend is only one striking example:

> Cada quien construye el mito del cuerpo como quiere, lee el cuerpo de Evita con las declinaciones de su mirada. Ella puede ser todo. En la Argentina es todavía la Cenicienta de las telenovelas, la nostalgia de haber sido lo que nunca fuimos, la mujer del látigo, la madre celestial. Afuera es el poder, la muerta joven, la hiena compasiva que desde los balcones del más allá declama: "No llores por mí, Argentina." (203)[12]

It is significant that in contrast to Posse's novel, Martínez does not strive for documentary validation. There is no reason to attribute any historical accuracy to the documents that exist; the memory of sources is a narrative generator beyond control or account; and institutional ruptures either destroy archives or corrupt them. Consequently, the narrator evokes nonexistent sources (for example, a grotesque polygraph name, Aldo Cifuentes), and his historical account has little to do with what one finds in "professional" sources (for example, Evita's putative role in the October 17, 1945, release of Perón from prison). There are some strategic typos (the sinister Spanish embalmer Ara appears alternately as Pedro and as José— bibliographies list his strange memoir under Pedro), and unlike almost every other book published on Eva, this one contains no photographs to give the sense of the "real" person.

The title of Martínez's novel is certainly perverse. It captures one cluster of beliefs concerning the figure of Eva Perón, beliefs that led to the request

Cover of Tomás Eloy Martínez's novel *Santa Evita*. Courtesy of Grupo Editorial Planeta.

(indeed, the demand) that the Catholic church canonize her; but here the reference is not to the veneration of a saintly miracle worker by her followers. One could well argue that the veneration of saints and their relics is a form of fetishism and that it has specific erotic dimensions (see Foster, *Textual Sexualities*, on the importance of Eva Perón for Argentine gay culture). Here, men who are part of the dictatorship's effort to dismantle the Peronista state become involved in a necrophilic obsession with the woman's embalmed body, and it is this obsession, which becomes indistinguishable from the veneration of a relic, to which the title refers.

Part of the neoliberal economic process in Argentina during the last five years has been a slavish imitation of forms of American packaging, and Martínez's novel slyly exploits the best-seller look: a glossy cover with a garish image of St. Evita looking like a third-rate Franciscanized Madonna dressed as perhaps the singer might envision her, and the title is in the large-letter embossed format that characterizes airport fiction. *Santa Evita* has been a best-seller because it is a brilliant novel. In the context of a new millenarian Peronista government, which has no use beyond superficial evocations of the legend of Eva Perón, it will be interesting to see what cultural resonances this novel provokes and whether it is indeed possible to liquidate the master narrative of Eva Perón or to recycle it for further popular cultural purposes.

Eva Perón's funeral in July 1952.

Left: Eva Perón speaking to the masses from the Casa Rosada balcony.

Middle: Eva Perón inaugurating a neighborhood built for the working people of Buenos Aries.

Bottom: Eva Perón inaugurating a Little League soccer tournament.

Eva Perón's cover photograph from her autobiography published in 1951.

One subtheme of Martínez's novel is the pilgrimage of Evita's body through the streets of Buenos Aires, like some sort of Wandering Jew or Flying Dutchman.[13] This clandestine voyage is as complex as Evita's public spectacle in life, and it is part of the truly fantastic nature of her story:

> En esos días, la Difunta regresó a la errancia que le causaba tanto daño: de uno a otro camión, en calles que nunca eran las mismas. La desplazaban al azar por la ciudad lisa, interminable: la ciudad sin trama ni pliegues. (274)[14]

Tulio Demicheli's 1987 docudrama, *El misterio Eva Perón* (The Eva Perón Mystery), in addition to being built around interviews with individuals associated with Evita and archival footage, contains interspersed reenactments of the futile attempts to hide her embalmed body somewhere in the city. While the reenactments of these events fractures the straight documentary value of the film, the visually presented story can be seen as a graphic, if artistically limited, complement to Martínez's novel.

There is perhaps no more universal feminine voice associated with Buenos Aires than that of María Elena Walsh, the author of some of the best children's stories and poetry to come from Argentina (she has recorded many of these poems to her own musical accompaniment) and a widely published "adult" poet as well. Walsh's adult poetry has only recently begun to be studied for its sociopolitical and feminist dimensions, and a queer reading of her interpretation of sexual identity is fully in order. Walsh's song "El País de Nomeacuerdo," which she sings as background music for Luis Puenzo's 1985 Oscar-winning *Historia oficial* (Official Story), is an example of her compositions that, while they may be attractive to children, also contain an adult message that transcends the interpretational horizons of the ostensible primary audience.

Walsh has also written narrative fiction, as well as theater, and is particularly skillful at embedding adult messages in a discourse ostensibly designed for children. I wish to refer here to her *Novios de antaño* (Sweethearts of Yesteryear), which was a best-seller in the early part of the decade. My interest in the novel is twofold. In the first place, it is the story of an English immigrant family that settles in the outskirts of Buenos Aires around the turn of the century. This family joins thousands of other new immigrant families in Buenos Aires and the littoral area during the period extending roughly between 1880–1930. It is a mass immigration every bit as vast as that of the United States during the same period, and it changes Argentine society, especially Buenos Aires, in the same profound ways. By the turn of the century, Buenos Aires will have begun to become increasingly a society of first-generation immigrants and their offspring. It is clear that urban culture in Buenos Aires and the second city, Rosario, is by now dominated by individuals lacking the historical Creole roots that characterize so many other, more Hispanic, Latin American societies. Unquestionably, the urban makeup of Buenos Aires changes considerably with the steady influx of immigrants, both as they negotiate for a space in the urban landscape and, more importantly, as they begin to have an impact on it. There is an extensive bibliography of immigrant groups in Argentina (see the photographic volumes published by Manrique Zago; Alvarez on Spaniards; Wolff on Jews; and Zago on Italians), and some bibliography of cultural production as it relates to them (for example, Onega on immigrants in general; Lindstrom and Sosnowski on Jews), although little in the way of specific correlations between urban culture and immigrant culture. As immigrant groups penetrate other geographic spaces than the ones to which they are assigned as new arrivals, and as they merge with social spheres that can do little to withstand the demographic weight of their presence, immigrant society comes to be Argentine society, particularly in the Buenos Aires and littoral regions.

In the case of Walsh's novel, the family she describes does not, like so many Italians and Jews, occupy some central but yet socially and economically marginal sector of Buenos Aires. Rather, they lie somewhere west of the Federal District in residential areas characterized by English-style houses and large gardens. The narrator's father takes the Ferrocarril Oeste into Plaza Once, where he works in the train line's central offices. Even though the family is able to enjoy the presumably greater comfort of suburban living not afforded to those who occupy immigrant ghettos in town, it is clear that their existence is tied to the city and to urban culture, particularly as culture, both high and low, and fashion are concerned. But the city is as much a place of mysterious, threatening danger as it is the source of the exciting things of life. The narrator describes an excursion into the city to see a doctor, and her ironic voice repeats the way in which provincial decency not only positions itself vis-à-vis the city, but also through the city, to the extent that it is the individual who is the one always to come to terms with the city:

> He viajado en tren con mis padres "para que otro doctor me mire la garganta." Bajamos en la estación de Flores donde, como siempre, contemplo curiosa y con nostalgia de reencarnada el pórtico de la casa de Marcó del Pont, que ha quedado sobre el andén como una escenografía mutilada por las vías.
>
> —No camines mirando para atrás.
>
> Es que creo ver a niños antiguos que juegan el gallo ciego entre las

columnas, figuritas que se animan desde el fondo de los tiempos, marionetas condenadas al oficio mudo.

Caminamos por calles sombrías hasta llegar a un consultorio desconocido donde el enfermero abre la puerta y se traza entre las orejas una mueca funesta que significa sin duda sonrisa para niños. [. . .]

—Antes la gente venía en carreta hasta aquí, a veranear en quintas—procura distraerme mi padre didácticamente—pero el Ferrocarril Oeste transformó todo esto en una ciudad, ya ves. La primera locomotora, "La Porteña," salió de Plaza Lavalle y llegó hasta aquí.

Y cuando espero escuchar el cuento de la misteriosa casa de la estación, el enfermero procede. (137)[15]

The second principal interest of *Novios de antaño* is the representation of masculinity. Of course, there is nothing new in noting that Buenos Aires is a thoroughly masculine society or that immigrant societies are thoroughly masculine. They are masculine not only in their reduplication of Old World hierarchies transposed to the New World, but also in the simple fact that because men are often the first to come to the New World and form a society before the arrival of other family members, a strong male bonding of comrades alone in a hostile environment has taken place. Part of the interest of Walsh's novel must necessarily be a feminist take on such dominance, whether or not it is understood in terms of any specifically marked sexual dissidence. One can argue, nevertheless, that the questioning of patriarchal structures is not just feminist. It is also sexually dissident, since it calls into question the compulsory heterosexuality that is a principal ideological mainstay of patriarchal privilege. It is this questioning, rather than any specifically "gay" content, that makes Manuel Puig's *La traición de Rita Hayworth* (Betrayed by Rita Hayworth) such an exemplary queer novel.

Walsh's narrator, in addition to scrutinizing the world according to her father, talks about the *novios*, the men who pass through the lives of the women in the novel. In an ironic fashion, she characterizes how, despite all of their individual differences, they are all inscribed within the same patriarchal mode. Of course, any man who was not, would, by definition, cease to be a man or would be an incomplete man, an *afeminado* (effeminate). These men, in an age before the emergence of some measure of women's urban independence, are the ones who own the streets of the city. More important, it is they who bring news of the streets to the enclosed world of women, and it is they who interpret that news for the women. While Walsh's novel is bemused and ironic, the tyranny of male privilege is hard to miss, as are the injustices, distortions, and cruelties it perpetuates. Like Puig's novel, Walsh's closes with a narrative sequence that is anterior to the main text. This ex post facto preface lays forth, in any exchange of letters (also a reference to Puig), the profound harshness of woman's lot in this masculine world.

But to the extent that the María of the novel is an autobiographical figure of María Elena Walsh, there is, if not an escape, a mutation in the relationship between women and the masculine world of urban culture. The author's triumphs in various realms of Buenos Aires, realms that her poetry and other writings comment on, is the sort of presence that her character, at the end of the principal narrative, has only begun to perceive:

> María siente el picor de la metamorfosis, que le brotan élitros al bicho canasto, que está exorcizando la insoportable etapa de sus mudanzas y sus duelos y que antes de que un aldabonazo la vuelva a la realidad encarnada en su propio padre venido a rescatarla y arruinarle el pastel, ha encontrado la salida del laberinto, el transbordo a lo desconocido, un pasadizo a la Europa de sus ancestros y de los más caros espejismos de su porvenir. (273)[16]

María Elena Walsh was associated with the production of Luis Puenzo's *Historia oficial,* the most widely seen film to come out of the period of redemocratization. It won an Oscar for the best foreign film of the year and provided at least one of its stars, Norma Aleandro, with the opportunity to make films in Hollywood. Aleandro and her other star, Héctor Alterio, were both known for their opposition to the dictatorship, and both had worked abroad because of the climate of censorship, which impacted very much on the film industry. The script of *Historia oficial* was prepared by Luis Puenzo and Aída Bortnik, herself one of the many women dramatists involved in the Teatro Abierto programs of the early and mid-1980s that defied censorship by staging cycles of one-act plays in which the challenge to censorship, to authoritarianism, and to the masculinist patriarchy (from the point of view of women and sexual dissidents) was very much in evidence. Walsh's contribution, which has been previously noted, was in providing the theme song, "El país de Nomeacuerdo."

Historia oficial is the story of a woman, Alicia, played by Norma Aleandro. Alicia has begun to become aware of growing opposition to the
military. A friend from her school days returns from exile after having been
arrested and tortured by the Argentine police, which contributes to Alicia's
growing alarm. Finally, she discovers that her own adopted daughter was
taken from an imprisoned woman and given to Alicia's husband as a prize
for his support of the dictatorship's financial schemes. Alicia, against the
violent objections of her husband, undertakes to discover the child's biological family, and this leads her to the Madres de Plaza de Mayo.[17]

The Madres have probably been the most important feminist movement
in Latin America. Organized to protest the disappearance of their children
and grandchildren, the group mounted an energetic public protest against
the government, marching weekly in front of the Casa Rosada, the government house, in the Plaza de Mayo. It is significant that the Madres brought
together women from all social classes. And it is also significant that the
Asociación de las Madres de Plaza de Mayo has become an important
political force in Argentina. It has continued to militate for closure on what
still remains a very open issue in the country, since many of the issues of
the disappeared have yet to be resolved, and to exercise influence in a wide
range of matters relating to human rights and women's rights (the bibliography on the Madres is extensive; see material by Agosín; Bouvard; Diago;
Fisher; Mellibovsky. Documentary films have also been made about the
Madres).

Historia oficial is ideologically a very problematical film (see Foster,
Contemporary Argentine Cinema, 38–54), precisely because of the way in
which the character of Alicia relates to the Madres. It is almost inconceivable that the wife of a man with close ties to the military regime could have
ended up aligning herself with very visible elements of resistance culture;
but, of course, this is part of the way in which cultural documents need not
be rigorously verisimilar toward opening up spaces of debatable meanings.
Alicia's principal point of contact is a modest provincial who turns out to
be the adopted girl's biological grandmother. Significant emotional bonding takes place between the two women, one that threatens to destroy
Alicia's marriage (the grandmother is played by the famous character actress Chela Ruiz). The film, however, leaves unresolved the fate of the
child, which is reasonable, since as much in the late 1990s as in 1985, the
fate of many of these children has been left unresolved, although most are

by now full-grown adults. The film also leaves unresolved—and this is more problematical—the fate of Alicia's relationship with her husband and the degree to which she will reconstruct her feminine identity around the interests of the Madres.

Both Alicia and the grandmother move freely in the public world, but with considerable differences. Alicia is a high-school teacher of history, which is ironic since she initially is ignorant, or pretends to be ignorant, of the details of the dictatorship; yet her preparation as a historian is valuable to her when she later undertakes to find her child's biological family. Because of her professional position and the business connections of her husband, Alicia moves in privileged worlds. Her entire social sphere confirms her sense of identity as an upper-middle-class woman.

Chela Ruiz's character, by contrast, moves in the world of the housekeeper of modest resources, and this fact is marked not only by her bearing but by her dress and speech. The world does not confirm an identity for her; the world belongs to others and she merely inhabits it, surviving as best she can. Nevertheless, at some point the movement of the Madres has given her a dramatically changed relationship to her social world, one in which she can not only have a profound comradeship with women of many different social classes, but a comradeship grounded in resolving the great sorrow of her life: the disappearance of her daughter, her son-in-law, and the child with which her daughter was pregnant at the time they disappeared (were disappeared by police thugs). Significantly, it is her world to which Alicia has begun to assimilate, and it is an assimilation that radically changes her relationship with her husband, as the ground of her relationship to a world of social privilege. It also radically changes her relationship with her adopted daughter. The spectator can only imagine its projection beyond the narrative frame of the film.

Concomitantly, the recovery of her friendship with her exiled school friend and the woman's-world intimacy she comes to share with her biological grandmother are elements in a radically changed relationship with other women. Alicia's identity is no longer identified with her husband, but with other women, no longer with one key person, but with a spectrum of other subjects. In this process, she moves from a secure world in which everything is in its place, to the world of the alien and unknown that is the daily lot of the vast majority of women outside the inner circles of social power. Among their many other forms of sociohistoric importance, the

Madres have brought women of social privilege into direct contact with the ways in which most women have always lived and experienced the social domains they inhabit.

By taking possession of the most politically significant public space in Argentina, the Madres impose a dramatically new meaning on a realm of considerable symbolism for the dominant sectors of power. In this, the Madres are following Peronismo's example, which radically reconfigures the uses of the Plaza de Mayo in the propagation and defense of its political ideology. But the Peronistas were reinforcing the policies emanating from the government house. The Madres's stance is oppositional and contestatorial. In the context of the political protest they articulate, they are seeking a sense of feminine self not controlled by the dominant and still essentially masculinist class. They are looking for a meaningful place in the world that women of modest means have always inhabited. Through Alicia's contact with the Madres, she learns a lesson deprived of her as a woman dependent on the masculinist patriarchy: how to "take" the city in defense of her own urgent needs as a woman and as a mother.

chapter 6

Jewish Buenos Aires

¿Pero acaso se pueden decir cosas de verdad en este idioma?
¿Acaso se pueden decir cosas de verdad, de las que salen de
adentro, de las que viven en las tripas: acaso hay palabras para
eso en castellano?
Castellano, bah: qué clase de idioma es ése.[1]
—Ana María Shua, *El libro de los recuerdos*

It makes little difference how one does the counting: Buenos Aires is home
to the largest Jewish community in Latin America and, by some estimates,
to the fourth largest in the world. In many ways paralleling the development of the New York Jewish community (indeed, many families have
their roots split between the two cities), that of Buenos Aires has moved in
one hundred years from being poor pariahs confined to marginal ghettos
to exercising enormous political, economic, and cultural power. Jews are
particularly prominent in the entertainment industry in Argentina. Like
their U.S. counterparts, they occupied emerging industries like radio, television, and the movies, which old Christian money considered to be beneath its interest and investment. Along with having availed themselves of
the state universities as a form of social advancement, they have also come
to exercise considerable influence in traditional entertainment industries
such as the theater and variety, as well as important sectors of the publications industry, including journalism.

There are, however, significant differences between the United States
and Argentina. In the first place, although there are Jews in other Argentine cities (Córdoba, for example), Jews and their institutions are concentrated preponderantly in Buenos Aires. In the second place, there is no
phenomenon similar to that of the migration of Jewish capital to other
parts of the United States, especially Los Angeles, which, with the establishment of the film industry there after World War I, began to emerge as
a serious contender to New York as a center of Jewish life and influence.

Moreover, as in the United States, most Jews in Argentina are of German and east European immigrant extraction. However, as in the case of many parts of Latin America, Mediterranean Jews arrived during the period of conquest and colonization. This has provided Argentina with a Sephardic substratum, which is lacking in U.S. Jewry, where Sephardic Jews mostly have no more history than do other groups. Finally, while one cannot discount abiding manifestations of anti-Semitism in the United States, the Jewish community in Buenos Aires continues to be especially vulnerable, as the bombing of first the Israeli embassy in 1992 and then the bombing of the Asociación Mutualista Israelita Argentina (Argentine-Israeli Mutual Aid Society) in 1994 demonstrates (Aizenberg uses this event for a pro-vocative meditation on Jews in Argentine sociocultural history). Federal police have heightened security around major social, religious, and cul-tural establishments, but Argentine Jews very much feel their exposure to political crosscurrents in Argentina and international conflicts played out through local affairs.

While there are prominent Jews in the economic and financial commu-nities, Argentine Jews have only since the return to democracy in 1983 been able to play a prominent role in politics, either as elected officials or as appointed high-level functionaries, and they continue to be absent from the official class of the armed forces. Until recent modifications in the Argentine constitution, the president was obliged by law to be Catholic. Even though this is no longer the case, it is unlikely a non-Christian would be elected president anytime soon. (Carlos Menem, the current chief of state, was raised a Muslim, although he converted to Christianity as an adult. It has been widely held that he converted only to meet constitutional conditions.) President Raúl Alfonsín, the first democratically elected presi-dent after the 1976–83 period of military tyranny, was forced to back down on the appointment of Marcos Aguinis as minister of culture. The Argen-tine Catholic Church and its supporters were unable to tolerate a Jew in such a position. Aguinis, who is of Sephardic origin and from the city of Córdoba, was an outspoken critic of the military, and he went on to head the government office for institutional redemocratization. Apparently, the identification of Argentina as a Catholic country, in which other ethnic-religious groups are "tolerated" (and then only with major exceptions), an identification underscored insistently by Church and military, could not be so easily suspended by constitutional democracy.

There continues to be the belief that Jews are not full Argentines, at least not if they practice religious Judaism and self-identify, no matter on what basis, as Jews. Ironically, it was not so long ago that this was the situation for Catholics in the United States, and discrimination based itself on the presumed higher allegiance to a foreign power, the papacy, which made American Catholics less American. Although one does hear in Argentina the proposition that Jews are more committed to the state of Israel than they are to Argentina, there is no national discourse over the foreign-power issue of the papacy, nor is there any movement to check the very real temporal powers of the Church, whose influence on the lives of all Argentines in alleged moral and social issues has not abated in the dozen years since the end of the military dictatorship the Church hierarchy endorsed mostly unreservedly.

Many fine studies exist on the Jewish contribution to Argentine literature and other forms of cultural production. Lindstrom has assembled a mosaic of Jewish writers in various genres while establishing an inventory of the issues and perspectives of Jewish-marked writing. Senkman focuses on Jewish identity in a detailed bibliography of texts by Jews and non-Jews. Sosnowski explores how what the predominantly non-Jewish culture of Argentine has perceived as disjunctive categories—Jew(ish) and Argentine—creates a specifically liminal consciousness. In narrower terms, Lockhart discusses Jewish essayists who have written on Argentine culture, with an emphasis on accounts of the authoritarianism, (neo)fascism, and military tyranny that so greatly impacted Argentine-Jewish society. Foster ("Argentine Jewish Dramatists") examines the participation of Jews in the Argentine theater, underscoring how the theatricalization of Jewish life and social issues provided for a sort of public communitarian display, both to predominantly Jewish audiences and to largely non-Jewish ones, that does not occur with privately consumed fictional writings.

Foster and Lindstrom's bibliography of published writings by identified Jewish writers in Argentina contains entries for approximately 350 individuals, while over 60 percent of the entries in the Lockhart dictionary of Latin American Jewish writing involve Argentines. Specifically intellectual and artistic figures are, of course, only a privileged sphere of Jewish life. Books like the historical survey of Weisbrot, Wolff's picture album, and Feierstein's general sociohistorical survey all contribute to constituting the larger backdrop about which Jewish authors and artists have written. While members of Argentina's Jewish community have had an enormous impact on the country's vital film industry—as actors, scriptwriters, directors, producers, technical support personnel, and owners of projection venues— there is as of yet no survey and analysis of their participation in one of the most extensive forums of popular and public culture in the country. (Feierstein, 408–9, provides a registry of Jewish names in the tango; elsewhere he talks about forms of cultural production. Moviemaking, however, is ignored.)

During much of the history of Jewish life in Argentina a specifically marked religious and social culture was not readily apparent in the public realms of urban space. Jews were as much ghettoized in Argentina as anywhere else. The urban village of Once (which has no official political status), intersected by Avenida Corrientes (better known in the eastern segment as the Broadway of Buenos Aires), has been the city's legendary home of Jewish immigrants since the turn of the century. Today, many institutions and commercial establishments associated with the Jews remain in the Once district. Corrientes and its side streets (mostly the five blocks south to Avenida Rivadavia, the principal east-west axis of the city; streets change names on either side of this bisecting avenue, which runs the entire length of the Federal District and on out into the Province of Buenos Aires) remain for the kilometer between Avenida Callao and Avenida Pueyrredón a vast middle-and lower-middle-class shoppers emporium tied to Jewish commercial interests, although Once is no longer the typical place of residence of Jews.

It is true that many older and poorer Jews may continue to reside in and around Once. However, beginning with Peronismo in the late 1940s, and especially as a consequence of the combined effect of democracy and neoliberal economics, there has been a massive emigration from Once to the posher neighborhoods on the northern fringe of the city, which is bounded by the Río de la Plata and the bedroom communities along the river to the northwest. The residential opportunities created in Once by this emigration have been taken by East Asians, predominantly Koreans, who are the new immigrant stock of the past couple of decades. That they are even more "foreign" than the eastern European Jews from whom they have bought or rent continues to mark Once as an urban site that is radically other vis-à-vis those areas of the city marked either by the dominant classes or by subaltern classes unified at the very least by their sense of being thoroughly "Argentine."[2]

The effect of the latter is, in a certain sense, a roughly drawn three-layer space of urban identity in Buenos Aires: (1) the hegemonic privileged classes to the north, with some pockets (Flores, Almagro) to the west of Once; (2) Once and its environs, located in the heart of the city and to the west of the government and banking district; this area is symbolically marked as the "Other," with its old and new Jewish inhabitants and East Asian occupants, who have only partially displaced the area's traditional Jewish association; and (3) the vast stretches of subaltern areas along the south side of the city, curving north into the west-central area beyond Once and the prestigious areas immediately west of Once. This characterization is, of course, very crude, since one suddenly comes upon tenement houses (*conventillos*) in the northern areas. And, between the middle-class and upper-middle-class Once neighborhoods there is a buffer zone that is one of the poorest and toughest areas of the city. The gentrification of the south side's zones (Boedo, historically associated with the anarchist and socialist movements of the city) and a certain Bohemian attraction for an artistic and intellectual set of Boedo or the old colonial area (San Telmo) combine to revise an image of the south side as strictly subaltern.

In terms of the modern social history of Buenos Aires, the customary opposition between the haves of the northern tier of the city and the have-nots of the remaining sectors was fragmented by Peronismo. With its populist bases, Peronismo not only curried the support of subaltern groups located in the south and central west, but it waged symbolic, if not always actual, economic and political war against the traditional oligarchy of the north. Moreover, Peronismo sought to encourage the development of a petite bourgeoisie that would provide it with political stability. The cry may have been in support of the *descamisados* (the shirtless), but until the shirtless could enter the bourgeoisie, their value was purely symbolic. The Jews were an immediately available group for this process. For the most part, they were unaccepted in any of the oligarchy's domains, except for certain groups of cultural producers who were afforded honorary elite status. An example is Alberto Gerchunoff, who assimilated to the hegemonic culture in his work on the literary supplement of the ultra-oligarchic newspaper *La nación* and who only wrote about Jewish culture to romanticize it (*Los gauchos judíos* [The Jewish Gauchos of the Pampas]) as part of the ideology of the 1910 centennial celebrations (Trentalance de Kipreos; Lindstrom, 51–60). The title of Gerchunoff's collection of sentimental tales betrays the sense of interpretation of Jewish life. It is not an irresolvable oxymoron (Jew vs. Gaucho). The Jew becomes a subset of the Gaucho prototype invested in the quintessence of Argentine rural and agrarian identity (as confirmed a decade later with Ricardo Güiraldes's *Don Segundo Sombra*, the definitive mythification of the Gaucho as spiritual master to the land-owning class).

The story of the Jews during Peronismo has been told by Weisbrot (227–40), who stresses the combined opportunity of the prosperity of the early years of Perón's government and the need to fill positions of power that would challenge and dilute the oligarchy offered to Jews, who were by then the sons and even the grandsons of the Jews persecuted during the Semana Trágica in 1919, which prefigured the Nazi Crystalnacht (see also Avni, 177–83). Much of the current Jewish bourgeoisie has its origins in the late 1940s. Although one can point to a sustained record of anti-Semitic discourse in Peronismo (Klich; Newton), Perón's opposition to the Catholic oligarchy and later to the Church itself provided important rapprochements between the Jewish community and Perón. In part, the anti-Semitism of the Catholic and traditionalist, neofascist military dictatorships between 1966 and 1981 derived as much from their opposition to the alleged Otherness of the Jews[3] as it did to the measure of support for Perón among middle-class Jews. Moreover, the sons of the latter were often the left-wing militants who in the early seventies defended Perón as a revolutionary harbinger (see, for example, the chronicle by the Jewish journalist Horacio Verbitsky of this support and its disappearance when Perón returned to Argentina in 1973 and resumed control of the government).

Issues relating to the relationship between Peronismo and the Jews, and to the Jews' presence in the urban landscape, are masterfully and ingeniously correlated by Mario Szichman in his 1981 novel, *A las 20:25, la señora entró en la inmortalidad* (At 8:25 Eva Became Immortal). The title of Szichman's novel refers to the death of Eva Perón, who died officially at 8:25 P.M. on July 26, 1951; the novel's character, Rifque Pechof, dies at the same time.[4] As a consequence of this unfortunate coincidence, it is impossible for Pechof's family to provide her with a proper Jewish funeral, including burial within twenty-four hours. Since the entire country comes to a standstill, they are unable to obtain the death certificate necessary for her burial and to contract the appropriate services as specified by strict Talmudic law.

Acutely experiencing their radical Otherness as second-class citizens, Pechof's family undertakes a long and arduous odyssey in order to get her buried in La Tablada, the Jewish cemetery outside Buenos Aires. As a synecdoche of the European tradition of forcing Jews beyond the pale, Jews, although they could live in Buenos Aires, could not be buried within the city limits. Szichman's novel is a surreal fugue that describes the Pechof family's agonies because they cannot comply with Talmudic law, despite the ostentatious public spectacle of the Christian burial of Eva Perón. Szichman's fugue is truly carnivalesque in its strategies of inversion of the established order: the codes of reality that explain and naturalize the structure of social life in Argentina, which, despite its revision by Peronismo, from the point of view of the Other, remain essentially the same. In the process of coming to terms with a relentless Christianity that permeates every crease and fold of the social text, the Pechofs take lessons in being Christian, in the vain hope that via such a transformation they will be able to manipulate the system from within and thus be able to comply with Jewish custom.

It is important to recall that Eva Perón's funeral—a public event that monopolized Argentine life for what those opposed to Peronismo felt was an interminable period—was far from the transformation of a private individual's body into a publicly displayed fetish. Rather, it was the logical and intrinsically necessary extension of the entire process by which Eva Perón became a markedly public persona, and it marks the violent, transgressive, strident ways in which she took possession of the city, and the nation, as a realm of personal performance. Eva Perón enacted not only the politics of Peronismo, but also the persona of Evita. I do not by this mean to evoke the hoary trope that all life is but a stage and all individuals are actors on it, nor that politics is essentially a form of vulgar theater, nor even less that, as much opinion has felt constrained to insist, Eva Duarte, the mediocre actress, could only become a star as Evita Perón, and her role as the wife of Juan Domingo Perón was the only first-rate starring role she ever played.

That Evita's public presence was inherently theatrical and/or a carefully staged performance may be true, but the point is not the textual organization of her spectacle; it is its impact on the city, such that Buenos Aires and Evita Perón became co-terminus with each other. This was as much true for those areas and sectors that supported her as it was for the virulent opposition she provoked, since the latter had nothing to offer but its opposition and could do no more than define itself on her terms. As a consequence, that which was not Peronista, that which could not become Peronista, or that which could only become Peronista in an imperfect, partial fashion was inevitably blanketed by Peronismo in the person of Evita. When the entire city is transformed into a funeral home to wake her death, it is only the casting in a different register of how for five years Buenos Aires belonged to Evita Perón.

Szichman's novel, glossing over the way in which some sectors of the Jewish community benefited from Peronismo, is especially eloquent in the overdetermined ways in which it represents a Jewish subalternity that stems generally from the anti-Semitism of Argentine society and specifically from the co-option of all symbolic capital by Peronismo in the person of Evita Perón (who is insistently only identified as "la señora"—her identity is so omnipresent that she need never be mentioned by name):

> El velorio de la señora convirtió a Buenos Aires en una ciudad de desarrollo detenido, enlazando dos épocas mediante el deterioro de algunos edificios y el añadido de obras en construcción que no pasaban de la etapa del encofrado.
>
> Los troleys y los tranvías fueron saliendo de circulación, lámparas de mercurio reemplazaron a las luces amarillas y el macadam cubrió el empedrado.
>
> A partir de esa muerte, Buenos Aires fue nocturna. La oscuridad concluía de un lado en la General Paz y del otro en el Riachuelo. Al pasar a la provincia, la gente levantaba la cabeza y veía el corte a bisel que separaba los dos cielos. (15)[5]

The experience of the Pechof family is not precisely that of the ghetto in its medieval or early Nazi-era sense. Many have written about the reelaboration of the ghetto experience in Buenos Aires, perhaps none in more pathetic tones than José Rabinovich, a paradigmatic immigrant author who wrote first in Yiddish and only later in Spanish. The title of his principal collection of stories, *Tercera clase*, which was published in Spanish translation in 1944, synthesizes the quality of immigrant life he describes (see Foster, *Social Realism in the Argentine Narrative*, 66–71). Although features of ghetto life emerge in *A las 20:25*, Szichman is writing from a different tradition than those for whom narrative is the opportunity to transmit a detailed sensory-based account of the texture of immigrant life. Szichman, however, seeks to examine, with his fugue-like variations, the sense of life as the Other for Argentine Jews. His grotesque and surreal narrative circumstances, while they do not correspond superficially with the sort of "picture" a writer like Rabinovich provides, does transmit the sense of frustration, outrage, and absurdity of an existence that is on many levels at variance with the established social codes. Jewish life is thereby always obliged to be dysfunctional in terms of the dominant structures—forced to observe the Christian Sabbath while at the same time sacrificing its own Sabbath in order to survive economically in a Christian society:

Jaime y Salmen fueron a la casa de Tajmer para aprender buenos modales. El millonario iba a presentar en sociedad a su futuro yerno, un goi que recibía coimas como inspector de la Impositiva. [. . .]

Jaime [espió] la fiesta. En el salón bailaban un tango.

—Mirá, esa es la música de mi ciudad. ¡Qué ganas de ser un malevo!—dijo Jaime admirado.

—Tajmer se está echando a perder con eso de invitar goim—señaló Salmen.

—Qué se va a echar a perder. Progresa. Y va a progresar más cuando deje de invitar idns. Fijáte qué pinta la del goi. Y ahora, fijáte en los nuestros. Mirá con qué facilidad nos quedamos pelados. Es suficiente ser un schnorer para que se te vuele la chapa. [. . .] El goi tiene un perro de paladar negro y con eso conquista el mundo. Vos podés ser Einstein, si querés, pero no valés nada al lado de este tipo. *¿Usted qué inventó*, le preguntaron a Einstein. *Yo inventé la radiactividad*, dice Einstein. *¿Tiene perro con paladar negro?* Y si Einstein no tiene perro con paladar negro, no sirve. Ni aunque invente diez radiactividades. Mirá a Tajmer. Se le cae la baba por el juzn. Mirá cómo se ríe el juzn. No muestra los dientes. Eso es tener paladar negro. (Szichman, 142–43)[6]

For *A las 20:25*, the way in which the public space of the city has unified in opposition to the Other is via the dominion imposed by Evita Perón. No matter how much she was an Other in her origins, and no matter how problematic her assumption of real and symbolic power may have been, she was for a crucial five years the hegemonic personification of Buenos Aires. In the passage cited, the Jew who holds the party and who is in the process of becoming a goi works for the government, an example of the aforementioned opportunities Peronismo began to offer Jews who entered the mainstream of Argentine life—at the expense of giving up their Jewish identity, of course. The grotesqueness of the reference to having a "paladar negro," which segues from owning a dog with such a palate to having one oneself is typical of the highly conceitful manner in which Szichman characterizes the relationships between the private lives of Jews and the public discourse of the city, between the ghetto and the dominant urban text.

The writings of Alicia Steimberg (b. 1933) engage the city in a totally different way. Steimberg hasn't written to be identified as a Jewish writer. Unlike Szichman, she has not created a dense narrative world centered on Jewish life and driven by a family saga extending over several generations (see, however, Schneider). Her novels are intensely urban, and many of her characters and situations are clearly Jewish. But more than anything else, her writing is marked by a sense of sacrilegious irony, irreverence, and smart-girl sassiness that can be generally identified as a Jewish—and, in this case, feminist Jewish—point of view. Steimberg has written short stories and novels, with her principal focus on the misadventures of middle-class women in their efforts to make their way against the odds of the city. These odds could be synthesized in terms of the masculinist codes that predominate as the ground zero of Argentine social life, although they are not always personified by male characters. Indeed, in her autobiographical first novel, perhaps the one most anchored in the immigrant ghetto, *Músicos y relojeros* (Musicians and Clock Makers), the household in which the narrator grows up is essentially the domain of women.

Yet it is clear that that domain serves to enforce patriarchal law, whether in its specifically Jewish form or as the prevailing social code, and forms of resistance are purely tactical skirmishes. In her second novel, *Su espíritu inocente*, Steimberg writes about being a Jewish student in the predominantly upper-middle-class, and therefore profoundly Catholic, teacher training school Lenguas Vivas, which specializes in language teaching (Steimberg is formally trained as an English teacher, and she worked many years as the translator of English-language fiction, mostly best-sellers). The fact that Steimberg was able to attend Lenguas Vivas in the early 1950s is the consequence of the changing fortune of Jews under Peronismo mentioned above. The title of the novel refers to a principal ideologeme of the school's anthem and the way in which a proper social education allows for overcoming the illusions, and dangers, of female innocence in the masculinist patriarchal jungle. Lenguas Vivas, for example, may continue to train mostly women (there are some men in the tertiary-level courses, which prepare graduates for secondary-school teaching), but there is no question that they are being trained to serve the state as its pedagogical agents.

La loca 101 (Madwoman 101) was published in 1973 during the brief period of cultural euphoria between the military's temporary withdrawal from power and Peronismo's return. The euphoria was short lived—the military resumed power in 1976, less than three years after turning the government over to civilian control. But while it lasted, some of the best of recent Argentine literature was published. Publishers were eager to bring out socially progressive and revolutionary culture from other Latin American countries as well. In large measure, in the period since the return to constitutional democracy in 1983, Argentine cultural production has yet to recover the sense of euphoria and creative intensity that characterized the early 1970s. Steimberg's novel was published by Ediciones de la Flor, one of the most important publishers, at the time, of innovative literature. Its list included as many non-Argentines as it did Argentines. Ediciones de la Flor published Enrique Medina's path-breaking *Las tumbas* in 1972.

In *Folio's* special issue on Latin American Jewish writers, Saúl Sosnowski speaks of Steimberg as "enhebrando pequeñas historias" (threading small stories). His comment is allusive in two ways. One, it stresses the "domestic" quality of Steimberg's writing. In contrast to the large social canvas that concerns a writer like Szichman, Steimberg's texts deal more with everyday, even mundane, matters. Whether or not it is paradigmatically feminist to back away from the great themes of masculinist culture—surely represented in Argentine literature by Domingo Faustino Sarmiento's *Facundo*, José Hernández's *Martín Fierro*, much of Borges' oeuvre, Julio Cortázar's *Rayuela* (Hopscotch),[7] and Ernesto Sabato's *summum* of Argentine social history, *Sobre héroes y tumbas* (On Heroes and Tombs)—the fact is that Steimberg focuses on details of experience that are synecdoches and metonymies of human existence. Such details may have a particular Jewish flavor about them, but they are more important for how they provide resonances to the commonplaces of daily life.

Secondly, Sosnowski's title stresses how Steimberg's writings are *petits récits*. Again, it may be a feature of feminist writing to renounce master narratives/narratives of the master, which is precisely the function of the forenamed texts, not only because they are by men and are attached to the dominant masculinist culture (Sarmiento as president; Hernández as a conservative lawmaker and wealthy landowner) and canonical figures (Cortázar as one of the four paragons of the so-called "boom" of the new Latin American novel of the 1960s; Borges as a literary giant; Sabato as a paternal moral conscience of his society [he headed the presidential commission on the disappeared, which published *Nunca más*, the official government report on the disappeared]), but also because they articulate interpretations cast as Big Issues and Major Themes.

For example, *La loca 101* is described as a novel. Yet, in 109 pages there are forty-four chapters. Each chapter is named in the index, although the names do not appear at the heading of the actual divisions. Most of the texts run two to three pages, with many shorter. Thus, Steimberg's novel possesses a loosely jointed continuity (a rejection of the sort of complex narrative structure of the latest modernist fiction of the midcentury boom) tied together by a feminine narrator who is unspecified beyond the suggestive nature of the title. In Argentine Spanish, *loca*, applied colloquially to a woman, means someone who is "daft" or "batty," but not strictly "mad" or "crazy." It is also used in the sense of someone who is overly talkative, sassy, unconventional, loud, nondemure—in a word, someone who is not sufficiently feminine in a conventionally reserved and self-effacing way. The result is a person who not only sees more than she should, but who talks openly about it as she should not, analyzing it aloud in a way that is highly improper.

What one receives, then, is one young woman's discomforting observations on the world around her. As Barr has stated, "the text reveals the author's underlying terror of everyday life. It is a bloody business to live where she lives" (*Isaac Unbound*, 59). In a society where there is an overdeterminedly constructed gender system, a woman sees things and experiences them substantially differently than a man does (assuming that individuals are conforming appropriately to the gender system). A *loca* will speak of that difference when, although her difference is not denied, she is supposed to keep it to herself. Steimberg's text functions both on the basis of that difference and on the fact that it is spoken out loud. As a result of her outspokenness, she does in fact make the transition from "daft" to "mad." The designation "101" refers to her identification within the insane asylum.

In chapter 11, identified in the table of contents as "La Pocha. Saludo al Ministro de Instrucción Pública," there is a juxtaposition between the importance of the adult masculine figures in their transit through public space and the virtual invisibility of the children. This is correlated with the transcendent nature of the very presence of the masculine figures in public and the nonsensical reference to the water-spouting frogs:

> Paseábamos por el Rosedal. Nos deslizábamos, casi sin tocar el suelo, por un camino de tierra anaranjada, bajo un cielazo azul, y yo avisté los cuatro sapitos de bronce que escupían agua en la fuente. Si se les tapaba la boca a tres de los sapitos, el cuarto largaba un chorro muy largo, un gran arco de agua que caía en el medio de la fuente. Eso hicimos yo y otros dos chicos desconocidos ante la mirada del guardián, que no se oponía a esta práctica, aunque sí a la del pasto pisar o las flores arrancar. Al rato vi que los mayores se habían alejado y corrí para alcanzarlos. No me prestaron atención porque por el camino venía Él, el Ministro de Educación, y papá lo saludó. El Ministro devolvió el saludo y siguió adelante con sus acompañantes. Cuando húbose alejado papá dijo: "Es el Ministro de Educación. Qué digo, es el Ministro de Justicia e Instrucción Pública." Y agregó: "Es jorobado de pecho y espalda." (35)[8]

The implication, underscored by the paternal voice, is that the children should be in awe of the authoritarian presence of the minister. Formal urban spaces such as the Rosedal serve as sites for the display of such social and political authority, but the children alter it by interfering in the symmetry of the decorative fountain. Moreover, that disruption, in addition to producing a grotesque image (grotesque because of the asymmetry of the one toad vis-à-vis the other toads, and the resulting disproportion of the stream of water it spouts), can be read as suggestive of urination. The allusion to the minister's physical deformity suggests the body configuration of a toad. Thus, the urinating toad becomes, in the disruptive act of the children, a figure of the minister, which should rather pass through the Rosedal in harmonious concert with its patriarchal formality.

In chapter 29, "Gato" (Cat), the quintessential phenomenon of the stray street cat seems to be evoked as a metaphor for life in the city, where the ghettoizing of cats, specifically identified here from a feminine point of view, refers to the processes of marginalization at work in the disposition of urban space:

Tanto las gatas de almohadón como las de alcantarilla pierden de vista a sus hijos al poco tiempo de nacidos. Los hijos de las gatas de familia se reparten entre los amigos de los patrones. Los hijos de las gatas de la calle corren suertes diversas: algunos mueren en manos de los chicos del barrio; otros vagan por las calles hasta que alguien los recoge y se los lleva a su casa, donde se convierten en gatos de estufa, o bien los lleva a algún Barrio para Gatos de los que funcionan en el Jardín Botánico o en cualquier jardín de hospital. (71)[9]

Buenos Aires and urban life have undergone enormous changes since the return to constitutional democracy in 1983. In addition to the public display of culture that was simply not possible during the period of military tyranny because of explicit or implied censorship, various programs to stimulate cultural production and to make works more available—notably through the Redemocratización project headed by Marcos Aguinis—added to the public display of culture (Aguinis). Buenos Aires has always been one of the world's major theater centers, with the public visibility of theater combined with the whole new cycle of filmmaking that took place. Although many traditional movie houses have disappeared with the emergence of video rental, new cinemas have also been built (especially the shopping-mall multiplex variety), and their marquees add to the open display of culture in the cityscape. Cultural events in outdoor venues complement the visibility of the various state-owned and private foundations that give culture a public face. The renewed impetus received by literary supplements after the end of the dictatorship reinforced their importance in Argentina as a form of providing a public forum for culture. Such was also the case with television and radio, which are as ubiquitous in Argentina as anywhere in the so-called First World.

The outpouring of culture under democracy and its importance as an element of public space was also enhanced by the dollarization of the Argentine economy and the imposition of unrestrained neoliberal economic policies, which has enabled a whole new formulation of foreign cultural influences in Buenos Aires, along with the changes they have meant for the city. American-style shopping centers, for example, provide a radically new forum for the insertion of culture into urban space, and so much of the modernization of the city has been in terms of practices and details borrowed from U.S. life, down to the detail of recently redressing the police force in New York blues.

One of the themes of cultural production in Argentina during the past decades has involved taking stock of what the changes in national institutional life and the neoliberal restructuring of the economy have meant in terms of daily life in the city. It has become commonplace to speak of Buenos Aires as a capital of postmodernity (Ferman) and to remark on the enormous contradictions that Argentines see themselves as living (a paradigmatic postmodern condition, beginning with the not inconsiderable gulf separating neoliberal desires from the difficult socioeconomics experienced by most people, who can only stare at the display of wares from outside on the mean street. A narrative production characterized by personal aimlessness and fragmented subjectivity exemplifies such a perception. Since the aimlessness cannot be attributed to the vagaries of an ad hoc government or the fragmentation claimed to be the consequence of the incoherences provoked by tyrannical repression, there is the sense that it stretches out into infinity as the basic condition of life in contemporary Argentina.

Where someone like Steimberg continues to produce a markedly puckish fiction that has moved away from daily life to alternative themes (see, for example, her 1989 *Amatista*, which won Spain's Editorial Tusquets prize for erotic fiction and was included in that publisher's La Sonrisa Vertical (Vertical Smile) series [Foster, "The Case for Feminine Pornography in Latin America"]), others focus on the texture of Jewish life under the changed conditions of urban life. For such writers, Jews may no longer be a privileged example of social subalternity, but they can in fact be at the center of structures of social and political power. Paula Varsavky's *Nadie alzaba la voz* (Nobody Raised His Voice) exemplifies this possibility. In a minimalist fashion, Luz Golman recounts, on the occasion of his sudden death on the plane carrying him from New York to Buenos Aires, the story of her father. Golman had been an important professor of physics at the University of Buenos Aires until his dismissal by the military dictatorship in 1969, which, in addition to the usual persecution of art and intellectual thought, considered science equally subversive (see note 3). Luz's life corresponds to the period of the dictatorship, and it is significant that her father dies at the time of the democratic elections in 1983. For her, the principal understanding of the consequence on society of the de facto government is his decision to pursue his career in New York, which means her separation from him. Although raised in settings of considerable material comfort—ample townhouses, country retreats, luxurious summer spas, international vacations in the United States, Brazil, and Europe—Luz's life is marked by spiritual desolation.

The title of Luz's account is both ambiguous and ironic. It is ironic because she is surrounded by people who do raise their voices, loudly and persistently—her family and friends, her elders and peers, the authorities and her intimates—all in the frantic scramble to assert the validity of their point of view and the primacy of their needs. But the title is also ambiguous. While it can refer to tone and volume of voice in the process of human intercourse, it also refers to speaking out against the social structures of family, education, and institutional authority that produce Luz's spiritual desolation. Her family comprises secular and cultural Jews who also have firm political commitments. But these commitments, which are never much in evidence (her father professes to hate Argentina, but he ends up making a considerable amount of money representing in New York the business interests of crass Argentines who became wealthy during the dictatorship), are inadequate to the task of alleviating Luz's alienation. Indeed, the only voice that would appear to have been raised in an acceptable fashion is her own, in the form of the narrative. Luz, however, is upper-middle-class, naively homophobic, and convinced that there is a difference between the authoritarian structures (the dictatorship, but also her family, specifically her mother, grandmother, and stepmother) that have separated her from her father and the unmediated ideal of her father's love for her. Here, the Law of the Father, which surrounds her in its other incarnations, is felt as a Lacanian absence because of her loss of its customarily most explicit embodiment.

While the Jewish elements in the novel are relegated to the general cultural ambiance (and Luz, as an upscale modern Argentine youth, is embarrassed when her father is given a generic Jewish burial), Freudian Oedipalism constitutes the crucial narrative core. Luz's desolation is as much due to her stifling existence in the Buenos Aires of the dictatorship as it is to the lack of any parameters—and, crucially, no consciousness, despite the privilege of her narrative act—to question the ways in which she must enact and enforce the will of her father. Luz is depressingly as much a nonfeminist as is possible, and Varsavsky's text only opens itself up to a feminist reading to the extent that the reader can assess the ironic gaps in Luz's account.

The novel assumes importance from the perspective of urban culture when Luz, as a young woman of considerable privilege despite the military dictatorship, is able to define herself repeatedly against the backdrop of the city. She moves between various residences, from the city to the beach and the countryside, from one shopping place to another, in school settings and the many other places where students meet, engaging always in a sort of pathetic fallacy whereby the sense of the city is a projection of her state of mind:

> Dejé de ir al colegio. En unos meses estaría en Nueva York, ¿para qué ir al colegio acá? Ni siquiera tomé la decisión de dejar. De pronto no fui más. No hubo ningún comentario al respecto, ni de mamá ni de papá.
>
> A los trece años, ya no creía en nada. En absolutamente nada. Era una escéptica total. Me habían traicionado en todo. No había quedado esperanza sin frustrar, ilusión sin decepcionar. Tampoco tenía más mi grupo de la primaria. No me quedaba nada en Buenos Aires. No me quedaba nada en la vida. [. . .]
>
> El domingo de la partida, mamá vino a despertarme. Me dijo que nos despidiéramos en ese momento. Que después sería peor. Que no quería acompañarme a Ezeiza. Le resultaría demasiado triste. Acepté. Que no me acompañara si no quería. Me daba lo mismo. No me parecía que me estuviera yendo. (68)[10]

Varsavsky's novel transmits the sense of Buenos Aires under the dictatorship in terms of the absence Luz feels because her father has been taken away from her by tyranny. However, his disappearance is not the one recounted by those Jewish writers who speak of the particular persecution of Jews by the Dirty War (Timerman; Kovadloff). The novel also transmits the sense of a privileged sector of Jews who, like Tajmer in Szichman's novel, have made a niche for themselves that will translate into economic and social power in the period after the dictatorship, which is Varsavsky's point of reference. Interestingly, the sections that deal with New York and the commercial and cultural details of the city are precisely those that become part of the neoliberal fantasy that will bring about key transformations in the city after 1983 and afford a new economic empowerment of Jews.

chapter 7

The Dirty Realism of Enrique Medina

Since the publication in 1972 of *Las tumbas* (The Tombs), a novel dealing with the reformatory experiences of a child abandoned by a single mother who cannot care for him (Foster, "Rape and Social Formation"), Medina has established himself as the major voice in Argentine literature of the urban lumpen proletariat. The author of more than twenty works of fiction (novels and short stories), chronicles, and children's theater, Medina was, during the military dictatorship known as the Proceso de Reorganización Nacional (1976–83), the author with the largest inventory of books banned by the censorship apparatus. *Las tumbas*, which has been one of the best-selling novels of contemporary Argentine fiction, was unavailable until the end of the dictatorship, and it was once again a best-seller after it was reissued.[1] This novel established the basic features of all of Medina's writing, and it is difficult to know which order of importance to assign to them.

Dirty Realism

Medina's determined effort to engage in "dirty realism" is understood as the commitment to describe the daily experiences of life with no attempt to euphemize them, either by turning away from certain aspects as somehow too gross to be related in literal terms or by supplementing them with a transcendent (social, political, religious) meaning that would detract from the imperative to examine the facts of life as unflinchingly as possible. Such a commitment is as much a defiance of the censorship imposed directly and indirectly on cultural production by tyrannical governments as it is a repudiation of the norm of good taste that usually serves as a de facto censorship with an obligation, precisely, to augment the depiction of reality with transcendent meanings.

Dirty realism also means a strict regard not just for what gets expunged from the "artistic" contemplation of the social record, but also the choice of which segment of the social record one focuses on. While it may not always be subaltern groups and marginal individuals—certainly there are plenty of dirty hidden stories to tell about the privileged sectors of society— those on which a writer like Medina will choose to focus are those social entities that, because their reality cannot be euphemized and transcendentalized, simply do not get reported on. Argentina has a long tradition of proletarian (Portantiero) and social realist writing (Foster, *Social Realism in the Argentine Narrative*), and there are many antecedents to Medina that can be mentioned: Roberto Arlt, Elías Castelnuovo, Leonidas Barletta, Bernardo Verbitsky, Bernardo Kordon, José Rabinovich, Alvaro Yunque, Max Dickmann. Various versions of a literature of commitment continue to produce other writers and artists, now enhanced by the strong presence of women's voices, whose work bears degrees of resemblance to Medina's project. Most of these writers, however, wrote during a time when writing about certain topics and using certain linguistic registers would have meant not being published or experiencing an unbearable degree of social opprobrium. Also, many writers of social commitment are, in fact, tied to a transcendent signifier (social revolution, the fulfillment of history, salvation through commitment itself) that imposes a supplementary level on their writing, as much as it may serve to distract them from executing a full account of the social record. The movement toward the transcendent signifier necessarily means leaving the concrete details of social life behind.

Medina has claimed that the discovery of Louis-Ferdinand Céline's books was a factor in his empowerment as a writer. His work showed Medina how one could write without yielding to a chimerical criterion of transcendence. Medina wrote with the goal of provoking the reigning principle of cultural decency in Argentina, such that works of his were banned. As a consequence, he was energetically condemned by sectors of the cultural press, and many bookstores refused to carry his titles (for example, the prestigious and ultraconservative Ateneo). The extreme circumstances of the dictatorships between 1966 and 1983 and the principle during the period of redemocratization of "Never Again" (*Nunca más* became the name of the best-selling report of the official commission on the disappeared) led to attempts to confront the social and political facts of national life. Such confrontation was accompanied by the changing appearance of those foreign cultural forces that, after the suspension of censorship, arrived in Argentina unmediated. These were important factors in providing some sort of final legitimacy to Medina's work. Currently, Medina does a weekly column for *Página 12*, the Buenos Aires newspaper that has published material of some of the country's most respected writers and intellectuals; my commentary on specific texts will be based on the published collections of his chronicles appearing since 1987.

Urban Context

Medina's attention has remained firmly anchored in the urban context, and he is probably the most important urban writer in Argentina at the present moment. Medina was for personal reasons obliged to remain in Argentina during the dictatorship, and he was throughout the period the recipient of many death threats. In the case of many writers who did leave Argentina, foreign residence often attenuated the precise outlines of their representation of Buenos Aires. In Julio Cortázar's *Rayuela* (Hopscotch), the city has more of an allegorical function vis-à-vis constants of Argentine social history than a specific lived environment. By contrast, Medina wishes very much to provide a sharply focused representation of urban life, although his characters are not drawn exclusively from the Argentine lumpen proletariat. (Many of his chronicles deal with foreign happenings; he has a particular interest in significant U.S. events because of the enormous idealization and selling of American culture as part of a whole range of venues in Latin America.) It cannot be said that Medina is exclusively a writer of the lower classes (for recent sociological research on marginal groups in Buenos Aires, see Montes de Oca). Medina is interested in other classes because of the need to examine the interrelationship of all social groups in order to understand a global power structure.

True, some of his memorable characters are from the working class or from a petite bourgeoisie that (often as a consequence of Peronismo) was working class in the last generation and in the present generation is barely hanging on to its social gains. One of Medina's most memorable characters is José María Gatica, the prizefighter who enjoyed the support of the Peróns. *Gatica* tells the story of a marginal youth lost in the city who makes it big, only to end up a broken wreck as the result of the pummeling taken in the ring. Gatica dies at the age of thirty-eight, when, drunk, he falls from the step of a moving bus he attempts to board and is run over, a symbol of a mortal cityscape (on Gatica's death, see Soriano). *Gatica* is a true story,

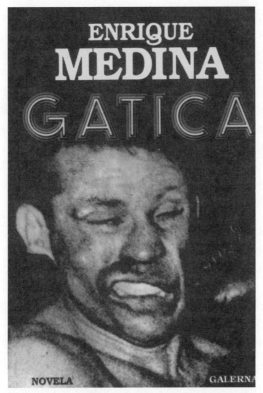

Cover of Enrique Medina's novel *Gatica*. Courtesy
of Enrique Medina.

while the young female characters of *Buscando a Madonna* (Looking for
Madonna) and *Con un trapo en la boca* (With a Rag in Her Mouth) are
fictional individuals on the cusp between the lower-middle class and the
abyss of complete social marginalization.

The character of *Buscando a Madonna* typifies the utterly aimless existence of a younger generation that has no viable space, at least in terms of
any sense of fulfillment in the social structure and, less so, as a woman (the
one-woman stage version, starring Emilia Mazer and directed by Mazer
and Carlos Demartino, had an enormous success in 1994). At least the
younger generation's parents had the military dictatorship and the larger
issue of social revolution to fight against. And, if they were directly committed, they had something against which to define themselves. Thus, Madonna is both a positive and a negative symbol, since she promises a female
and feminist (and perhaps lesbian) social agency, while at the same time

she is a skillful media creation of the American culture that is transforming the country as part of a neoliberalist venture of a commercial elite. The woman of *Con el trapo en la boca,* by contrast, has quite a bit more agency, and the novel is the story she tells to, apparently, a female lover about the violence she has suffered at the hands of a masculinist society. The story is particularly colored by military authoritarianism, and its principal point is how she counters the aggressions of a male lover by castrating him as a rather definitive farewell gesture.

The sense of Buenos Aires and its social actors in Medina's novels is indeed intense, and he has very much of the meaning of the relationship of the individual to society described by Greimas:

> It is true that in examining the practice of subject-citizens, along with individual roles, we were able to identify social roles by which individuals participate in collective tasks. Consequently, we can say that these social roles are "lived" in one way or another and that these social activities are significant for the individual. But such an analysis cannot be pushed too far, if only because social activities are participatory, each role and each program being inscribed within the framework of collective practice that goes beyond them. (151)

One well-crafted movie made from his fiction is *Perros de la noche* (the novel is from 1977; the film, directed by Teo Kofman, is from 1986 [Foster, *Contemporary Argentina Cinema* 109–23]). It deals with a brother and sister who lose even their shack in a slum settlement when their mother, who has managed to hold the family together, dies. In a sort of reversal of the paradigmatic trek into the big city from the outskirts and the provinces, the two hit the road in order to survive. The sister tries to get work as a striptease dancer (one of Medina's early novels, and perhaps one of his very best on life in a dark and dank Buenos Aires created by the military, is *Strip Tease;* Foster, "Bare Words and Naked Truths"). Her brother, who raped her, presents himself as her agent. After she has been forced to participate in what becomes virtually a snuff film (Medina plays on the allegations that the military sponsored the production of pornography, including snuff films, using women who had been kidnapped or detained), she finally rebels against her brother's exploitation when they return to Buenos Aires, where the slum seems almost like a mecca to her.[2] The movie is, of course, able to visually place the story of these urban heirs of Hansel and Gretel against the backdrop of the city in a way that the novel can only suggest. But without ever falling into local-color practices that would betray the presence of a transcendent signifier, Medina holds the materiality of Buenos Aires firmly in the foreground as the specific sociohistorical reality in which his characters are enmeshed. The forces, personal and impersonal, that move this reality are given metonymic expression in the details of the city they have created and in terms of which the daily lives of individuals, whose resources are limited almost to the vanishing point, play themselves out—most exemplarily under the sign of terrible violence that those structures impose.

Language

One of the most distinctive features of Medina's writing concerns the registers of Spanish he employs. His own prose as a narrator has striven to be a model of academic writing, and this is admirably demonstrated in the care that he takes with the composition of his texts, in both stylistic and discursive terms. However, the speech of his characters is another thing, and it is here where one most tangibly understands the meaning of dirty realism. Of course, dirty realism also characterizes the narrator's voice, simply in terms of the matters chosen to be described in the detached, almost clinical terms of mainline journalistic prose. But Medina's characters express themselves with what one can take as a painfully accurate sociolinguistic documentariness. Especially in the case of female characters, his writing is based on the attempt to provide an image of recorded speech such as one might obtain from linguistic fieldwork. Such speech is "dirty" because of the multiple ways in which it violates dominant linguistic taboos. It is also dirty in the way in which the social world Medina evokes is dirty. Unable to comply with the model of social propriety endorsed by those who exercise symbolic power, either because that very exercise impedes the access to symbolic power by vast sectors of the populace, or because the model espoused has little to do with the material conditions of life, Medina's characters are confined to spaces that are considered dirty, and they talk accordingly.

Violence

Violence is a slippery term, particularly when used to refer to something other than deliberate physical harm done to another person's body. It has become customary to speak of certain uses of language and discourse as constituting forms of social violence, especially where epithets on the basis of race, ethnicity, gender, and sexual preference are involved, and it has been argued that verbal abuse is of a whole with physical assault. Concomitantly, the concept of structural violence has been proposed to explain how certain social structures are intrinsically violent toward those who are obliged to live them. Thus, slavery is violent in the ways in which torture is used as a means of control, but slavery is also violent because it is predicated on the denial of personal liberty, no matter how benevolent the treatment of the slave may be.

Medina's books are filled with violence, no matter how such a concept is defined. There is violence in the sense of gross bodily harm, such as the castration of a man by a lover fed up with the sustained abuse she has received from him. There is certainly violence in the sense of language used as an instrument of assault, whether the object is the reader (an individual of some degree of social standing and, therefore, complicitous with symbolic power, by virtue of being able to read literature) or another character, whom the reader overhears the language directed against. And, finally, there is structural violence. Medina shows the physical suffering of individuals both as a consequence of specific circumstances, such as military dictatorship, and as the result of the oppression created by generalized social structures. He implicitly argues to the effect that one form of violence begets another and that some dimension of legitimacy ought to be assigned the dirty language of dirty realism.

All four of these aspects of Medina's work define a very specific interpretation of urban life, both in terms of the particular spaces inhabited by the lumpen proletariat and, beyond those spaces, their interaction with other sectors of Argentine society. It is important to note that Medina has scant interest in focusing exclusively on the marginal *barrios* (neighborhoods) and *villas miseria* (slums) of the city. The nature of social life is such that the inhabitants of these sectors, in their struggle for survival, go out into the world and interact with those who exercise symbolic power, either in a way that is tolerated (as docile labor) or in ways that provoke outrage (as criminals, activists, or lone individuals who engage in random and insulting acts of social resistance). Thus, Medina's characters range over the entire urban domain. By contrast, the higher the symbolic power of individuals, the more circumscribed their movement in the city tends to be. In this way, the extent of their interaction with the city as a whole confirms Medina's interest in interrelating the violence by which the lumpen proletariat is victimized with the global social structures that produce, legitimate, duplicate, and overdetermine that violence.

Medina began writing chronicles essentially urban in scope after the return to constitutional democracy in 1985. Since the mid-1980s he has published six collections of his columns from *Página 12*. These columns belong to a long tradition of journalistic micronarratives, and the chronicle is considered a literary genre in many Latin American societies. Practitioners like Mexico's Carlos Monsiváis and Brazil's Luiz Veríssimo are very popular authors, and each has staked out his own particular cultural space. Whereas Medina has focused on the dirty realism of the megalopolis, Veríssimo composes droll human-comedy sketches underlain by a serious contemplation of the chaos and tribulations of urban life—the inherent ridiculous, surrealistic, grotesque texture of daily existence. Monsiváis is the most scholarly of the three, and he has used his columns both to analyze with considerable subtlety the dynamics of life in the largest city on the planet, with an emphasis on the elements of popular culture in terms of which that life is essentially conducted, and to provide an interpretation of Mexican cultural institutions that is grounded in an understanding of historical and social forces. Monsiváis's texts are often not as narrative as Veríssimo's and Medina's, but together the three constitute a cultural phenomenon taken much more seriously in Latin America than in the United States.

One of Medina's obvious predecessors is Roberto Arlt (1900–1942), whose *aguafuertes* (etchings) series—*Aguafuertes porteñas* (Buenos Aires Etchings), *Aguafuertes españolas* (Spanish Etchings), *Aguafuertes uruguayas* (Uruguayan Etchings)—gave definite literary status to the chronicle. Like Medina, Arlt also practiced a form of dirty realism, although Arlt was more interested in the petite bourgeoisie than he was in the parents of Medina's lumpen proletariat. Arlt, too, was criticized for his use of language, but more for the patois of immigrants (*lunfardo* in the broad sense, and with specific reference to Italian immigrants) than for any vulgarity. Indeed, Arlt seems at times to be an armchair philologist as he analyzes the semantic scope of words and phrases and charts their incorporation into Argentine metropolitan Spanish. Arlt was important for constructing a specific space for urban literature in Argentina at a time when it was still believed that authentic national culture could not be found in the city, where immigrants were rapidly distorting and corrupting whatever was left of the Creole inheritance, but rather in the countryside, the repository of tradition, as in the case of Ricardo Güiraldes's *Don Segundo Sombra,* one of the principal entries in a bibliography of rural mythification (ironically, Arlt worked at one time as Güiraldes's personal secretary).

Medina's first collection of essays cleverly marks with its title the transition from the period of military dictatorships to institutional democracy, under whose aegis Medina is not only able to reissue books that had been banned, but to practice the sort of critical commentary to which he has devoted himself for the past ten years. *Desde un mundo civilizado* (From a Civilized World) refers to a traditional oligarchic trope, to the effect that we live in a civilized world (the one created by the oligarchy) and we should conduct ourselves as such (the rule of decency, decorum, acceptance of the status quo). In Medina's text, this trope, with the irony of the title, appears as it does over a nineteenth-century cut depicting violent mayhem. It is the first step in subversion, and it points in two directions. First, it points to how we do not live in a civilized world. If such a world did in fact exist, there would have been no military dictatorship in Argentina (for the oligarchy and their adherents, the military is a confraternity of gentlemen: so Jorge Luis Borges said, at least with respect to Pinochet, although he later recanted this sort of effusion). Consequently, there would be no social marginalization in the country, no gross economic injustice—precisely the stuff of Medina's chronicles. Second, the title points to how Medina's texts, in their very existence as cultural production, break with the gentleman's academic agreement as to what constitutes decency in writing: a violent and uncivilized discourse to challenge a violent and uncivilized social experience. By echoing the civilized tenet that we inhabit a civilized world from which the manifestations of a dirty reality are regrettable deviations, Medina explores how they are, quite to the contrary, exemplary vignettes of a society in which the individual is constantly at the mercy of a dynamic of structural violence that masks itself with the illusion of civility and law and order.

In terms of the need in Argentina in the mid-1980s both to denounce a national structural violence that made military tyranny possible and even welcome and to overcome the tendency for a country that had at that time emerged from a recent ignominious past to view itself as a pariah among self-reputedly civilized nations, *Desde un mundo civilizado* exemplifies the attempt, from the position of cultural production, to redefine a national consciousness on the basis of a broader analysis of sociocultural dynamic than the denunciatory testimonial (Foster, "Los parámetros de la narrativa argentina"). Since many of the texts deal directly or by implication with recent actual events that have appeared on the front pages of the newspaper, Medina is also demonstrating the ability of literary narrative to provide a more probing inquiry into the motivations and consequences to the individual of acts and events that journalism can profitably chronicle. Specifically, Medina frequently focuses on the interior processes of the so-called agents of violence in order to suggest their compulsions as well as to portray the psychological impact on them of their actions.[3]

Although neoliberalism has brought a renovation of equipment and the implementation of differential service, the *colectivo*, the most common form of surface transportation, remains ubiquitous in the streets of Buenos Aires. The Buenos Aires subway system, the first in Latin America, is efficient but limited, and suburban trains are, since privatization, on the way again to becoming a major form of transportation between the city and the suburbs. But within the city, where most people cannot afford the equally ubiquitous and superb taxi service, the vast network of buses is what basically moves workers, students, and shoppers. Few cities of Latin America have as rich a folklore surrounding the bus as does Buenos Aires, where brightly colored vehicles stand out against the generally drab background of the city, and where the driver's area is typically highly personalized with icons of cultural identities: a picture of Gardel, a pennant of a soccer club, a holy card of the Virgin of Luján, patron saint of travelers, perhaps a picture of one's mother, not to mention stickers that announce with caustic and aggressive wit a particular view of society and mankind. Even Borges, not much of a fan of popular culture aside from the tango, wrote about the stickers during his early vanguard local-color phase, although with reference to an earlier exterior placement on vehicles ("Las inscripciones de los carros"; see also Folino's delightful book, in a series titled "Cuadernos de la nostalgia" [The Nostalgia Notebooks], *Chofer buena banana busca chica buena mandarina* [A Banana Driver Seeks a Tangerine Chick (banana = handsome; tangerine = pretty)]).[4]

Medina, however, has no interest in the folklore of the *colectivo* or in the sort of nostalgic registry provided by Folino. His text "El colectivo" is a nightmarish metaphor of the tumultuous nature of collective life.[5] Indeed, the very word *colectivo* refers to the fact that it is a collective mode of transportation. Like an urban ship of fools, it brings together a social sampling of individuals from the city and places them in uncomfortable and therefore potentially violent contact with each other. The text is written in brief sentences, most of which are four or five words in length, and few are more than ten. The staccato beat of the text is clearly meant to capture the frenetic and jumpy pace of the bus, its abrupt starts and stops, and the harried circumstances in which everyone travels. Nerves can never be anything other than frayed, and the bus driver is in a constant state of apoplexy. Civility is impossible in such circumstances, and the individual, implacably subjected to the indignities of mass transit, can do nothing more than become a conduit for indignities committed against the person of fellow travelers.

The brief text has a number of recurring motifs, one of which is a policeman whose hand rests on the butt of his holstered gun. This image is stated four times in seven pages, and one's conclusion is that it marks the ineffective authoritarianism of Argentine society. The symbols are always present of police power, but such power, whatever else it can do for/to the citizenry, cannot impose civility, and the policeman is no more safeguarded from indignities at the hands of the passengers than anyone else. "El colectivo" is a metaphor of Argentine society in the sense that it models the low level of human comfort that is imposed by an anonymous and ugly urban experience. Echoing the hoary commonplace of travel as a figure for the human transit of life as a journey filled with trying experiences, Medina underscores how these passengers are condemned, like the Flying Dutchman, to travel eternally by horrendous modes of public transportation: "Para el colectivo. Por suerte llegamos a la estación dice una. Tomarán el tren y otro colectivo y otro colectivo y otro colectivo. Toda la vida" (134).[6]

In order to reinforce the ship-of-fools image, the author, in addition to sketching a sociologically representative inventory of urban personages, relies on metonymies of dirty realism to highlight the incivility that flourishes in this quintessentially urban nightmare: "El hombre le ha dado un golpe a la mujer. En el costado y con disimulo. Sus ojos giran huracanados. Ella intenta calmarlo. ¡No se puede bajar por adelante! Gritan. El colectivero no abre la puerta hasta que dicen que es la embarazada" (133).[7] Or: "Y por si fuera poco alguien grita: ¡Abran la ventanilla por favor! Fue un pedo sordo y despiadado" (132).[8] During the period of military dictatorship, one category of American movies that could be shown without restrictions or censorship belong to Hollywood horror movies of the *Carrie* and *Friday the 13th* possession, stalker, slasher variety. It is possible to argue that such horror fantasies, which have little if any correspondence to lived human experience and to actual social reality, serve by design or accident to distract the viewers from the verifiable horrors of daily life outside the theater. Latin American culture production has rarely attempted to vie with U.S. skills at producing science fiction, horror films, and action flicks, especially now that the majority of the inflated budgets goes to the sophisticated technology of special effects. Horror and related genres of Latin American cultural production have instead relied on accurate documentaries of sociohistoric interpretation. Such interpretations, of course, are not free of ideological circumscriptions. However, a contemplation of their interpretive project within the context of an adequate understanding of how ideology always drives interpretation provides the occasion for a sustained public debate over the substance of daily life. From this point of view, Medina's chronicles paint much more of an authentic horror story than any Hollywood film ever could. Certainly, there are those who would insist that Hollywood's work can be read as rich and suggestive allegories of the terrors of existence that bourgeois normalcy and decency insists on glossing over. Yet Medina's point seems to be that, thanks to the effects of military tyranny and an abiding social authoritarianism, there is no glossed-over surface to allegorize.

Published five years after *Desde un mundo civilizado*, *Es Ud. muy femenina* (You Are Very Feminine) and *Deuda de honor* (Debt of Honor) continue to practice something like a narrative radar mission in which the author scrupulously seeks out metonymic incidents of contemporary Porteño life. True, many of Medina's texts continue to report on incidents from other parts of Latin America and the United States, as though he were concerned that his lens of dirty realism was not confined exclusively to Argentina. Medina also continues his carefully measured usage of a third-person, indirect free style. This modality often represents a special challenge to the foreign reader because of the cultural and linguistic information that it typically presupposes and that the brevity of the text is unable to elaborate on. What is especially effective about the indirect free style, however, is that it challenges the reader to accept the legitimacy of the spoken consciousness of individuals whom "decent" or "genteel" readers have difficulty accepting as anyone whose view of the world on either microcosmic or macrocosmic terms they might be willing to accept. That is, Medina's indirect free style functions to create a measure of legitimation for the radical Otherness of dirty realism for the literate reader. Since Medina's characters and their consciousness are drawn from a wide array of social classes, from the miserable and the marginal to the powerful, it is not simply a question of entering and sharing the perspective of the forgotten members of society, but of scrutinizing the hidden dirty face of those who are among the most prominent and influential.

Medina's success as a writer has been based in large part on his ability to firmly grasp the tenor of the moment. Thus, even as his texts represent a panoply of constants about Argentine social life as it is showcased in Buenos Aires, especially the self-satisfied and self-serving pretenses of a moral superiority that have justified that country's worst history of oppressive institutions, they are also artfully in tune with shifts in a first instance of social consciousness. This is what gives *Deuda de honor* a particular stamp of originality. Well into the current Carlos Menem administration, with all the unremittingly harsh realities associated with the recapitalization of the national economy, any gesture toward a resistant culture of localized strategy of human dignity has disappeared from these chronicles. In previous collections, although there have been texts that examine the bleakest aspects of the human social drama, there were also narratives that demonstrated something like successful efforts at resisting institutional humiliation and the constituent elements that make such a resistance possible. None of this is present in *Deuda*. Text after text slips into place in a mosaic of failure and despair on the one hand and cynical manipulation on the other as reflexes of the total disappearance of the optimism associated with the redemocratization of Argentine society in the 1980s.

Boedo is a legendary working-class neighborhood on the south-central side of Buenos Aires, famous for its proletarian cultural roots which, in a facile ideological binary, have customarily been juxtaposed to the north side of elite writers like Borges (Barletta). However, like Borges, Medina is particularly interested in issues relating to masculinity and the blindness it creates in the individual with regard to the violence of his conduct. In "El crimen del barrio Boedo" (The Crime in Boedo) the reader follows the interior discourse of an individual jailed for killing the mother and sister of

the woman he suspects of being unfaithful to him. Before or after killing
Patri's sister—and he insists that it was not his intention to kill the two
women, but only to insist energetically on their telling him where Patri
was—he rapes her. When through the bars of his cell the prisoner is tossed
a dead rat with a message around its neck, "Las muertas que mataste, te
saludan,"[9] the prisoner hangs himself.

Medina needs provide no judgment here, not against the codes of machismo, not against the justice and jail system, not against the journalism
whose impersonal account of the murder the prisoner reads as he picks his
teeth with a fork after eating. But where there is a space of assessment
opened up is in the juxtaposition between the assumptions of the newspaper report and the criminal's reaction to it. The criminal, caught up in the
reasoning process that involves his relationship with Patri, the reasons for
his attempt to find her, the fatal altercation with her sister and mother, the
taking out on them of his anger, and the alienation of his almost virtual
disengagement with the reader, finds little of himself in the newspaper
report:

> "*Según el relato de los testigos, un hombre al que luego se identificó
> se apersonó en la agencia d acompañantes donde trabajaban junto a
> Patricia y le reclamó a ésta que volviera a unirse a él sentimental-
> mente. Ante la negativa de la joven . . .*"¿Qué saben los diarios? ¿Qué
> sabe la policía? ¿Qué saben los testigos, los análisis microscópicos y
> los jueces y . . . ? Mira las fotos. Están al costado de la página. No las
> quería ver a pesar de que la policía ya se las había mostrado. Las mira
> detenidamente. (76)[10]

As though the prisoner had little to do with what he reads about in the
paper, or as though what was being reported were not what really happened, the anomie of the prisoner is confirmed by the fact that, in reading
the story, he is particularly interested in making sure his name is spelled
correctly: "Con el tenedor busca su nombre. Sí, está bien escrito" (78).[11]
This apparently insignificant detail, which from one point of view marks
his psychotic disengagement from the crime, has the value of humanizing
him: among the millions of inhabitants of Buenos Aires, only a limited
percentage have Hispanic names, and the need to confirm one's identity by
making sure a name is spelled correctly is not an insignificant detail for a
miserable urban outcast.

There is clearly no suggestion of cultural resistance in "El crimen del barrio Boedo." Locked in the codes of masculinity and sealed in the anomie of the outcast condition provoked by the violence pursued in conformity with those codes, the prisoner appears to commit suicide. Suicide is certainly one form of cultural resistance, as Western culture has known at least since Cato's defense of it in antiquity. However, Medina's text, as a chronicle, is too short to allow for the sort of psychological build-up to such a decision that would make it evident as a condition of despair leading to the considered decision to take one's life as a gesture of defiance and escape. One suspects here that suicide is meant to signify a degree of individual will, as a correlate of the prisoner's separation from the image of him in the newspaper report and the importance for him to ascertain that his name is spelled correctly. At the same time, as an interpretation of the implacable violence of social life, of which the prisoner is less "victim" in any liberal sense than the transparent embodiment, Medina's text demands a cruel investment on the part of the reader. As a reflex of urban life, the prisoner cannot be set aside for the reader via the process of "humanizing" him as a victim. Victimization disengages individuals and turns them into unique human cases whose tragedy we contemplate from a distance, relieved that we are not in their shoes. By contrast, the individual who is a reflex of an entire social dynamic, by virtue of not being individuated and therefore engaged from the multitude, becomes a synecdoche of that multitude, and his anonymous case—we never learn his name that he is so concerned to see spelled correctly—can be the case of anyone. The illusion of the greater misfortune of the subaltern individuals is only an illusion: one does not embody social codes as an act of social agency. Social codes embody the individual, who has little choice in fulfilling their demand, and the consequences are repeatedly every bit as appalling as Medina's chronicle demonstrates. In a certain sense, the individual exists only to carry out the social code, and any unique subjectivity the individual is alleged to possess is a recurring fallacy of our cultural ideologies. It is along these lines that Medina often chooses not to individuate his characters. When they do have names, such as the lover, Patri, or her sister, Miriam, they are of no particular importance, which in turn only underscores how they are undifferentiated ciphers of an unalleviatingly and mercilessly dirty urban landscape.

There may be no sense in which *autism* is used in less than strictly clinical terms to describe the sort of acute alienation of an individual who, without being socially marginal in the way uninstitutionalized psychotics are, manifest alarming symptoms of being out of synch with society at large. Such malcoordination may, on the one hand, reveal something like an innocence derived from the inability or the unwillingness to accept the unyielding cynicism of the outside world. On the other hand, it may manifest certain profound limitations in the ability to understand the demanding subtleties of being attentive to the needs, the worldview, and, of course, the limitations of others.

José María Gatica (1926–1963) was probably the most controversial figure in the history of the Argentine ring, fighting ninety-four matches, of which he won eighty-five, with only seven losses and two draws.[12] Unfortunately, the fight of his life, against Ike Williams in New York, with the full backing of the Peronista propaganda machine, was the most spectacular of his losses. It was a downward turn in his career and his life at a time when, given the opportunities and the support available to him, he should have been a stunning triumph. Gatica was never able to shake the family and friends who sponged off him mercilessly, and he was caught up in the high life of the postwar and Peronista boom years in Argentina, especially the cabaret scene in Buenos Aires. Unfortunately, he was never able to grasp the conditions of discipline that would have made him a truly great fighter, and he died at thirty-eight, a down-and-out drunk run over by a city bus.

Gatica is an important title to consider for the urban culture of Buenos Aires, something that is readily apparent in the 1993 film by Leonardo Favio, *Gatica, el mono* (Gatica, the Monkey; for a review, see Beceyro). Favio's film has many things wrong with it; an almost sycophantic evocation of Gatica's relationship with the Peróns; a mawkish deathbed scene between Gatica and the dying Evita that is totally unhistoric; a clumsy attempt to impose an auteurist style on the filming, especially the scenes dealing with the deadening pummeling of Gatica's later fights; and the lack of any sense of sociohistorical interpretation. Yet there is a careful attempt to evoke both the popular-culture identities of Gatica and the importance to his life of elements of the urban landscape. Gatica was a rough-and-tumble kid who lived the streets of Buenos Aires during the so-called Década Infame (Infamous Decade), the period of Argentina's first military

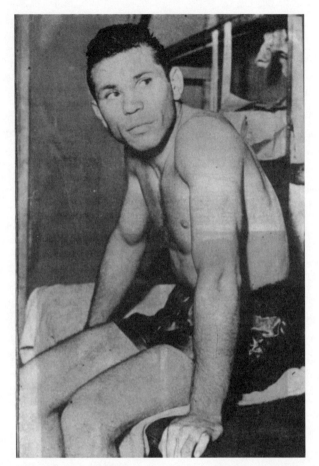

Boxer José María Gatica revealing both his popular origins
(his physical features) and his psychological alienation (his
inability to face the camera). Courtesy of Enrique Medina.

dictatorship, which was driven by various elements of fascist inspiration.
Gatica's rise corresponded to the rise of Peronismo, which overtly and
energetically favored popular culture, especially forms that could be used
as public display, thereby constituting extensions of a Peronista political
rally. The enormous growth of the mass media during the prosperous 1940s
and early 1950s meant greater forums than ever in radio, print journalism,
and newsreels. Television was to come at the tail end of the Peronista

period, but Gatica was pretty much washed up by then. In general, the growth of such forums has meant a significant increase in the public display of popular culture, and this is even more so in the case of populist Argentina (see Ciria; Geltman). Favio, who has been a long-time Peronista supporter, is reasonably interested in enhancing the sort of nostalgic look at the heyday of Peronismo a picture like *Gatica, el mono* permits.[13] Indeed, the greatest value of Favio's picture, in which it is clear, and rather suspect, that he equates Gatica's decline with the decline of Peronismo, or makes an allegory of the other, is in the nostalgic evocation of the urban spaces, mostly marginal, even when they included posh cabarets, inhabited by Gatica during his short and brutal career.

By contrast, Medina's novel, *Gatica,* which was published the same year as Favio's film, wastes no time in also setting up Gatica as an icon of both the freewheeling corruption of the Peronista years in Argentina and of the enormous distance between the cultural myths of Argentine society and the grinding inexorableness of the false promises. Surely, on the basis of this novel, as allegorical as Favio's film, but in a more critically negative way, one cannot expect of Medina any desire to defend Peronista ideology or its hagiography.

Gatica, like Peronismo, truly believes that he is the best that ever was. At the same time, he senses he is being used, that he has no effective control over his body or the conduct of his life, that he is merely a cipher in a political machine with no substance in terms of human dignity. Thus, Gatica is made to serve Medina's overall interpretive project regarding the dirty realism of Argentina: Gatica may be made to believe that he is in control of his own life, that, with his talent and his ensuing fame, he has gained a measure of social agency and can, in fact, attain a position of social respectability that must naturally accompany his professional accomplishments. But the novel is relentless in demonstrating that it is all smoke and mirrors, that Gatica could never rise above the slime of his original social condition, and it is to that slime that he will in the end return—or at least to the biblical dust in which he rolls after being run down by a bus. The scene in which Gatica is hit by the bus reminds us of the social symbolism that, in the essay commented on above, Medina had attached to the Buenos Aires *colectivo;* except in this case its client-victims are outside as well as inside:

Se levanta, va hasta el mostrador, paga todo, vuelve a decirle chau a los amigos y sale muy tambaleado. Busca un taxi. Hace señas y no le paran porque debido a la dificultad que le produce la pierna enferma y a su confusión mezcla de vino y grapa, camina como espantapájaros sacudido por la tormenta. Gatica los insulta. Ve un colectivo lleno que lo puede llevar y, esquivando autors que a su vez lo esquivan, corre a treparse. Se aferra de un pasamano; bien, a pesar de que la gente amontonada en el estribo es demasiada. Salvo el intento del dedo índice, con la otra mano no logra agarrarse debido a los dos muñequitos que se la ocupan. En un pequeñísimo lugar consigue poner un pie. El tipo que está colgado delante de él intenta subir un escalón, el colectivo en marcha inesperadamente adquiere velocidad y el tipo se echa algo para atrás haciéndole perder el equilibrio a Gatica que, cayendo, porque una mano sola no lo puede sostener, ve al hombre subir por fin el escalón al mismo tiempo que la puerta se cierra de un latigazo. Cae, Gatica, sobre los adoquines; casi sin soltar los muñequitos. El colectivo hace el cuarto de giro para doblar la esquina y las ruedas traseras brincan sobre el cuerpo asombrado. (*Gatica*, 301–2)[14]

The novel is constructed around segments that move between a characterization of Gatica's unarticulated thoughts (he probably articulates no more than a dozen or so utterances directly in the course of the novel) and a recitation in the image of the hard-bitten yet occasionally sensationalist and sentimental sports-page prose of the period of the circumstantial facts of Gatica's life and career. Gatica's life is unquestionably an allegory. But it is a terrible and thereby effective account of a capitalist society in which the destiny of the individual has hardly any consequence at all. In this sense, Gatica is put forth as an Argentine lumpen-proletariat everyman. Medina wrote his novel at a time when Argentina was beginning to move once again into the throes of institutional incoherence imposed by a neoliberalist economic adventurism and government by decree, with a president for whom the ethos of sports (with every trace of its disingenuousness covered over by an unrelentingly brutal, masculinist rhetoric) is the quintessence of the Argentine national character. In this regard, it is instructive to refer to the lamentable chronicle of the soccer superstar Diego Maradona (see Medina's chronicle, "La mesa está tendida"). There can be little doubt that Medina intends *Gatica* to be read as an accurate barometer of the deep social deceptions spoken through the main character's often almost incoherent flow of consciousness.

But to return to the matter of the presence of Buenos Aires, Gatica, by transcending the streets of the city, if only momentarily and falsely, confirms the importance of urban popular culture and its spaces for the construction of an itinerary of important facets of Argentine self-identity. Since Medina has no interest in romanticizing the Buenos Aires cityscape, he has no occasion to dwell on its importance in defining significant moments in Gatica's life. The city is simply there, and its spaces are where what Medina's story about Gatica takes place, for no other reason than that there is nowhere else for it to take place. Gatica may have had access to privileged spaces, as Evita certainly did, but for both of them, life was where people (or *the* people) were. The spaces of the lumpen proletariat and their extensions—cafés, bars, cheap restaurants, sports rings, dance halls, dives, and the like—were the places Gatica was most at home.

chapter 8

Sara Facio As Urban Photographer

Photography by women obeys in large measure the general outlines of feminine/feminist cultural production: the opportunity to have a voice from the perspective of women's experience and to contribute to the vast project of creating women's history. Even when female cultural producers are not aware of seeking such a participation, or even when they are, in terms of their personal projects, adamant about not seeking such participation, alleging that they wish to be viewed as cultural producers without any gendered inflection, they are, nevertheless, when viewed from the perspective of the dominant practice of such participation, making, despite themselves, a significant contribution. For, surely, the desire not to be viewed as a feminist cultural producer, like the desire not to be viewed as gay or as Latin American or as Afro-American cultural producers, is itself an important statement within and with reference to a project for forging feminine/feminist cultural products. Put differently: any cultural production by a member of a subaltern group is necessarily involved with subaltern identity, whether or not it wants to be, and with the project to construct alternatives to subalternity.

There is another way in which women's photography is particularly feminist, and that is in the way in which it provides opportunities for the gaze and, in fact, legitimates it. As feminist criticism has routinely argued, women are the object of the gaze, but rarely its agents. Or, when women are its agents, it is as surrogates of the masculine/masculinist gaze: women take the place of patriarchal men in exercising the gaze as part of the exercise of social control, and the corrective role they play as a consequence of what that permissible gaze allows them to discover either enforces the codes of the patriarchy or enforces the position allowed to women within it. For example, when a woman uses the gaze allowed to her

to control her man's sexual conformity, she is enforcing not only his compliance with masculinity in a general way but also the advantages that
accrue to her as the partner of a properly sexualized man.

Any gaze other than the ones specifically allotted to women is transgressive. A certain amount of restrained transgression in this regard is allow-
able, such as the gaze of the sexually adventurous woman whose eroticiza-
tion of the male body enhances a man's sense of masculinity before her
(resulting in greater sexual capital for him), before society (resulting in
greater social capital), and before himself (resulting in greater psychological capital). Such a gaze must be strictly monitored, however, because the
over-eroticization of the male body, even if it does not run the risk of
queering that body (since excessive gaze is a motif associated with homoeroticism and the need to display and be seen displaying the body as part
of a demonstration of identity, as a form of seduction, and as a validation
of sexual agency), can indicate that the woman has assumed a position of
visual control that can always end up in the humiliation of the male.

Cultural production, especially that production which has been con-
ferred the status of an element in the restructuring of women's roles in a
society, involves vast new realms for the exercise of the gaze, since it can
safely be assumed that "seeing" in the fullest sense and in all of its dimensions is essential to the production of culture of any ideological significance. Just as women's theater and women's filmmaking involves a prioritized display of women's bodies, of women's experiences, of women's
history, photography involves a prioritized seeing. One could certainly
argue that photography, like painting or like culture in general, involves
the representation, the display, as the primary circumstance of existence of
the cultural product at issue. But, as theoreticians of photography have
argued, photography is first of all an act of seeing, and the photograph is a
semiotic field in which what is portrayed is, in fact, an occurrence of "seeing being seen." As we see the photograph, we are not just seeing a slice of
reality being represented. Rather, the photograph is a staging of the
photographer's act of seeing, and the photography is the process of seeing
as much as, if not more than, the product of what has been seen. This is the
force of Barthes's significant metaphor of the *camera lucida*: The photograph is, in reality, what is the real camera, and what we think of as the
technical instrument is only a resource for the creation of the processing
camera that is the photograph.

Moreover, since photography is always based on the freeze-frame (even the photographic sequence is still a series of discrete frozen frames), it marks, in ways in which film or television, which involve the illusion of the presence of life in motion before our very eyes, even when we know that it is not really taking place there on the screen, a distancing, and therefore an interpretive recodification, from lived life that we usually associate only with such highly mediated products as poetry and fiction. All cultural production, of course, involves extensive mediation, but some products, like film and television or theater, work off the illusion that life is really there before our eyes, while literature, through the complex medium of written language, can never involve the sensation of presence. Derrida has taught us this very well, shattering definitively any possible belief in a literary realism. Photography is like literature in this regard, despite the popular belief that it too holds life up to our unmediated gaze. The point of theorizing about photography continues to be how that genre of cultural production is, ironically, as complexly mediated as it is semiotically transparent.

Latin America has a long tradition of women artists—Mexico's Frida Kahlo is, to be sure, one of the continent's most famous names—and, as a recent show in the United States has shown, Latin American feminist painters now constitute an especially vigorous presence. Yet photography, like filmmaking, has counted on few women, which is undoubtedly due as much to the enormous cost of materials and production as it is to access to technical resources. Sara Facio was trained in fine arts and began working in photography in the mid-fifties. After studying with Annemarie Heinrich, she worked in the photographic studios of Luis D'Amico, and until the mid-eighties collaborated closely with his daughter Alicia (see Rosenbaum, 302). In 1973, Facio and María Cristina Orive founded the publishing house La Azotea. La Azotea has published an extensive bibliography of her works first with D'Amico and then, after the dissolution of their artistic partnership, her now-extensive solo work (concerning D'Amico's work, see Gimbernat de González). Facio has been important in the development of resources for professional photographers in Argentina, and she now curates the FotoGalería of the Teatro Municipal General San Martín in central Buenos Aires, one of the major theater complexes in Latin America, which in addition to the photography gallery—in reality an ample passageway to the city's Centro Cultural that lies behind the San Martín—hosts musical events and art film cycles (career information on Facio is provided by Scimé; Potenze).

Facio has been primarily an urban photographer. Although she and D'Amico published a work in conjunction with Julio Cortázar, *Buenos Aires Buenos Aires*,[1] in which the cityscape is featured, her work has dealt especially with individuals who are either identified with the city of Buenos Aires (well-known writers, artists, and personalities) or who are anonymous everymen portrayed as integral elements of the city as a human space. As one might expect, Facio has had a particular interest in women. One of her recent publications, *Retratos 1960–1992*, contains considerable material relating to women. One section, "Las hechiceras" (The Temptresses), is of particular interest: "Esta serie traduce devoción por sus personajes. Mujeres modelo admiradas por lo que realizaron en sus respectivas disciplinas. Se las ve bellas, fuertes, únicas" (37).[2]

Facio does not explain what she means by *hechicera*, although she certainly must be aware of the resemanticization feminism has given the concept of the witch in Western culture. Where traditionally the witch was understood by patriarchal society to be the agent of the Devil—indeed, his concubine—the word was used to denominate any woman who could be legitimately persecuted for her alleged moral deviation. While subsequent cultural interpretations understood that such persecution was in reality a punishment for social dissidence (see Arthur Miller's *The Crucible*), it was a feminist reading of women's history that underscored how the witch was always the woman who had placed herself beyond patriarchal control, especially a woman who spoke from the margins of masculinist society against its control of women whose behavior constituted an overt defiance of compulsory heterosexism (old maids, the sexually promiscuous, "cruel" mothers, and, most especially, lesbians). Mary Daly's writing has particularly underscored the need to promote the figure of the witch, the wild woman spinning beyond the control of patriarchal and straight society (see *Gyn/ecology*, for example).

Facio's figures unquestionably fulfill the guidelines set out by Daly and feminists who revindicate the witchly vocation of strong women. They range from a strong-presence actress like Norma Aleandro to Griselda Gambaro, one of Argentina's leading playwrights, whose works are indeed terrifying for their stagings of the implacable dynamics of patriarchal power. Also included are María Luisa Bemberg, one of Latin America's first successful feminist filmmakers; the urban singer Susana Rinaldi; and the folklore singer Mercedes Sosa. Sosa's music is a Latin American paradigm of songs of social protest underlain by a firm ideological commitment to the importance of traditional material, projected through the presence of a powerful Mother Earth figure. Aída Bortnik, the scriptwriter of Luis Puenzo's *Historia oficial,* the film Norma Aleandro starred in that brought her, through the Oscar the film won, to international attention, is also photographed, along with actress Cipe Lincovsky and non-Argentines like the major British poet Doris Lessing and the French feminist philosopher Simone de Beauvoir. Facio's fellow photographer María Cristina Orive is photographed with her camera, and dancer Iris Saccheri is featured in three takes, and in two she is indeed Daly's whirling woman.

In her presentation note, Facio goes on to write: "Algunas 'Hechiceras' inspiraron la necesidad de *darles color*, no mediante una toma con negativo color, sino pintando zonas caprichosamente elegidas. Imposible imaginarlas en blanco y negro" (37).[3] Facio works exclusively in black and white, and what she is referring to here is the way in which, working off of an old photographic tradition of colorizing black and white photographs, she has colored her prints by marking over them in broad strokes with transparent markers. This provides the photographs with a marked painterly texture that emphatically underscores the mediated nature of photography: if black and white is less "realistic" than color photography (which is why it is the preferred medium of art photographers), such a painterly texture, by being in such contrast to color photographs because of the way in which color has been applied in a nonrealistic way, increases the element of nonrealism.

By adding color to some of the photographs, Facio dramatizes certain elements that she has already highlighted in her composition of the frame, and it is a highlighting, especially in her use of garish colors, that further dramatizes the exceptional nature of these women as feminist models. This is especially true in the case of Facio's close friend María Elena Walsh (who writes the postscript [69]), one of the most respected woman writers in Argentina and known internationally for her children's narratives and poetry (she has recorded much of the latter as songs), as well as her "adult" poetry and narrative writings (Foster, "María Elena Walsh"). Facio provides Walsh with a framing within the frame. That is, in addition to the border of the photograph as the material cultural product, Walsh's image

María Elena Walsh, by Sara Facio.

within the frame is specifically reframed. This is done by a double border drawn with a marker. The double border, in addition to the details of added coloration, makes this an exceptionally interesting example of the way in which the added highlighted coloring of some of Facio's photographs of the *hechiceras* calls special attention to Walsh. This befits Walsh's important place in contemporary Argentine culture as a figure of resistance to authoritarian culture. Walsh is particularly well remembered for a sarcastic essay she wrote against the military dictators, "Desventuras en el País-Jardín-de-Infantes" (Misadventures in the Kindergarten Country). The essay, as the title indicates, plays off her association with children's literature, although in this case the association is a particularly grim one.

Facio captures her subjects in many different types of poses, but it is particularly notable that many of the women face the eye of the camera directly, a pose that has them engaged in an ocular communication with the photographer, as though therefore sharing meanings and identities

Norma Aleandro, by Sara Facio.

with her, and that gives the sensation that the viewer of the photograph is participating in that communication, whether as a stand-in for the photographer, as somehow a part of her world, or as someone to whom the photographer has yielded her place in the act of communication. Such a (re)duplication and triangulation may be fairly smooth in the case of a presumed ideal female/feminist/feminine-identified spectator, but it is clearly potentially upsetting for a viewer who falls outside of such a subject positioning. Admittedly, spectators who cannot approximate female/feminist/feminine-identified culture may simply choose to ignore it, as opposed to the aggressive repudiation others may prefer to engage in, especially professional critics who cannot subscribe to a gender-marked production (as though culture in general were not masculine/masculinist marked always and already).

The full frontal gazes are those of Aída Bortnik (although she seems to be looking slightly away from the camera), Norma Aleandro, María Luisa Bemberg (although hers is just a degree off angle, meaning that she appears both to be confronting the camera and to be gazing away from it), Susana Rinaldi, Celeste Carballo (this is the one photograph which is truly aggressive from a conventional point of view; Carballo is photographed from the breasts up, with her hands clasped behind her head, revealing her unshaven underarms and prominent nipples; around her neck she is wearing on a chain or thong the international peace symbol made popular in the 1960s), Cipe Lincovsky, María Elena Walsh (the one gaze that is categorically nondefiant and marked by warm tenderness), Simone de Beauvoir, and an unnamed woman. One will immediately grasp that these women, all Argentines, with the exception of Beauvoir, are known for their transgressive nature as individuals and as cultural producers.

I would like to examine a little more fully the image of Norma Aleandro, in part because of her important position in Argentine film and as an

María Luisa Bemberg, by Sara Facio.

Argentine actress who has now worked extensively abroad. For those familiar with her persona as an actress, it is impossible to see this photograph and not think of female roles she has played (ones that are both significantly feminist, as the protagonist who acquires a historical consciousness in *Historia oficial*, and ones that are quite unfavorable to feminist issues, as the patriarchal enforcer wife of the man who refuses to continue working in Fernando Ayala's 1969 *La fiaca;* it is impossible not to imagine her distinctive voice, whose loud and grating quality is the antithesis of conventional demure femininity. I realize there are sociolinguistic issues involved with regard to voice quality and its cultural and gender meanings, but Aleandro is part of a group of Argentine women actresses who have made a specialty of wielding a notably "harsh" voice, women like Thelma Biral, China Zorrilla (actually Uruguayan, but with a long record of work in Argentine productions), Bettiana Blum, Soledad Silveira, and Luisina Brando.

In addition to Aleandro's direct gaze into the eye of the camera—and understanding that this is a semiotic point of reference for the photograph and not the camera as instrument—Facio's photograph is notable for the way in which the actress's abundant hair spills off beyond the top and two side borders of the frame. This means that her hair, as a signature feature of her persona, as an iconic trait of femininity, as a highly charged erotic fetish, and, because of its texture, as a sign of her dynamic body, stretches off into infinity without discernible control or proportion to the head and upper torso that is featured in the photograph. Moreover, the way in which her hair is styled, in a long upward sweep off her forehead and out in opposing directions from her crown, suggests the wild woman of radical feminist conduct. I do not mean to attribute to Norma Aleandro political and social commitments that are not those of her personal identity. Rather, I mean to point out ways of legitimately interpreting the structure of elements captured by Facio's photograph, since what is involved here is less the viewer's interpretation of the historic Norma Aleandro than it is Sara Facio's interpretation of that woman.

In this interpretation, in addition to the overpowering distribution of the woman's hair, there are deeps shadows around her face, so much so that her right check is an eclipsed moon, and the right side of her neck is completely absent from the neckline of what she is wearing. By contrast, the left side of her face and neck is precisely marked. In this way, her face, partially ill defined, hovers in a dark background that gives it emphatic prominence. Her barely closed eyes (the lids occlude part of the iris) and her barely open mouth suggest an expressive use in the moment of the taking of the picture that lies behind the frozen image. It would be easy to say that this picture captures a woman in movement. More important is to stress how it captures the enormous and energetic vitality of Aleandro that is an integral part of her acting presence.

In none of these photographs is the urban context directly portrayed. Nevertheless, it is evident that these are urban women. The professional activities and their public persona are those of urban women. The Argentines portrayed here, with the exception of Mercedes Sosa, whose enormous success has, nevertheless, occurred in the urban context that voraciously consumes musical performances, are women from Buenos Aires and environs. They participate in the public life of the megalopolis, and they count on the typical vehicles of the city for the distribution of their cultural production. These women include Bemberg, Aleandro, and Lincovsky in film; Gambaro and Bortnik in theater; Rinaldi, Walsh, and Sosa in musical performances; and Orive in her own urban-based photography. For the Argentine spectator familiar with the work of these women and familiar with the roles they play in the life of the city, the urban dimensions evident in traces of the photographs (hairstyles, body language, clothes, and articles of adornment) hardly need be stated explicitly through details of background setting for the photographic images.

Humanario (a neologism: Humanarium), produced in collaboration by Sara Facio and Alicia D'Amico,[4] with an essay by Julio Cortázar, carries a colophon stating that printing was completed on March 26, 1976.[5] This date was two days after the most recent neofascist military dictatorship assumed power in Argentina. Such a coincidence is extremely ironic, since this collection of photographs deals with the mentally ill. As Cortázar explains in an essay structured as carefully as a Renaissance sonnet, the condition of mental illness is to a large extent an internal condition of human life. I would suggest that, in the sense that the title of this collection must be understood, mental alienation is an integral part of the human condition; some individuals, however, are categorically marked by a semiosis of mental illness that marginalizes them from society and that is used to incarcerate them. What is terribly ironic about Cortázar's explanation of the Moebius strip of sanity/insanity is how he understands that the pathologicization of alienation is a part of authoritarianism, and that, as the Sr. Ministro says in Carlos Somigliana's *El Nuevo Mundo* (The New World), one of the cycle of one-act plays of the event known as Teatro Abierto, which in 1981 defied military censorship, "La locura es una efermedad que sólo afecta a los opositores" (260).[6] Cortázar writes:

> Siempre he sentido que alejándose de esa zona contigua entre cierta locura y cierta cordura, los locos y los cuerdos se asemejan simétricamente en su proceso de ser cada vez más locos y cada vez más cuerdos. Finalmente, lo que pierde a ciertos locos es la forma insoportable que para la sociedad asume su conducta exterior; los tics, las manías, la degradación física, la perturbación oral o motora, facilitan rápidamente la colocación de la etiqueta y la separación profiláctica; es lógico, es incluso beneficioso para el loco, es [*sic*: en?] una sociedad que aplica las reglas de su juego con las que nadie está autorizado a jugar. Pero en el otro extremo de esa simetría, allí donde la razón va siendo cada vez más razonante y razonable, donde la conducta exterior no solamente no ofende a la ciudad sino que contribuye a exaltarla y a enriquecerla, basta mirar de cerca para descubrir a cada paso la otra alienación, la que no sólo no transgrede las reglas del juego sino que incluso las estatuye y las aplica. (13)[7]

In an authoritarian society, the mechanisms of alienation become maximally internalized, such that individuals become agents of their own self-regulating adherence to the implacable "rules of the game" Cortázar alludes to. Therefore, madness is the circumstance of a body marked by signs of its inability to internalize self-regulatory control—to even imagine it or apply it with the degree of success necessary to "pass" in an "ordered" society. If passing is what lesbigays and queers must do in a homophobic society to escape regulatory and punitive violence (in many societies, sexual dissidents are routinely accused of being mentally ill and treated accordingly), or what people of (Other) color must do in a racist society, sanity is also a form of passing in a society in which the concept of rationality becomes a strategy for marking a differentiating subset as crazy. The twin strands of madness and authoritarian society were brought together in an Argentine cultural product like Eliseo Subiela's 1987 *Hombre mirando al sudeste*, a film made as part of the redemocratization of the country

Gazing, by Sara Facio and Alicia D'Amico.

after the period of the neofascist tyranny, and Hugo Soto's character is a perfect embodiment of Cortázar's proposition.

Humanario is divided into three sections: women, men, young people. Perhaps it is because of Facio and D'Amico's feminist allegiances, or perhaps because it is the sacred status given women in a society like Argentina, where being a mother—and it is assumed unless proven to the contrary that all women are mothers—is the only unalloyed condition available to women. If to marry is for a woman to secure a stable position in the patriarchy, to be a mother is to make it permanent. Only if a woman turns out to be a bad mother does she lose the guarantees of respect that exalted social title brings with it. Indeed, in the case of the woman featured on pages 30–31 of the album, one is immediately struck by the bands she wears on both of her ring fingers. It is not conclusively clear that they are wedding bands (significantly called *alianzas* in Argentina), but it is safe to assume they are.

Such signs both connect this woman with a role of important social identity and create a dimension of pathos for the spectator by virtue of her severance as an institutionalized patient from the spheres in which she might properly exercise that role. It is important to note that mental institutions, like Argentina's vast Instituto Borda (where *Hombre mirando al sudeste* was filmed), are urban phenomena. Or, put differently, an integral part of urban culture is the mental institution to which marginal social subjects are confined. Outside the urban realm, those judged to be mentally ill (the classification in these terms of social subjects is less rigorously applied in nonurban settings) are confined by their own families (compare with the Victorian motif of the madwoman in the attic [Gilbert and Gubar]— in Argentine culture, the grandmother of Camila O'Gorman in María Luisa Bemberg's 1984 *Camila* is confined for political reasons, but she is also treated like a madwoman); ignored or tolerated (the local crazy in Héctor Olivera's 1984 film *No habrá más penas ni olvido*); or shipped off to the insane asylum in the city.

Facio-D'Amico's subject is given social identity by her ordered clothing: a nice turtleneck and carefully buttoned jacket and her decently cut hair held in place by a feminine scarf. She grips the frame she is looking through as if it were the window jamb of her own home: her fingers are relaxed and evenly distributed as though belonging to someone at peace. The femininity of the woman's appearance and the social markers of her role in society as revealed by the rings she wears are not specifically urban, but the institution she occupies is. It is in this way that we understand there is an urban context surrounding her inscription in this particular space she inhabits, which is the inside of a mental institution. Perhaps if the photograph were not included in this album, one would assume that the heavy wooden slats through which she peers were those of a barn or rustic hut, or perhaps of even a slum dwelling on the urban periphery.

But the viewer knows the woman is confined to a mental institution and that those wooden slats, which appear to be framing her face but which, because of their distribution for security purposes, actual crop it, are instruments of her forced confinement. While there may be some measure of "intelligence" in the woman's mouth, the camera catches her eyes in what is, in Cortázar's formulation, the external sign of her alienation. Her right eye looks straight into the camera, while her left eye wanders ever so slightly above the center line and turns inward. Of course, something other than the strict alignment of the eyes may be a problem of motor coordination that is congenital, disease induced, or the result of the aging process. Outside the context of this collection, a viewer might first assume a physical problem before reading the woman's eyes as betraying mental illness. And for that matter, her eyes may not even be a sign of mental illness. But social semiosis works with overdetermined signs. Signs have more than meaning as they occupy a structure of semantic meanings; it is a principle of semiosis that no sign has a meaning in and of itself: meaning is a function of a position in a network of signs. Signs also participate in subsets of redundancy, although what is properly called overdetermination is much more than a question of signs with equivalent meanings that echo and emphasize each other. Overdetermination involves signs not quite semantically equivalent to each other that, by their enmeshment in recurring structural patterns, end up impinging on each other and transferring fields of meaning between them—something like placing in a similar position in lines of poetry (for example, in key end-line positions) words like *amor* and *furor*. These two words are not synonyms, but when rhymed together in positions that link them (such as at the end of the last line of balanced quatrains in a sonnet), meaning spills over between them. In terms of social semiosis, anything can be turned into a meaningful sign and customarily is (even if Freud did say that sometimes a good cigar is just a good cigar). There is a tendency to group signs together in order to extract a maximum meaning: the sign of femininity is not just one detail, but a whole constellation of signs that speak to each other and reinforce synergetically a specific social meaning. By the same token, the presence of one prominent sign may provoke the scansion for other confirming signs, such that other details on view are converted into signs that fit into the a priori meaning for which confirmation is being sought. Knowing that the woman in this photograph is confined to a mental institution requires the viewer to find something to confirm that fact. Where other individuals in this album are portrayed in poses considered to be eloquent markers of insanity (for example, the women huddled into a corner on pages 36–37; one is barefoot and the other appears to be wearing unlaced men's slippers), this woman appears to be relaxed, and therefore the viewer asks how it is that she is confined. In this context the line of sight is drawn to the eyes, always the inevitable initial point of reference for photographs of human subjects aware they are being photographed, whereupon the unaligned eyes of the woman offer themselves as the "conducta social" for this woman's acute mental state.

Many of Facio's and D'Amico's photographs involve repeating frames, either identically (60), from different angles (64), or via an interplay between close-ups and wide-angle shots. The photographs on pages 21–23 constitute a sequence in which the first is a depth shot of a woman hunched over on the floor of a room or on the ground of an enclosed space. On page 23, there is a wide-angle shot in which the foreground of the first photograph—a space (perhaps a door or gate) between two walls that provides a frame for the woman sitting down—becomes the background for a patio in which we see the bodies of various women strewn around as though in a stupor. The photograph on page 22 does not "fit" the layout of the other two in any obvious way, although, placed between them, it appears to be a different angle of the same patio of the second one.

If the first photograph is an eloquent representation of the alienation of the seated woman, placing her in the context in the third one and, by extension, in the second one of a large group of alienated women gives the impression of a society of alienated zombies. The other women are mostly in fully supine positions (one is standing and one appears to be walking, while others may be stretching or twitching), while the one framed by the presumed doorway is seated in a hunched-over position, lost in the dark depths of her illness (between the two photographs, her position is reversed, as though saying that from whatever angle she is viewed she is the same madwoman). What makes this sequence particularly chilling is the way in which it almost seems to be a metaphor for those who will be gassed and killed by the ensuing Dirty War put into place by the tyrants of the 1976 coup, who, to be sure, were only following up on the state terrorism that had already been installed by the constitutional president, Isabel Perón, during the two previous years of her administration. To be sure, most of the killing took place outside of direct public view; although, so great was the government's and executioners' sense of impunity, some victims were executed in buildings and houses, with little regard for whether or not there were witnesses. The parallelism here is twofold: (1) the female mental patients tossed out on the ground like rag dolls as read in terms of the thousands of prisoners strewn about the holding rooms of the clandestine prisons of the military, often in a state of shock following torture; and (2) these same prisoners as social discards as read in terms of "discarding" the overflow of the clandestine prisons, which were constantly taking in new prisoners during the height of the Dirty War at the end of the 1970s, by dumping the prisoners alive and semiconscious from airplanes over the estuary of the Río de la Plata. Ricardo Bartís, in his play *Postales argentinas (sainete de ciencia-ficción en dos actos)* (Argentine Postcards

Untitled, by Sara Facio and Alicia D'Amico.

[Science-Fiction Operetta in Two Acts]), imagines the bottom of the Río de la Plata, dried up in the year 2043, as a vast fossil bed of the Dirty War. In terms of Cortázar's comment about how those who are identified as mentally ill are an extension of the "sane" who are able to hide their madness(es), one can say that the persecutions of the Dirty War constitute nothing more than an alternative reading of the bodies of social subjects in order to identify the signs of political madness, and in order to apply to those bodies the practices of imprisonment, torture, and, ultimately, discard by death.

Perhaps the most famous collaboration between Facio and D'Amico came in 1968 with the publication of *Buenos Aires Buenos Aires*, which is also accompanied by texts by Julio Cortázar (concerning the latter's textual contribution to the book, see Roy-Cabrerizo). Although published during the first round of neofascist dictatorships in the mid-1960s, censorship during those years was nowhere near the level it reached a decade later, and, moreover, this collection does not have the political implications that underlie *Humanario*. Too, Julio Cortázar, whose profile as an unflinching critic of neofascism has yet to attain the stridency it had in the 1970s, particularly with the publication in 1973 of *El libro de Manuel*, an album of resistance struggle, provides only occasional poetic texts; lacking is the sort of introduction that will provide an ideological interpretation of social madness that orients a reading of *Humanario*.

Yet *Buenos Aires Buenos Aires* is more than a series of nostalgic images of the sort that accompany the literary texts in *Buenos Aires, mi ciudad* (Buenos Aires, My City), which is from the halcyon years before the 1966 coup and a period of enormous cultural productivity: indeed, it is in 1963 that Cortázar's novel *Rayuela* appears, one of the major literary documents of the period. *Buenos Aires Buenos Aires* is remarkable for its sensitivity to the daily life of the city. In contrast to an enormous amount of photography that memorializes the so-called Paris of the Southern Hemisphere, this collection appears almost to be a photographic accompaniment to *Rayuela*. Cortázar's novel problematizes the continuities in the Argentine imagery of Buenos Aires and Paris by having his characters reenact again and again the routines of daily life in the lower-middle-class neighborhoods of the city, where monuments are vague shadows in the distance of the centers of power. Facio's and D'Amico's work is equally insistent on maintaining a focus on everyday life. Significantly, when monumental cityscapes do appear, such as a stunning aerial view of Plaza San Martín, one of the most patrician monuments in the entire city, there is the absence of human presence, as though the space were an architectural model rather than a vibrant lived human space. As such, it is contrasted with numerous photographs of bustling human spaces—streets and intersections, highways, parks and beaches, stadiums, cafés and bars, subway platforms and exits. Even another aerial view (rooftops of typical urban apartment buildings) bears the signs of human presence, even if no actual persons appear in the photograph: television antennas, laundry hung out to dry, telephone and electrical lines, rubbish, patio furniture. There are, of course, some images of the skyline that give the sense of the city's immensity. But the fact that these traditional "tourist" images are outnumbered by photographs of everyday people going about everyday lives only serves to distance the former as part of the economical apparatus that controls those lives.

What is particularly significant is the contextualization of *Buenos Aires Buenos Aires* as a project carried out during the military dictatorship of the late 1960s. Apart from structures of persecution, repression, and censorship, a military dictatorship provides an overwhelming masculinization. To be sure, societies are masculinist to begin with, and the markers of patriarchal power are overt and omnipresent. But military dictatorship enhances the workings of masculinism, and the signs of it are given greater meaning (overdetermined) to evoke this semiotic concept again. In fact, to the extent that the military comes to power because there is the belief that patriarchal power has been diminished ("by lack of patriotic will," for example) or undermined ("by foreign ideas"), a characterization that is frequently accompanied by rhetorical interpretations that stress the contrary signs of nonmasculinism/feminization, military intervention is customarily cast as a necessary and salutary remasculinization: the reorganization and reaffirmation of the masculinist must occur to restore a transcendent national character whose greatest manifestation is to be found, precisely, in the signs of the military institutions.

There is, of course, no appearance of the military, nor any sign of the dictatorship, in these photographs. There is, however, a number of photographs that interpret the masculine culture of Buenos Aires. I do not refer specifically to those many photographs in which men are shown engaged in the tasks of daily life. These photographs are certainly marked by masculinism in the sense that the rigid codes of sexual difference in Argentine society carve out separate realms for men and women, realms that have little chance for intersection. Thus, neighborhood bars and the workplace in general are virtually exclusively male domains. Photographs on these themes are substantially different; they are documents with a socially significant meaning different from that of those in which men and women appear together, such as on the street or in cafés and other similar public spaces. Concomitantly, a photograph of a woman modeling a dress in a boutique window under the gaze of another woman in the street illustrates that windows are such a customary feminine space, the spectator finds nothing unusual about it. Such differences are so much a part of the normalized social landscape that they seem totally "natural." Thus, an interpretive interest would lie elsewhere: the exertions of the human body in the imperious circumstances of work, the details of middle-class elegance

Assembled, by Sara Facio and Alicia D'Amico.

as seen in the highly textured details of the boutique, both its internal details as well as its spatial location as seen in the background beyond the windows (probably the very elegant Plaza Vicente López in Barrio Norte). Such class contrasts, especially since *Buenos Aires Buenos Aires* tends to focus on working individuals, provide for a dimension of analysis in which sexual difference is lost.

Yet sexual difference is present in Facio's and D'Amico's photographs. One of the truly exceptional examples is a two-page spread taken across the street from the Baños Públicos Nueva Pompeya, a public bath. In Buenos Aires in the 1960s, as in other Latin American cities, there still existed Roman-style public baths. In addition to providing a place for complete bodily hygiene—something lacking in the often primitive and congested bathroom facilities of tenement houses—these baths also constituted a privileged male domain of undeniably homosocial dimensions. Indeed, the gay bathhouses that emerged in major world cities in the 1960s were nothing more than an extension into the explicitly homoerotic homosocial world of the public baths that may have often supported male-male contacts for sexual activity.

The two-page spread of Baños Públicos Nueva Pompeya is the most explicit because the presence of a female photographer is inscribed into the photograph. This is evident by the faces of the men congregated alongside the entrance to the baths. There are eight men photographed. One is standing alone, looking off to the right, while the other men interact directly with the camera. Two men are clearly commenting on the photographer; one is gesturing and his mouth is partially open, as though speaking. The second man listens to him as he looks toward the camera, which can easily be assumed to be the topic of conversation. Next, there is a group of three men. Two are looking toward the camera, while a third is turned toward the men, as though commenting on what they are seeing. Finally, two men stand apart from the other men and from each other (the second is cropped off by the right edge of the photograph). They are clearly studying the photographer. It is customary for individuals to face a camera and to interact with the camera's eye by addressing, if only implicitly, the photographer on the other side of the instrument. It is also customary for subjects to be somewhat bemused at being photographed. From the point of view of a criterion of social invisibility—the ability to conform with the norms of a society to the extent that one is invisible, beyond scrutiny and therefore safe from the humiliation accorded the misfit—to have one's picture taken in public, as either a planned event or a surprise occurrence, is to suspend that sought-after invisibility. The photograph becomes a liberating experience by virtue of that suspension; but the act of being photographed also involves a measure of threat, since the camera alludes to the controlling gaze of society that ensures social conformity, as seen specifically in the phenomenon of the surveillance camera. Certainly, scopic vigilance was an issue during periods of military control of society.

In this photograph, the roles are reversed. It is not a case of the camera's authoritative gaze producing discomfort and subjugation in the individual photographed. Quite the contrary. The faces of these men show a condescending humor at being photographed by women. Not only are gender roles especially marked here by virtue of the extraordinarily unusual circumstance of a camera in the hands of women, but the camera has gone to seek men out in what is an exclusively male preserve.

There are, of course, public baths for women, and there are baths for both men and women, like those of the traditional Spanish Hotel Castelar in downtown Buenos Aires. Baños Públicos Nueva Pompeya, however, is in one of the most modest neighborhoods of Buenos Aires. As a consequence, the collision of gender roles represented by the conjunction of photographer and subject is complicated by the collision of class roles: two obviously middle-class urban women taking photographs of men who are clearly marked as lower class and, barely two decades after the first Peronista government encouraged non-European provincials to flood Buenos Aires, with the features customarily subsumed under the racist epithet of *cabecita negra*. Indeed, the man who shows the most ironic attitude toward the female photographers (second from left) is the one who is most marked by his subaltern class status. This photograph is, therefore, quite unusual in the collection *Buenos Aires Buenos Aires*. Gender is certainly present in the other plates in the book in terms of gendered roles being portrayed (and it is appropriate to work from the assumption that the human body is always multiply marked for gender, even when this is not immediately apparent), whether or not one can make an issue out of the gender of the photographers. But it certainly is here: the expression almost of distaste on the face of the man standing directly below the sign identifying the establishment is as much as to say "What the hell are you doing here?"

There is another double-page photograph remarkable for its inscription of gender. Facio and D'Amico rarely worked with montages, choosing rather to concentrate on highly structured compositions that fill a full page or a double page. However, *Buenos Aires Buenos Aires* contains one print that is an assemblage of sixteen images of men in public spaces, a sort of registry of middle-class Porteño manhood. All of the men are dressed for work in combinations of the traditional middle-class Argentine masculine uniform: white shirt, tie, a suit or pants and sport jacket, perhaps a vest or a pullover, and, should the weather demand it, a raincoat. Although the pictures are in black and white, color would make little difference, since blacks, grays, and navy blues predominated dress at the time. Only one man (perhaps a student) appears without a tie, which at that time could have barred his entrance into certain places; certainly the lack of a jacket would have resulted in a categorical prohibition.

Men, A, by Sara Facio.

Men, B, by Sara Facio.

All of the men are clearly middle class: students, executives, responsible office workers, businessmen. Many are notably handsome, in a well-kept and well-nourished sense, and the cut of their clothes is a mark of their prosperity. Moreover, most are caught in full stride, and their body language exudes confidence and security in their masculinity and social position. All are photographed in public places, mostly on the street, and almost half of them are smoking, a customary badge of masculine authority. Although it is only absolutely clear for one of these men, it would be safe to assume that most are sporting a wedding ring, another categorical marker of masculinity achieved and maintained at a time of intransigent compulsory heterosexuality, where to occupy any position of symbolic capital required the trappings of the presumed social stability of marriage.

Finally, it is difficult to overlook the fact that all sixteen of the men are framed in "full-body cuts." That is, the frame of their respective photographs is cropped to match proportionally the bulk of the masculine figures. For photographers accustomed to shooting subjects against detailed backgrounds, these cuts are surprisingly spare. One's first impression is their phallic outline, which matches the Buenos Aires obelisk that popular urban lore repeatedly identifies as the city's most masculine icon (the obelisk, one of the city's most famous monuments to the site of the first raising of the national flag in Buenos Aires, is barely present in any of these photographs). However, a less pop-Freudian view is that the photographs look like identity shots. Although identity photos are usually limited to the head and shoulders and usually consist of rigid poses, Facio's and D'Amico's photographs are cropped in a fashion similar to such photos, which brings them into the same semantic field. If identity shots, in turn, serve an official function—to identify a person for security purposes, as well as for the workplace, school, clubs, driving, voting, and the like—there is an "officialization" of the men in these shots as sober and self-confident members of a male-dominated and relentlessly masculinist society. In this way, the mocking attitude of the men outside the Baños Públicos Nueva Pompeya can be understood not as simple bemusement at the presence of women photographers, but as resentment at an invasion of their public, but nevertheless thoroughly privileged, space. What is clearly evident is that, despite the enormous class difference between the identity photos of middle-class men and the photograph of the men outside the public bathhouse, both sets of men are united in the privilege of their control of public space on which the women photographers spy as nonparticipant observers. When the former look toward the camera, they do it with all the self-confidence that men of their class are likely to have; the mockery of disdain of the latter surely masks their social marginalization.

The role of woman as an onlooker in a male world is evident in another photograph in *Buenos Aires Buenos Aires*. In the photo, a young and attractive young woman is at her window watching the world go by. She has the ability to engage in the contemplation of public life, but her window is covered by sturdy grillwork, and there are shutters that allow light and air to pass through but do not permit viewing. Much has been made of the independence and liberty of Argentine women, especially in Buenos Aires, and especially following the role modeled by Eva Perón. Unquestionably, Porteño women have a public visibility and social agency unmatched virtually anywhere else in Latin America. Nevertheless, Argentine society is no less a domain of masculinist privilege—and even less so during the period of neofascist tyranny—than anywhere else. Facio's photographs may show transgressive women in all their splendor as *hechiceras*, but nowhere in her work, either alone or with D'Amico, is there a sense of women as social agents in a public domain—at least not as a direct and integral part of the photographic image. This is perhaps the most feminist dimension in all of Facio's photographic work.

Notes

1. *Porteño* means "relative to the port city of Buenos Aires."

2. The statement is not completely accurate with regard to political weight, at least as far as military coups are concerned: because of Córdoba's industrial center, the armed forces have always found it necessary to secure control over Córdoba. To be sure, union activity and related agitation (such as the massive uprising against the military dictatorship in 1970 known as the Cordobazo) make such control of this city crucial to a military government's power. Moreover, Rosario has a long tradition of literary reviews and academic research. The best publisher of monographs in the area of cultural studies, Editorial Beatriz Viterbo, is located in Rosario.

3. There are no books that highlight Buenos Aires' "literary haunts" (another frequent urban genre), such as there are for New York (Maurice, *New York;* Edmiston and Cirino), Paris (Maurice, *Paris*), Madrid (Baker; Lacarta; *Biografía literaria de Madrid*), Los Angeles (Fine), and the American city in general (Gelfant; Sharpe and Wallock). As interesting and useful as works like these are, they do not, however, analyze the spatial figuration of the city in cultural production. See, however, the language textbook prepared by Lewald. Concerning the importance of the plaza in Latin American society, see Low.

CHAPTER 1

1. Mafalda's universe is that of Latin America in its most developed metropolitan sectors. From many points of view, it is a Latin universe, and this means Mafalda is much more comprehensible to American readers than many characters in U.S. strips. Moreover, Mafalda is, in the final analysis, a "hero of our age." One should not think this definition is an exaggeration for Quino's pen-and-ink character.

2. *Mafalda* is not a progressive strip; rather, its criticism takes place within the limits tolerated by the system. Not only does it not question the system, but its timid commentaries help maintain the farce commonly known as "freedom of the press."

3. Did I tell you that my problem with lack of communication is my inability to communicate?

4. Yííííííííííík-crash: nonseparable proposition customarily prefixed to certain idiomatic expressions.

5. The world's really a handkerchief!

6. Then, one should lodge a complaint with the cleaners.

7. Literally, "misery town."

8. Looking out the train window is like seeing the country on TV.

9. It's too bad TV has better programs than the country.

10. Oh! And those poor people! What a rundown little shack!

11. "Picturesque," little girl, "picturesque."

12. What a naive bunch, no?

13. Little children!

14. A perfect shave. An impeccable shirt. A delicious cup of coffee. An excellent cigarette.

15. And here's where things stop being like in the ads.

CHAPTER 2

1. Literally means "dirty war," the military operation of extermination in 1976–79 of all traces of guerrilla activity and armed resistance to the military dictatorship that ousted María Estela (Isabelita) Martínez de Perón in March 1976.

2. *Cocoliche* is the "interlingua," the amalgam of the native dialects of the Italian immigrants and local Spanish; it is made particularly rich by the many similarities between Spanish and Italian that allow for more continuity between them than occurs between languages not related in terms of linguistic genealogy (e.g., Spanish and Yiddish).

3. *Nona.* Good morning.
Carmelo. Grandma! What are you doing up?
Nona. I'm here to eat my breakfast.
Carmelo. What breakfast?
Nona. My breakfast. It's morning.
Carmelo. What morning? It's 10 P.M.
Nona. [*Angry.*] But, what about the light?
Carmelo. [*Looking at Chicho.*] What light?
Nona. [*Angrier.*] The light! Daylight!
Carmelo. It's the electric light, Nona. Look. [*He raises the curtain looking out on the patio.*] Can't you see it's nighttime?
Nona. But I'm hungry.
Carmelo. You finished eating just fifteen minutes ago.
Nona. Fifteen minutes ago? That's the reason. Do you have a bite of baloney?
Carmelo. It's time to go to bed, not to eat. Come on, off you go to bed.
Nona. [*Sitting down at the table.*] Well, since we're here, my breakfast.

4. As someone who has played the role of Nona in two productions (the role has customarily been played by a man, which underscores the grotesqueness of Nona's character), I always knew that this line would be greeted by laughter.

5. Go get stuffed! I want some french fries.

6. *La nona* by Héctor Oliveira in 1979; *La fiaca* by Fernando Ayala in 1969.

7. *Madre. [After looking at him and shaking her head several times. In a scolding tone.]* Is this how I taught you? Huh? Answer me! *[Néstor fiddles with the end of the cover.]* So many years of struggling! And what for? For you to pay me back like this? Missing work like a bum? *[Néstor does not answer. The mother looks at Marta, who motions for the former to follow her.]*

8. *Jauregui. [Without stopping.]* Please, ma'am! The science of human relations allows us to grasp profoundly the problems, anxieties, and aspirations of the worker and the employee. It is an activity that obliges us to plumb all aspects of their personality and, as a consequence, to understand all the errors, defects, and deviations that, as human beings, they normally experience. In this way, we share with them, we establish a warmer relationship, one less commercial. We are able to have each worker, each employee, feel that he is part of the company. Fiagroplast is not an abstraction for them, something cold and distant. No. Rather they feel themselves protected and supported, and they feel that the company belongs to them, as though it were their second home. [. . .] A model employee like your husband must be given special consideration. Fiagroplast cannot abandon him in a situation that is so abnormal, so *[he can't remember]* . . . critical. The object of my visit is to guide him, to help him recover for his own personal well-being and that of the whole community.

9. *Peralta. [In a childish tone, disillusioned.]* Fuck it. (*Ta* is short here for *puta* [whore]; its reduction has a euphemistic quality.)

10. *Néstor.* Fiagroplast does not exist, Peralta! It's a vacant lot, full of kids playing soccer!

Peralta. [Shouting.] The lot's not there anymore! The kids are guys like us! They're all inside working! And I'm not at a desk! What am I saying, Vignale? They're going to fire me! They're going to fire me!

Néstor. [Desperate.] Don't be a pansy, Peralta! Stay and play with me!

11. *[The women, taking note of the manager's cordial and friendly tone, have drawn closer more readily. Néstor attempts to stand up and speak, but can't.]*

Mother. Just look at him, he's speechless.

12. *[Writing with a yellow carpenter's measuring stick on a piece of newspaper and looking every now and then around him.]* 45 years old today, I traverse a Buenos Aires in its last dying gasps. The bonfires of the survivors on the street corners illuminate the ancient skeletons of my former neighbors. There is a breeze and there are ashes in the air. Everything seems to remind me of a law of the blood: you must write.

13. *[Falling into an ambiguous ecstasy, she drops the letters, leans back and looks straight ahead.]* Your father! Oh, your father! How much he loved you! He was the best man that ever lived. Saturdays and Sundays did not exist for him, and his goodness was not ruled by the calendar. *[He has fallen asleep, and the mother smacks the table to awaken him.]* He was always ready to put you on his

shoulders and take you for a walk around the lumber yard. Oh, his love was a bottomless pit! Those were the days. . . . [*Bandoneón music.*] The streets were filled with the light and fragrance of the sun and of grapes sweetening on the vine on every corner. The songbirds trilled their melody better and the bells sang their song in the breeze. [The *bandoneón* is a double-reeded squeeze-box that is square with buttons on both sides, permitting more complicated chords than the piano.]

14. [*Carrying her (Pamela Wilson, the beautiful florist) in his arms.*] How beautiful Buenos Aires is! Black! Black and brilliant like an omen of death! [*He sets Pamela down on the floor.*] Here we are, at the old La Noria port, just like yesterday, and I discover everything now, on the verge of death. Goodbye, Pamela, my little girl, my dream, I'm sorry I didn't realize before that I loved you. Goodbye, mother, wherever your indomitable spirit may be. Buenos Aires, my beloved land. Goodbye, dear lifelong pals. Goodbye, dead things. I depart for your shores, orange sea of Buenos Aires. [*He makes a ball of his papers, throws it, and then mimics his body falling.*]

15. I am Héctor Girardi! I am Argentine!

CHAPTER 3

1. The tango is manly.

2. For example, the Insight City Guide for Buenos Aires (Hoefer) includes an essay by Judith Evans ("Meet Me at the Café," 119–21).

3. It is important to note at this juncture that these comments are overgeneralizing about the tango, to the extent that they refer principally to the "classical" tango of Buenos Aires associated with Carlos Gardel.

4. Sunday mornings in Plaza Dorrego in the old colonial area of Buenos Aires, San Telmo, one may see couples performing the tango as a spectacle for tourists and clients as part of the antique flea market that takes place there.

5. The order of names involved in the composition of tangos will be first the lyricist and then the author of the music.

6. Hey, fellow, we share your pain.

7. Woman who abandoned me.

8. A bit of neighborhood there in Pompeya, asleep alongside the embankment, a lantern balanced on the wall, and the mystery of a good-bye cast off by the train. Dogs barking at the moon and love hidden in a doorway, toads croaking in the lagoon, and a *bandoneón* in the distance.

Neighborhood of tango, moon, and mystery, distant streets, what are they like? Old friends who today I can no longer recall, what has become of them, where are they now?

Neighborhood of tango, what became of Juana, the blonde I loved so much? Does she know I've suffered thinking about her from the day in which I left her?

Neighborhood of tango, moon, and mystery, I see you once again in my memory.

A chorus of whistles there on the corner, the gang filling up the grocery store, and the drama of the pale neighborhood girl who never got out to see the train.

Thus do I evoke your nights, neighborhood of tango, with the trucks pulling into the warehouse. And the moon splashing in the mud, and, far off, the voice of the *bandoneón*.

Neighborhood of tango, moon, and mystery, I see you once again in my memory.

9. Literally, "ranch song," the Mexican equivalent of country-western music.

10. When I was a little boy, I would look at you from the outside like those things you can never quite attain, my nose against the window, blue with cold, and it was only later that I lived it as my own. Like a school in all things, when I was a child you surprised me with a cigarette, the faith in my own dreams and the hope for love.

However can I forget you in my lament, small Buenos Aires café? You're the only thing in life that reminded me of my mother. In your miraculous mix of profound men and suicides I learned philosophy, dice, gambling, and the cruel poetry of thinking no more about myself.

You give me a handful of friends in spades who now animate my hours. José, the one with a dream, Marcial, still believing and waiting, and skinny Abel, who is now departed but still guides me. I cried one afternoon on your tabletops the first time I was deceived in love. I was born to suffering. I drank my years away, and I gave myself up without a struggle.

11. A grocery store that is pink like the back of a playing card glowed, and in the back of the store men discussed a game of *truco* [a card game like poker]; the pink grocery store took flower like a neighborhood tough, already the owner of the corner, already hard and full of resentment.)

12. The first small organ sounds across the horizon in its wheezy manner, its Havana, its Italian sound. The men in the lumber yard are firm in their support of Yrigoyen, while a piano somewhere plays tangos by Sabordi.

13. Where have they all gone? asks the elegy of those who are no more, as though there were a region where Yesterday could be Today, Even, and Still.

14. Today, beyond time and fateful Death, those dead live in the tango.

They are in the music, in the strings of the stubborn, laborious guitar, which weaves in the happy *milonga* the feast and innocence of courage.

15. That gust, the tango, that prank, defies the burdensome years; made of dust and time, man lasts less than the light melody, which is only time. The tango creates a cloudy, unreal past that is in some way certain, the impossible memory of having died fighting, on a corner on the outskirts.

CHAPTER 4

1. We can, therefore, imagine the other spaces that would be appropriate for us [in addition to bars], such as social organizations, libraries, clubs, gyms, movie houses, and theaters—in sum, all that a free and lively community is able to create.

2. It is necessary to abstain from exalting the triumph of evil over good, the dissolution of the family, the betrayal of the Fatherland, the vituperation of the forgers of national identity, the mocking of physical defects, sexual deviance, or eroticism.

3. What one can refer to concretely is Article 11 of the text of the Constitución de la Ciudad de Buenos Aires that went into effect in 1996: "Se reconoce y garantiza el derecho a ser diferente, no admitiéndose discriminaciones que tiendan a la segregación por razones o con pretexto de raza, etnia, género, orientación sexual, edad, religión, ideología, opinión, nacionalidad, caracteres físicos, condición psicofísica, social, económica o cualquier circunstancia que implique distinción, exclusión, restricción o menoscrabo." (The right to be different is recognized and guaranteed, and discriminatory practices that promote segregation for reasons or with the pretext of race, ethnicity, gender, sexual orientation, age, religion, beliefs, opinion, nationality, physical characteristics, psychophysical, social, economic condition or any other circumstance that implies difference, exclusion, restriction, or belittlement will not be allowed.)

4. An important contribution to the public visibility of homoeroticism in Argentina is the monthly publication *NX* (formerly *Nexo* [Nexus]), subtitled *Periodismo gay para todos* (Gay Journalism for Everyone) and published since 1994. It is a slick magazine costing six dollars per issue, and like many such European and American publications, it contains articles, informative notes, reviews of pertinent cultural productions, ads, personals, and the all-important map of clubs and bars. What is especially significant is that as part of the project to "naturalize" gay culture in Argentina (understood to include lesbians as well as gay males), *NX* depends heavily on reproductions of foreign images and styles, as though such a continuity with international materials, in a country with an obsession to be *à la page* in terms of international styles, legitimates local homoeroticism.

5. Spanish offers few alternatives. *Queer*, whether as a bridge term for male and female or as a separate ideology that questions gender construction, and is thus juxtaposed to gay/lesbian in their sense of political and historical identities, has no good equivalent. In Argentina *gay* has come to be used as a common noun and adjective, although the marginalization of women makes *lesbiana/lésbica* often necessary for clarification of a subset of identities. Finally, I would argue that, in its usage in Argentina, *gay* has moved less from specifying a subaltern identity than it has to assuming the semantic range of *queer* in both of the senses noted above.

6. The transition to accepted visibility has not gone completely smoothly. Under an influence attributed to a new and conservative Catholic minister of the interior, police harassment of gay places and gay public presence has taken a dramatic and disconcerting upswing. The details of this renewed persecution are included in Montes de Oca (207–8).

7. I know of no lesbian-marked film to have been made in Argentina, although one could certainly read many films as raising, by implication or explicitly, les-

bian issues (Raúl de la Torre's 1982 *Publis angelical*), just as other films can be alleged to insinuate male gay issues (Mario Soffici's 1958 *Rosaura a las diez* (Rosaura at 10 O'Clock) (see Brant, "Marco Denevi" on the original Denevi novel). I am discounting Héctor Babenco's 1985 *Kiss of the Spider Woman*, although it was made by an Argentine director working in Brazil and was based on the 1976 novel by exile Argentine writer Manuel Puig; however, I did treat it in *Contemporary Argentine Cinema* (123–35). Although primarily filmed in prison (also a societal microcosm and one in which homosexual rape, as opposed to homoerotic desire, is an instrument of social control), the main gay character, now also a collaborator of social revolution, moves briefly through a major urban space, dressed stereotypically as a gay man, before being gunned down by the police.

Argentina has, however, come forth with, to the best of my knowledge, the first Latin American AIDS film, Diego Musiak's *Fotos del alma* (1995). The film focuses more on the issue of AIDS discrimination and persecution than on the details of how the main character may have ended up HIV positive. Even if any gay identity for him is left unexplored, it is a gay man who comforts him.

8. I have written elsewhere about Luis Humberto Hermosillo's 1984 *Doña Herlinda y su hijo* (Doña Herlinda and Her Son), which is also based on a consideration of the private versus the public and in which there is a crucial explicit representation of the acts of homoerotic desire (Foster, "Queering the Patriarchy in Hermosillo's *Doña Herlinda y su hijo*").

9. It is important to remember that in 1973, at the height of the guerrilla movement, the beginnings of a gay movement in Argentina, the Frente de Liberación Homosexual, declared its support for the Peronista left and the Montoneros.

10. See Foster, "Teatro norteamericano" for a discussion of recent gay American theater on the Avenida Corrientes commercial circuit.

CHAPTER 5

1. Being a woman in Buenos Aires—now that's a hell of an undertaking.

2. *Marianismo* is the cult of the Virgin Mary and of a manner of social being that replicates themes associated with a specific institutionalized interpretation of Mary, including submission, obedience, diligent motherness, reserve, and chastity. The latter includes not only absolute premarital chastity, but a non-sexualized compliance with the demands of the matrimonial bed.

3. For example, in Marting, almost 25 percent, the largest representation, of authors examined is made up of Argentines. Moreover, Argentine representation is only a little under twice what it is for Mexican writers. Brazil is not included.

4. The array of women-oriented magazines is truly impressive. Five may be listed as among the most widely read in the late 1990s: *Para ti* (Editorial Atlántida), *Luna* (Editorial Perfil), *Mujer única* (Editorial Publitec), *Pronto* (Editorial Publitec), *Mía* (Editorial Perfil).

5. And some have chosen to write and publish outside of Latin America. Luisa Valenzuela is a casebook study of the Argentine writer who, one could argue, has a greater reputation in the United States than in Argentina. Not only have many of her texts been published in the United States in English translation, but her *Novela negra con argentinos* was first published in 1990 by Ediciones del Norte of Hanover, New Hampshire. The novel is especially interesting because of the story it has to tell, somewhat along the lines of Liliana Cavani's *Night Porter*. A group of Argentine exiles, all apparently with sinister and tortuous pasts, re-create stories of the late 1970s Dirty War in the streets and lofts of New York City. Valenzuela effectively captures the threatening nature of New York's marginal stories, and correlates their urban presence with the stories her characters bring to New York from their Argentine past.

6. Liliana ceased to fight at a certain time of the night. She was unable to read, unable to sleep, unable to stand how she felt. She remained lying down, watching the darkness through her window. She took leave of her senses at a certain moment and allowed herself to be carried along by the darkness. He mind drifted along strange paths, weird philosophy, and stupid thoughts. At a certain point the sky began to turn light, in spite of everything, and then she got dressed. She brushed her teeth, avoiding the mirror—she didn't want to see. Giving it little thought, she grabbed a coat and went out into the street. She hesitated in the doorway, struck by the light and the frosty air. She put dark glasses on and stepped down to the sidewalk. It seemed as though she'd spent weeks in her apartment, when it had only been a night of sleeplessness. An eternal night. The street was empty, the odor of the air still intact. In the dawn's silence, the trees, with extraordinary punctuality, were beginning to turn green, despite the cold. Silence. A blue car went by in the distance along Callao Avenue, and a boy and girl dressed in black and with shaved heads walked by in silence.

Saturday, very early in the morning. What was she doing in the street? She was surviving, nothing more. She crossed the plaza at an angle. The jacaranda trees were blooming shamelessly, despite the cold. She walked into a coffee bar that she found open and ordered a cup of coffee.

7. The second most prominent woman in modern Argentine cultural history is Victoria Ocampo, who was (without, it would appear, the lesbianism) something like an Argentine version of Gertrude Stein. A cultural maven whose roots lay with the oligarchy, she published for more than thirty years the intellectual and literary review *Sur* and its book imprint, which she founded in 1931. Ocampo dominated a national and Porteño literary scene virulently opposed to Peronista populism. It is significant to recall that Ocampo's sphere of influence, while it included most of the major figures of the Porteño cultural scene, included residences on the fringes of urban Buenos Aires: her city home in the almost suburban (at the time) Palermo; her estate in the bedroom community of San Isidro, along the Río de la Plata outside of Buenos Aires; and her summer cottage in the upper-class (at the time) watering hole south of Buenos Aires on the ocean, Mar

del Plata (Villa Victoria is now a museum and cultural institution in what has become very much a middle-class and urbanized Mar del Plata).

8. We will spare the reader Evita's comings and goings, her frequent visits to factories, schools, hospitals, unions, athletic and cultural clubs. Her energy was superhuman. Let us say only that we could fill entire pages with just the description of such activities. Authors like Marysa Navarro [author of the most important feminist interpretation of Evita], Fermín Chávez, and so many others have gone to the trouble of following her day by day. We have preferred to leave this astonishing quantity of inaugurations, presentations, declarations, and travels as a backdrop, in order to concentrate on the image of a woman who grows, develops, affirms herself . . . and makes speeches. (The published English translation is not quoted here, as it deviates significantly from the original Spanish.)

9. There are several technical problems with *Eva Perón: La biografía:* the bibliography is dreadfully organized, the text continually makes reference to sources that are undiscoverable, and an index is sorely lacking. Finally, Dujovne Ortiz has Evita trying in vain to be received by Queen Elizabeth when, of course, the queen at the time was Elizabeth's mother, Mary.

10. Perón commuted between the residence and Congress in a convertible. Eva could hardly stand up straight. But for this last role, she did not want to be sitting next to a standing Perón. So they gave her more morphine. They also created a plaster support in which they had her stand. Her large fur coat hid the belt holding her to the window placed behind the driver. Some said that they had plastered her right arm, too, for despite her weakness, she constantly waved to the crowds, never resting her arm. (*Eva Perón: A Biography*, 272.)

11. A president of the Republic said to me: "We are all that corpse. It's the country" (365).

12. People construct the myth of the body however they please, read Evita's body with the grammatical declensions of their gaze. She can be anything and everything. In Argentina she is still the Cinderella of television serials, the nostalgia for having been what we never were, the woman with the whip, the celestial mother. Outside the country, she is power, the woman who died young, the compassionate hyena who declaims from the balconies of the beyond: "Don't cry for me, Argentina." (*Santa Evita* [English translation], 186.)

13. Denise Chrispim Marín was interviewed on Eva Perón in the "Mundo" section of the July 30, 1995, Sunday edition of the *Folha de São Paulo*. The interview is accompanied by a detailed map of the peregrinations of Evita's cadaver, including almost a dozen different sites where it was kept in Argentina.

14. During those days the Deceased resumed the wandering that was causing her so much harm: from one truck to another, down streets that were never the same. They moved her at random through the flat, endless city: the city without a weft or folds. (*Santa Evita* [English translation], 254.)

15. I went by train with my parents "so another doctor could look at my throat." We got off at the Flores station where, as always, I looked with the

curiosity and nostalgia of someone reincarnated, at the doorway of Marcó del Pont, which is found on the platform like a piece of scenery mutilated by the tracks.

"Don't walk looking over your shoulder."

The fact is I think I see the bygone children playing blindman's bluff among the columns, little figures that are animated from the depths of time, marionettes condemned to a silent office.

We walk through the somber streets until we reach an unknown doctor's office where the male nurse opens the door, a sinister grimace between his ears that undoubtedly means a smile for children. . . .

"People used to come here by wagon, to their summer places," my father attempts to distract me with such information, "but the Western Railway changed all of this into a city, as you can see. The first engine, La Porteña, departed from the Lavalle Plaza for her."

And just when I expect to hear the story about the mysterious station house, the nurse proceeds with what he has to do.

16. Mary can feel the itching sensation of metamorphosis, that elytras are coming out on the basket bug, exorcising the unbearable stage of her mutations and her mourning and before a clanging of a bell can bring her back to the reality incarnated in her own father, who has come to rescue her and ruin things for her. She has found the exit from the labyrinth, the transfer over to what is unknown, a move to the Europe of her ancestors and the very costly reflections in a mirror of her future. (The basket bug derives from a large larva that attaches itself to the leaves of trees; it is considered an important pest in the Buenos Aires region.)

17. The Mothers of Plaza de Mayo (the square in front of the Casa Rosada [Pink House], the Argentine government house) began to march weekly to demand information about their disappeared children during the military's antisubversion arrests in the late 1970s; many of the people arrested were never heard from again. Their protests went on to include other disappeared family members. Significantly, in the face of the decision by subsequent democratic governments not to pursue to their final consequences investigations against the military regimes for human rights violations, the Mothers have continued to march and claim that they will do so until every disappeared person is accounted for.

CHAPTER 6

1. Do you really think you can say anything in this language? Can you really say things that are true, things that come from down deep inside, from your very guts? Are there words in Spanish for such things?

Spanish—give me a break. What kind of language is that?

2. Mention must be made of another group of immigrants in Buenos Aires: individuals from neighboring Latin American countries. Such individuals may have once come for political reasons (Paraguay in the early 1950s; Brazil after the 1964 coup; Chile and Uruguay after coups in 1973; and so on). But today they

constitute mostly a migrant laboring class that works illegally in factories, sweat-shops, and construction sites, often for substandard wages and in marginal circumstances. Political exiles, who were often professionals and semiprofessionals, have become quite integrated into the patterns of Buenos Aires life, while at the same time, migrant laborers such as the Paraguayans (the population in Buenos Aires is reputed to outnumber the population of the Paraguayan capital, Asunción) are often very much of an ostracized lumpen proletariat.

3. Witness the infamous denunciations during the early years of the Proceso of the triumvirate of Jewish scourges on Western civilization: Marx for questioning economic structures; Freud for questioning the sexuality and, by implication the patriarchal family; and Einstein for proposing a relativity that was interpreted as challenging absolutes in religion, politics, and the like.

4. *A las 20:25* is one in a series of novels in which Szichman uses the Pechof family, of Polish origin, to represent the life of Jews in Argentina. Other novels in the sequence include *Crónica falsa* (False Chronicle; 1969), *Los judíos del mar dulce* (Fresh-Water Jews; 1971), and *La verdadera crónica falsa* (The True False Chronicle; 1972). See overview comments by Meter; Barr, *Isaac Unbound*, 85–105.

5. The funeral of the lady put Buenos Aires into suspended animation. Past and future were linked by the deterioration of some buildings and the addition of a few new ones that never went beyond the stage of frames and scaffolds.

Trolleys and streetcars went out of circulation. The pallor of vapor lamps replaced the yellow glow of street-lights. Cobble-stoned streets were paved over.

From the moment she died, Buenos Aires became a night city. The edge of darkness fell on Avenue General Paz on one side, and on the Riachuelo on the other. Whenever they travelled to the provinces people raised their heads and saw the sharp cut that separated the two heavens. (Szichman, *At 8:25 Evita Became Immortal*, 5.)

6. Jaime and Salmen went to Tajmer's house to learn good manners. The millionaire was presenting his future son-in-law to society. He was a goy who took bribes as inspector of Internal Revenue. . . .

Jaime [watched] the party. The guests were dancing a tango in the hall.

"Look, that's the music of my city! How I wish I were a neighborhood tough!" Jaime said with admiration.

"Tajmer is lousing up his life with this business of inviting goys," Salmen pointed out.

"What do you mean lousing up his life? He is improving it. And he will improve it even more when he no longer invites yids. Look at the goy, how great he looks. Now look at the yids. See how easily our hair falls out. All you've got to be is a *schnorrer* and you end up bald. . . . The goy has a dog with a black palate, and with it he conquers the world. You can be Einstein, if you want, but you're not worth a thing next to that guy. *And what did you invent?* they ask Einstein. *I invented radioactivity*, Einstein says. *Do you have a dog with a black palate?* And if Einstein doesn't have a dog with a black palate, good-bye. Not even if he invented ten radioactivities. Look at Tajmer. He's drooling over that *chuzin*. Look at the *chuzin*. He smiles without showing his teeth. That's what it means to have a black palate." (Szichman, *At 8:25 Evita Became Immortal*, 137–38.)

7. Cortázar, of course, wrote *petits récits avant la lettre* in the texts of *Historias de cronopios y famas* (Stories of Cronopios and Famas). When his short stories were gathered together in *Relatos* (Stories), the *Historias* were not included.

8. We were walking through the Rose Garden. We were gliding along, our feet almost not touching the ground, over an orange dirt path, beneath a large blue sky, and I spied the four small bronze toads that spit water into the fountain. If you covered the mouths of three of them, the fourth would give of a very long jet, a large arc of water that would fall in the middle of the fountain. I and two other kids I didn't know did this under the gaze of the caretaker, who did not object to this practice, although he did object to anyone walking on the grass or picking the flowers. After a while I saw the older ones had moved on and I ran to catch up with them. They paid no attention to me because He was coming up the path, the Minister of Education, and Dad greeted him. The Minister returned the greeting and continued on with his companions. When he was some distance away, Dad said: "That's the Minister of Education. I mean, he's the Minister of Justice and Public Instruction." And he added: "He's hunchback both in front and back."

9. Both the pillow cats and the alley cats end up losing their young from sight soon after they are born. The young of family cats are given away to friends of the owners. The young of alley cats have various kinds of luck: some die at the hands of neighborhood kids; others wander the streets until someone takes them in, where they become stove cats or until they are taken to some Cat Neighborhood like the kind you find in the Botanical Gardens or on the grounds of any hospital.

10. I stopped going to school. In a few months I would be in New York, so why go to school here? I didn't even make the decision to stop going. Suddenly I ceased to go. No one said anything about it, neither my mom nor my dad.

At thirteen, I no longer believed in anything. In absolutely nothing. I was a total skeptic. They had betrayed me in everything. I had no hope left unfrustrated, no illusion left undisappointed. I also no longer had my grade school group of friends. I had nothing left in Buenos Aires. I had nothing left in life.
. . .
Mamma came to wake me up the Sunday I left. She told me we should make our good-byes then, because it would be harder later and she didn't want to go with me to Ezeiza Airport. I agreed. She didn't have to go with me if she didn't want to. I didn't care. It didn't seem to me like I was leaving.

CHAPTER 7

1. There is a 1991 film loosely based on the novel, but it had no commercial success and received scant critical attention.

2. At the end of the novel he dies, but in the movie she pummels him as a sign that she is no longer under his control.

3. A particularly notable feature of Medina's collection is the decision to dedicate each one of the thirty-six texts to a group of individuals with whom he as a writer and as a citizen identifies. The result is the evocation of a broad network of men and women (and children) with a shared commitment to knowing how the world is, despite what the hegemonic discourse would maintain is hardly a civilized place, yet by extension to knowing how such knowledge can contribute to the forging of a decent society. (The hegemonic discourse, of course, is likely to find many uncivilized in the world, but only as a deviation from its privileged norms.)

4. Unfortunately, I know of no Argentine film set on a *colectivo* (bus), not at least of the importance of Luis Buñuel's 1951 *La ilusión viaja en tranvía* (Illusion Travels by Trolley), made as part of his Mexican cycle and, like the 1950 classic *Los olvidados* (The Forgotten; released in English as *The Young and the Damned*), so eloquent in revealing Buñuel's fascination with the Mexican cityscape. Neville D'Almeida's *A dama do lotação* (The Lady on the Bus; 1978) showcases Brazil's Sônia Braga (*lotação* is the Brazilian Portuguese word for *colectivo*). Santiago Carlos Oves's *El verso* (The Shtick; 1995) concerns the sort of ambulant salesman who finds hawking cheap wares (penknives, ballpoint pens, comic books, coloring books) on city buses, and several scenes take place on *colectivos*.

5. It is interesting to compare a similar version of the bus with a Chilean writer of dirty realism, Pedro Lemebel. In his text "Coleópteros en el parabrisas," we read: "La micro es una lata de sopa que revuelve los intestinos. Un pastiche de eructos, flagos y peos que colorean el duro tránsito que se desbarranca a la periferia" (72).

6. The train stops. Someone says we're lucky to have reached the station. They'll take the train and one bus and another and another. For their entire life.

7. The man has struck the woman. In her side so no one can see. His eyes range wildly. She tries to calm him down. You can't leave by the front! They shout. The driver does not open the front door until they tell him she's the one who's pregnant.

8. As though it weren't bad enough, someone yells, "Open the window, please." It was a silent and unrelenting fart.

9. The women you killed send their greetings.

10. *According to the witnesses' story, the man later identified showed up at the escort agency where they and Patricia worked, demanding that the latter resume romantic relations with him. When she said no. . . ."* What do the newspapers know? What does the police know? What do the witnesses know, the microscopic examinations, and the judges, and . . . ? Just look at the photos. They are along the edge of the page. He didn't want to see them even though the police had shown them to him earlier. He looked at them closely.

11. He uses the fork to find his name. Yes, it's spelled correctly.

12. There is little information available about Gatica, despite his popular cultural importance. See information in Barrera on the history of boxing in Argentina; Montes provides a earlier (and trite) novelized account of Gatica; Ramírez includes a section on Gatica (41–43).

13. Note that Favio underscores the nickname Mono (= monkey). Gatica himself would have preferred to be called Tigre (= tiger), and for this reason, Medina avoids using the former. Such nicknames, still widely used in Argentina, are synecdochal and metonymic in nature and that they can refer to features that may be as much viewed as affectionate as pejorative.

14. He gets up, goes over to the counter, pays for everyone, returns to say good-bye to his friends, and stumbles out the door. He looks for a taxi. He waves at them, but they do not stop because the difficulty he has with his sick leg and the confusion resulting from wine and schnapps make him walk like a scarecrow shaken by the wind. Gatica swears at them. He sees a crowded bus that he could catch and dodging cars that in turn dodge him, he runs to jump on board. He grabs a rail––great, because there are too many people jamming the running board. Except for the attempt with his little finger, he's unable to grab on with his other hand because of the two dolls he's carrying. He manages to put his foot down in a tiny space. The guy hanging on in front of him tries to climb up a step, the bus in motion suddenly picks up speed, and the guy throws himself a bit, which causes Gatica to loose his balance. He falls because one hand is not enough to hold on, and he sees the guy finally make it up the step at the same time the door snaps shut like a whip. Gatica falls to the pavement, almost without letting go of the dolls. The bus swings out to turn the corner and the back wheels bounce over the astonished body.

CHAPTER 8

1. According to María Elena Walsh in her introduction to Facio's and D'Amico's *Fotografía argentina* (Argentine Photography), the presentation of this book was prohibited by the military government because it contained texts by Cortázar.

2. The series is pregnant with devotion for its characters. Model women admired by what they have done in their respective disciplines. They are seen as beautiful, strong, unique.

3. Some "temptresses" inspired the need to "give them color," not in the sense of a color negative, but by painting areas chosen at random. It would be impossible to imagine them in black and white.

4. Facio and D'Amico signed their work together, as a single artistic unit. Although some sources have made separate attributions, Facio prefers to continue to consider this work a single unit (personal communication via e-mail, April 29, 1997).

5. Facio's and D'Amico's retrospective album, *Fotografía argentina* (Argentine Photography), identifies the photographs reproduced in *Humanario* as dating

from 1966, a gap that is due to the fact that they were taken in 1966 but were never shown or published until ten years later.

6. Madness is an illness that only affects members of the opposition.

7. I have felt that, by separating oneself from that contiguous zone between madness and a certain sanity, madmen and the sane look like each other symmetrically in their process of being ever madder and ever saner. Finally, what ruins things for certain madmen is the intolerable way their exterior form strikes society. The tics, manias, physical degradation, oral or motor clumsiness allow for an immediate labeling and prophylactic separation. It's to be expected, and it is even beneficial for the person who is mad, in a society that applies the rules of its game that no one is authorized to play. But on the other extreme of this symmetry, there where reason is ever more reasoning and reasonable, where exterior conduct not only does not offend the city, but contributes to exalting and enriching it, it is enough to look closely to discover the other alienation at every turn, that which not only transgresses the rules of the game, but also brings them into being and applies them.

Bibliography

Absatz, Cecilia. *¿Dónde estás, amor de mi vida, que no te puedo encontrar?* Buenos Aires: Espasa Calpe, 1995.

Acevedo, Zelmar. *Homosexualidad: Hacia la destrucción de los mitos.* Buenos Aires: Ediciones del Ser, 1985.

Agosín, Marjorie. *Círculos de locura: Madres de la Plaza de Mayo* (Circles of Madness: Mothers of the Plaza de Mayo). Fredonia, N.Y.: White Pine Press, 1992.

Aguinis, Marcos. "Evolution of a Democratic Argentine Culture." In *The Redemocratization of Argentine Culture, 1983 and Beyond,* edited by David William Foster, 7–9. Tempe: Center for Latin American Studies, Arizona State University, 1989.

Aizenberg, Edna. "Jewish Gauchos and Jewish 'Others,' or Culture and Bombs in Buenos Aires." *Discourse* 19, no. 1 (1996): 15–27.

Albert Robatto, Matilde. *Borges, Buenos Aires y el tiempo.* Río Piedras, P.R.: Editorial Edil, 1972.

Albuquerque, M. A. *Antología de tangos.* 8th ed. México, D.F.: Medina, 1970.

Almaguer, Tomás. "Chicano Men: A Cartography of Homosexual Identity and Behavior." *Différences* 3, no. 2 (1991): 75–100.

Altamiranda, Daniel. "Jorge Luis Borges." In *Latin American Writers on Gay and Lesbian Themes: A Bio-Critical Sourcebook,* edited by David William Foster, 72–83. Westport, Conn.: Greenwood Press, 1994.

Alvarez, Gerardo, ed. *Los españoles de la Argentina.* Buenos Aires: Manrique Zago Ediciones, 1985.

Archetti, Eduardo P. "Multiple Masculinities: The Worlds of Tango and Football in Argentina." In *Sex and Sexuality in Latin America,* edited by Daniel Balderston and Donna J. Guy, 200–216. Albany: State University of New York Press, 1996.

"Argentina." In *Escenarios de dos mundos: Inventario teatral de Iberoamérica,* 1:123–97. Madrid: Centro de Documentación Teatral, 1988.

Armus, Diego. "La idea del verde en la ciudad moderna. Buenos Aires, 1870–1940." *Entrepasados; revista de historia* 5, no. 10 (1996): 9–22.

Avellaneda, Andrés. *Censura, autoritarismo y cultura: Argentina 1960–1983.* Buenos Aires: Centro Editor de América Latina, 1986.

Avni, Haim. *Argentina and the Jews; A History of Jewish Immigration.* Translated by Gila Brand. Tuscaloosa: University of Alabama Press, 1991.

Baker, Edward. *Materiales para escribir Madrid; Literatura y espacio urbano de Moratín a Galdós.* Madrid: Siglo Veintiuno de España, 1991.

Barletta, Leonidas. *Boedo y Florida; Una versión distinta.* Buenos Aires: Ediciones Metrópolis, 1967.

Barr, Lois Baer. "Alicia Steimberg." In *Jewish Writers of Latin America: A Dictionary,* edited by Darrell B. Lockhart, 499–504. New York: Garland, 1997.

——. *Isaac Unbound: Patriarchal Traditions in the Latin American Jewish Novel.* Tempe: Center for Latin American Studies, Arizona State University, 1995.

Barrera, Ulises. "Una década entre las cuerdas." *Todo es historia* 120 (1977): 150–60.

Bartís, Ricardo. "Postales argentinas." In *Otro teatro después de Teatro Abierto,* compilation and side-bar texts by Jorge A. Dubatti, 5–23. Buenos Aires: Libros de Quirquincho, 1990.

Beceyro, Raúl. "La exclusión: Sobre *Gatica, el mono,* de Leonardo Favio." *Punto de vista* 46 (1993): 23–25.

Bhabha, Homi K. "DissemiNation: Time, Narrative, and the Margins of the Modern Nation." In *Nation and Narration,* edited by Homi K. Bhabha, 291–322. London: Routledge, 1990.

Biografía literaria de Madrid. Edited by Matilde Sagaró Faci. Madrid: Editorial El Avapiés y Luis Cossío, 1993.

Blumenfeld, Warren, ed. *Homophobia: How We All Pay the Price.* Boston: Beacon Press, 1992.

Borges, Jorge Luis. "Las inscripciones de los carros." In *El lenguaje de Buenos Aires,* edited by Jorge Luis Borges and José E. Clemente, 49–59. Buenos Aires: Editorial Emecé, 1968.

——. *Obra completa.* Buenos Aires: Emecé Editores, 1974.

Borges, Jorge Luis, and Silvina Bullrich. *El compadrito: Su destino, sus barrios, su música.* Buenos Aires: Compañía General Fabril Editora, 1963.

Bossio, Jorge Alberto. *Los cafés de Buenos Aires.* Buenos Aires: Editorial Schapire, 1968.

Bouvard, Marguerite Guzman. *Revolutionizing Motherhood: The Mothers of the Plaza de Maya.* Washington, D.C.: Scholarly Resources, 1994.

Brant, Herbert J. "Marco Denevi." In *Latin American Writers on Gay and Lesbian Themes: A Bio-Critical Sourcebook,* edited by David William Foster, 34–37. Westport, Conn.: Greenwood Press, 1994.

——. "The Mark of the Phallus: Homoerotic Desire in Borges' 'La forma de la espada.'" *Chasqui* 25, no. 1 (1996): 25–38.

Brown, Stephen. "'*Con discriminación y represión no hay democracia*': The Lesbian and Gay Movement in Argentina." Paper presented at the meeting of the Latin American Studies Association, Guadalajara, April 17–19, 1997.

Buenos Aires, mi ciudad. Photographs by Sameer Makarius. Buenos Aires: Editorial Universitaria de Buenos Aires, 1963.

Calvera, Leonor. *Mujeres y feminismo en la Argentina*. Buenos Aires: Grupo Editor Latinoamericano, 1990.

Campra, Rosalba. "Buenos Aires infundada." In *La selva en el damero; espacio literario y espacio urbano en América Latina*, edited by Rosalba Campra, 103–17. Pisa, Italy: Giardini Editori, 1989.

Camusso, Cristina. *Mujer: Un camino de emancipación*. Buenos Aires: Búsqueda Editora, 1991.

Cañizal, Eduardo Peñuela. "Quino: Uma proposta de leitura." *Vozes* 69, no. 3 (1975): 37–48.

Carlson, Marifran. *¡Feminismo! The Woman's Movement in Argentina from Its Beginnings to Eva Perón*. Chicago: Academy Chicago Publishers, 1988.

Carreira, André. "Teatro callejero en la ciudad de Buenos Aires después de la dictadura militar." *Latin American Theatre Review* 27, no. 2 (1994): 103–14.

Castro, Donald S. *The Argentine Tango As Social History, 1880–1955: The Soul of the People*. Lewiston, N.Y.: E. Mellen Press, 1991.

Ciechanower, Mauricio. "Entrevista a Joaquín Lavado (QUINO). Mafalda: Esa famosa y tremenda criatura." *Plural* 2a época 209 (February 1989) : 62–73.

Ciria, Alberto. *Política y cultura popular; La Argentina peronista, 1946–1955*. Buenos Aires: Ediciones de la Flor, 1983.

Cirne, Moacy. "Mafalda: Prática semiológica e prática ideológica." *Vozes* 67, no. 7 (1973): 47–54.

Collier, Simon. "The Popular Roots of the Argentine Tango." *History Workshop: A Journal of Socialist History* 34 (fall 1992): 92–100.

Corbatta, Jorgelina. "El tango: Letras y visión del mundo." *Hispanic Journal* 15, no. 1 (1994): 63–72.

Cossa, Roberto. *La nona*. Bound with Carlos Gorostiza, *Los hermanos queridos*. Buenos Aires: Sociedad General de Autores de la Argentina, 1980.

Cruz, Jorge. *Genio y figura de Florencio Sánchez*. Buenos Aires: Editorial Universitaria de Buenos Aires, 1966.

Daly, Mary. *Gyn/ecology: The Metaphysics of Radical Feminism*. Boston: Beacon Press, 1978.

D'Amico, Alicia, and Sara Facio. *Retratos y autorretratos; escritores de América Latina*. Buenos Aires: Ediciones Crisis, 1973.

D'Amico, Alicia, Sara Facio, and Julio Cortázar. *Buenos Aires Buenos Aires*. Buenos Aires: Editorial Sudamericana, 1968.

Diago, Alejandro. *Conversando con las Madres de Plaza de Mayo: Hebe, memoria y esperanza*. Buenos Aires: Ediciones Dialéctica, 1988.

"El día que me quieras." *Página 12* 10 (December 5, 1996): 2–3.

Donat, Patricia, and John D'Emilio. "A Feminist Redefinition of Rape and Sexual Assault: Historical Foundations and Sexual Change." In *The Other Americans: Sexual Variance in the National Past*, 191–203. Westport, Conn.: Paeger, 1996.

Dorfman, Ariel. "Borges y la violencia humana." In *Imaginación y violencia en América*, 38–64. Santiago de Chile: Editorial Universitaria, 1970.

Dujovne Ortiz, Alicia. "Buenos Aires." In *Critical Fictions: The Politics of Imaginative Writing*, edited by Philomena Mariani, 115–33. Seattle: Bay Press, 1991.

———. *Eva Perón: La biografía*. Buenos Aires: Aguilar, 1995.

———*Eva Perón: A Biography*. Translated by Shawn Fields. New York: St. Martin's Press, 1996.

Eco, Umberto. "Mafalda la disconforme." Foreword in *Mafalda: y digo yo* . . . , by Joaquín Salvador Lavado (Quino). Barcelona: Noveno Arte, 1974.

Edmiston, Susan, and Linda D. Cirino. *Literary New York: A History and Guide*. Boston: Houghton Mifflin, 1976.

Evans, Judith. "Tango." In *Buenos Aires*, 147–51. Singapore: APA Publication/ Insight Cityguides, 1988.

Facio, Sara. *Retratos 1960–1992*. With an introduction by María Elena Walsh. Buenos Aires: La Azotea Editorial Fotográfica, 1992.

Facio, Sara, and Alicia D'Amico. *Fotografía argentina 1960–1985*. With a prologue by María Elena Walsh. Buenos Aires: La Azotea Editorial Fotográfica, 1985.

Facio, Sara, Alicia D'Amico, and Julio Cortázar. *Humanario*. With an introduction by Dr. Fernando Pagés Larraya. Buenos Aires: La Azotea Editorial Fotográfica de América Latina, 1976.

Feierstein, Ricardo. *Historia de los judíos argentinos*. Buenos Aires: Editorial Planeta Argentina, 1993.

Ferman, Claudia. *Política y posmodernidad: Hacia una lectura de la anti-modernidad en Latinoamérica*. Miami: Iberian Studies Institute, North-South Center, University of Miami, 1993.

Fernández Bitar, Marcelo. *Historia del rock en Argentina: Una investigación cronológica*. Buenos Aires: Ediciones El Juglar, 1987.

Fine, David, ed. *Los Angeles in Fiction: A Collection of Essays*. Rev. ed. Albuquerque: University of New Mexico Press, 1995.

Fisher, Jo. *Mothers of the Disappeared*. Boston: South End Press; London: Zed Books, 1989.

Folino, Norberto. *Chofer buena banana busca chica buena mandarina*. Buenos Aires: Ediciones de la Flor, 1974.

Forster, Merlin H. "Buenos Aires: Culture and Poetry in the Modern City." In *Buenos Aires: 400 Years*, edited by Stanley R. Ross and Thomas F. McGann, 127–41. Austin: University of Texas Press, 1982.

Fossati, Franco. *Il fumetto argentino*. Genova: Pirella Editore, 1980.

Foster, David William. "Argentine Jewish Dramatists: Aspects of a National Consciousness." In *Cultural Diversity in Latin American Literature*, 95–150. Albuquerque: University of New Mexico Press, 1994.

———. *Argentine Literature: A Research Guide*. 2d ed., rev. and expanded. New York: Garland Publishing, 1982.

———. "Argentine Sociopolitical Commentary, the Malvinas Conflict, and Beyond: Rhetoricizing a National Experience." *Latin American Research Review* 22, no. 1 (1987): 7–34.

———. "Bare Words and Naked Truths (Enrique Medina: *StripTease*)." *The American Hispanist* 12 (1976): 17–19.

———. "The Case for Feminine Pornography in Latin America." In *Bodies and Biases: Sexualities in Hispanic Cultures and Literatures,* edited by David William Foster and Roberto Reis, 246–73. Minneapolis: University of Minnesota Press, 1996.

———. *Contemporary Argentine Cinema.* Columbia: University of Missouri Press, 1992.

———. *Currents in the Contemporary Argentine Novel.* Columbia: University of Missouri Press, 1975.

———. "The Demythification of Buenos Aires in the Argentine Novel of the Seventies." In *Alternative Voices in the Contemporary Latin American Narrative,* 60–106. Columbia: University of Missouri Press, 1985.

———. *Espacio escénico y lenguaje.* Buenos Aires: Editorial Galerna, 1998.

———. "El lenguaje como vehículo espiritual en *Los siameses* de Griselda Gambaro." *Escritura* 8 (1979): 241–57.

———. "Lenguaje y espacio escénico: El italiano en dos textos teatrales." *Revita de crítica literaria latinoamericana* 45 (1997): 55–65.

———. "*Mafalda*: The Ironic Bemusement." In *From Mafalda to Los Supermachos,* 53–63. Boulder: Lynne Rienner, 1989. An earlier version appeared as "Mafalda: An Argentine Comic Strip." *Journal of Popular Culture* 4 (1980): 497–508, which in turn was based on the note "Mafalda . . . the Ironic Bemusement." *Latin American Digest* 8, no. 3 (1974): 16–18.

———. "María Elena Walsh: Children's Literature and the Feminist Voice." In *Cultural Diversity in Latin American Literature,* 73–94. Albuquerque: University of New Mexico Press, 1994.

———. "'Narrative Rights' in the Argentine Tango." *Symposium* 37 (1983–84): 261–71.

———. "Los parámetros de la narrativa argentina durante el 'Proceso de Reorganización Nacional.'" In *Ficción y política: La narrativa argentina durante el proceso militar,* 96–108. Buenos Aires: Alianza Editorial; Minneapolis: Institute for the Study of Ideologies and Literature, 1987. Also in *Revista letras* [Curitiba] 37 (1988): 152–67.

———. "Paula Varsavsky." In *Jewish Writers of Latin America: A Dictionary,* edited by Darrell B. Lockhart, 551–52. New York: Garland, 1996.

———. "Playful Ecphrasis: María Elena Walsh and Children's Literature in Argentina." *Mester* 13, no. 1 (1984): 40–51.

———. "Prolegomenon to an Investigation of Regionalism in Argentine Literature." *Hispanic Journal* 14, no. 2 (1993): 7–19. Also in *Violence in Argentine Literature: Cultural Responses to Tyranny,* 13–57. Columbia: University of Missouri Press, 1995.

———. "Queering the Patriarchy in Hermosillo's *Doña Herlinda y su hijo.*"

In *Sexual Textualities: Essays on Queer/ing Latin American Writing*, 64–72. Austin: University of Texas Press, 1997.

——. "Rape and Social Formation: Enrique Medina's *Las tumbas*." In *Violence in Argentine Literature: Cultural Responses to Tyranny*, 75–97. Columbia: University of Missouri Press, 1995. Also in a shortened form as the introduction to Enrique Medina's *Las tumbas*.

——. Review of Enrique Medina, *Gatica. World Literature Today* 66, no. 2 (1992): 311–12.

——. *Social Realism in the Argentine Narrative*. Chapel Hill: North Carolina Studies in the Romance Languages and Literature, 1986.

——. "Teatro norteamericano/teatro gay en Buenos Aires." *Teatro XXI* 2, no. 2 (fall 1996): 5–7.

——. *Textual Sexualities: Queer/ing Latin American Writing*. Austin: University of Texas Press, 1997.

——. *Violence in Argentine Literature: Cultural Responses to Tyranny*. Columbia: University of Missouri Press, 1995.

Foster, David William, and Naomi Lindstrom. "Jewish Argentine Authors: A Registry." *Revista interamericana de bibliografía* 41, nos. 3, 4 (1991): 478–503; 655–82.

Fuentes, Carlos. "Jorge Luis Borges: La herida de Babel." In *Geografía de la novela*, 32–55. México, D.F.: Fondo de Cultura Económica, 1993.

Fuskova, Ilse, and Claudina Marek. *Amor de mujeres: El lesbianismo en la Argentina, hoy*. Buenos Aires: Planeta, 1994.

Fusková-Kornriech, Ilse, and Dafna Argov. "Lesbian Activisim in Argentina: A Recent but Very Powerful Phenomenon." In *The Third Pink Book: A Global View of Lesbian and Gay Liberation and Oppression*, edited by Aart Hendriks et al., 80–85. New York: Prometheus Books, 1993.

García de Fanelli, Ana, Mónica Gogna, Elizabeth Jelin. *El empleo femenino en el sector público nacional*. Buenos Aires: CEDES, 1990.

Geirola, Gustavo. "Juan José Hernández." In *Latin American Writers on Gay and Lesbian Themes; A Bio-Critical Sourcebook*, edited by David William Foster, 188–91. Westport, Conn.: Greenwood Press, 1994.

Gelfant, Blanche Housman. *The American City Novel*. Norman: University of Oklahoma Press, 1954.

Geltman, Pedro. "Mitos, símbolos y héroes en el peronismo." In *El peronismo*, edited by Carlos Pérez, 109–37. Buenos Aires: Carlos Pérez, 1969.

Gené, Juan Carlos. *Cosa juzgada*. Buenos Aires: Granica, 1970–76.

Gerchunoff, Alberto. *Los gauchos judíos*. Buenos Aires: J. Sesé, 1910.

Gilbert, Sandra M., and Susan Gubar. *The Madwoman in the Attic: The Woman Writer and the Nineteenth-Century Literary Imagination*. New Haven: Yale University Press, 1979.

Gimbernat de González, Ester. "La fotografías de Alicia D'Amico: Cambiando las reglas del juego." *Confluencia* 9, no. 2 (spring 1994): 3–4.

Gobello, José. *Nuevo diccionario lunfardo.* Buenos Aires: Corregidor, 1990.

Goloboff, Gerardo Mario. "La ciudad de Borges." In *La selva en el damero: Espacio literario y espacio urbano de América Latina,* edited by Rosalba Campra, 215–23. Pisa, Italy: Giardini, 1989.

Gomes, Renato Cordeiro. *Todas as cidades, a cidade.* Rio de Janeiro: Rocco, 1994.

Greimas, Algirdas Julien. *The Social Sciences: A Semiotic View.* Minneapolis: University of Minnesota Press, 1990.

Güiraldes, Ricardo. *Don Segundo Sombra.* Buenos Aires: Editorial Proa, 1926.

Hernández, Pablo José. *Para leer a Mafalda.* Buenos Aires: Ediciones Meridiano, 1975.

Hoefer, Hans. *Buenos Aires.* Insight City Guides. Edited by Kathleen Wheaton. Singapore: APA Publications, 1988.

Jáuregui, Carlos. Interview with Patricia Narváez and Alejandro Cruz. In *La maga,* August 28, 1996, 32–33.

Jelin, Elizabeth. *La mujer y el mercado de trabajo urbano.* Buenos Aires: El Centro de Estudios de Estado y Sociedad, 1979.

Jelin, Elizabeth, and María del Carmen Feijóo. "Presiones cruzadas: Trabajo y familia en la vida de las mujeres." In *Del deber ser y el hacer de las mujeres: Dos estudios de caso en la Argentina,* 143–234. México, D.F.: El Colegio de México/PISPAL, 1984.

Jockl, Alejandro. *Ahora, los gay.* Buenos Aires: Ediciones de la Pluma, 1984.

Jones, Gareth A. "The Latin American City As Contested Space: A Manifesto." *Bulletin of Latin American Research* 13, no. 1 (1994): 1–12.

Kaiser-Lenoir, Claudia. *El grotesco criollo: Estilo teatro de una época.* Havana: Casa de las Américas, 1977.

Katz, Jonathan Ned. *The Invention of Heterosexuality.* New York: Penguin, 1995.

Klich, Ignacio. "A Background to Perón's Discovery of Jewish National Aspirations." *Judaica latinoamericana: Estudios histórico-sociales,* 192–223. Jerusalem: Editorial Universitaria Magnes, Universidad Hebrea, 1988.

Kovadloff, Santiago. "Los chicos y la dictadura." In *Argentina: Oscuro país; ensayos sobre un tiempo de quebranto,* 39–47. Buenos Aires: Torres Agüero Editor, 1983.

Kunckel, Dietrich. "The Latin American Metropolis." In *The Metropolis in Transition,* edited by Ervin Y. Galantay, 319–41. New York: Paragon House, 1987.

Kusch, Rodolfo. *Geocultura del hombre americano.* 2d ed. Buenos Aires: F. García Cambeiro, 1976.

Lacarta, Manuel. *Madrid y sus literaturas.* Madrid: Avapiés, 1986.

Lara, Tomás, and Inés Leonilda Roncetti de Panti. *El tema del tango en la literatura argentina.* 2d ed. Buenos Aires: Secretaría de Cultura, Secretaría de Estado de Cultura y Educación, 1970.

Lavado, Joaquín Salvador (Quino). *A mí no me grite.* 4th ed. Buenos Aires: Siglo XXI Argentina Editores, 1973.

——. *Mafalda.* 10 vols. Buenos Aires: Ediciones de la Flor, 1966–74. Volume 2 is titled *¡Así es la cosa, Mafalda!*

——. *Mafalda inédita.* Buenos Aires: Ediciones de la Flor, 1989. Includes as an unpaginated appendix the *Declaración de los derechos del niño, comentada por Mafalda y sus amiguitos para la UNICEF.* Originally published in Bogotá by Editorial Retina in 1977.

——. *Mafalda: Y digo yo . . . .* Barcelona: Noveno Arte, 1974.

——. *Quinoterapia.* Buenos Aires: Ediciones de la Flor, 1985.

——. *Sí, cariño.* 2d ed. Buenos Aires: Ediciones de la Flor, 1988.

——. *Toda Mafalda.* Buenos Aires: Ediciones de la Flor, 1993.

Lemebel, Pedro. *La esquina es mi corazón.* Santiago de Chile: Editorial Cuarto Propio, 1995.

Lewald, H. Ernest. *Buenos Aires: Retrato de una sociedad hispánica a través de su literatura.* Boston: Houghton Mifflin, 1968.

Lindstrom, Naomi. *Jewish Issues in Argentine Literature: From Gerchunoff to Szichman.* Columbia: University of Missouri Press, 1989.

——. "Oral Histories and the Literature of Reminiscence: Writing up the Jewish Past." In *The Jewish Diaspora in Latin America; New Studies on History and Literature,* 89–100. New York: Garland, 1996.

Litvin, Aníbal. *Los más abiertos chistes de homosexuales.* Buenos Aires: Ediciones de la Urraca, 1995.

López Badano, Cecilia. *Violencia de género en los medios de comunicación social argentinos. Apuntes sobre la historia de un imaginatio popular disciminatorio.* Buenos Aires, forthcoming.

Low, Setha M. "Cultural Meaning of the Plaza: The History of the Spanish-American Gridplan-Plaza Urban Design." In *The Cultural Meaning of Urban Space,* edited by Robert Rotenberg and Gary McDonogh, 75–93. Westport, Conn.: Bergin & Garvey, 1993.

Lumsden, Ian. *Machos, Maricones and Gays: Cuba and Homosexuality.* Philadelphia: Temple University Press, 1996.

Madrid, Lelia. "'Fundación mítica de Buenos Aires' o la utopía de la historia." *Bulletin of Hispanic Studies* 69, no. 4 (1992): 347–56.

Mafud, Julio. *Sociología del tango.* Buenos Aires: Editorial Américalee, 1966.

Manrupe, Raúl, and María Alejandra Portela. *Un diccionario de films argentinos.* Buenos Aires: Ediciones Corregidor, 1995.

Martínez, Alberto B. *Baedeker of the Argentine Republic.* 4th ed. New York: D. Appleton, 1916.

Martínez, Tomás Eloy. *Santa Evita: Novela.* Buenos Aires: Biblioteca del Sur/ Planeta, 1995.

——. *Santa Evita.* Translated by Helen Lane. New York: Alfred A. Knopf, 1996.

Martínez Estrada, Ezequiel. *La cabeza de Goliat: Microscopia de Buenos Aires.* Buenos Aires: Club del Libro A.L.A., 1940.

Marting, Diane E., ed. *Spanish American Women Writers: A Bio-Bibliographical Source Book.* Westport, Conn.: Greenwood Press, 1990.

Marzullo, Osvaldo, and Pancho Muñoz. *El rock en la Argentina: La historia y sus protagonistas*. Buenos Aires: Editorial Galerna, 1986.

Massey, Doreen. "Politics and Space/Time." *New Left Review* 196 (1992): 65–84.

———. *Space, Place and Gender*. Cambridge: Polity Press, 1994.

Matamoro, Blas. *La ciudad del tango; Tango histórico y sociedad*. Buenos Aires: Editorial Galerna, 1982.

Maurice, Arthur Bartlett. *New York in Fiction*. Port Washington, N.Y.: Ira J. Friedman, 1899/1900; reprint 1969.

———. *The Paris of the Novelists*. 1919. Reprint, Port Washington, N.Y.: Kennikat Press, 1973.

Medina, Enrique. *Desde un mundo civilizado*. Buenos Aires: Editores Milton, 1987.

———. *Deuda de honor*. Buenos Aires: Editores Milton, 1992.

———. *Gatica*. Buenos Aires: Editorial Galerna, 1991.

———. "La mesa está tendida." *Página 12*, May 26, 1991, 25.

———. *Las tumbas*. Buenos Aires: Ediciones de la Flor, 1972.

Mellibovsky, Matilde. *Círculo de amor sobre la muerte*. Buenos Aires: Ediciones del Pensamiento Nacional, 1990.

Meo Zilio, Giovanni, and Ettore Rossi. *El elemento italiano en el habla de Buenos Aires y Montevideo*. Florence: Valmartina, 1970.

Mercader, Martha. *Solamente ella*. Buenos Aires: Bruguera, 1981.

Meter, Alejandro. "Mario Szichman." In *Jewish Writers of Latin America: A Dictionary*, edited by Darrell B. Lockhart, 504–8. New York: Garland, 1997.

Miller, Neil. *Out in the World: Gay and Lesbian Life from Buenos Aires to Bangkok*. New York: Random House, 1992.

Montes, Hugo. *El "Mono" Gatica y yo*. Buenos Aires: Corregidor, 1978.

Montes de Oca, Eva. *Guía negra de Buenos Aires: Marginación en la gran ciudad*. Buenos Aires: Grupo Editorial Planeta, 1995.

Morse, Richard M., and Jorge E. Hardoy, eds. *Rethinking the Latin American City*. Washington, D.C.: The Woodrow Wilson Center Press; Baltimore: Johns Hopkins University Press, 1992.

Mott, Luíz. *O lesbianismo no Brasil*. Porto Alegre: Mercado Aberto, 1987.

Murray, Stephen O. *Latin American Male Homosexualities*. Albuquerque: University of New Mexico Press, 1955.

Navarro, Marysa. *Evita*. Rev. and expanded. Buenos Aires: Editorial Planeta Argentina, 1997.

Newton, Ronald C. "German Nazism and the Origins of Argentine Anti-Semitism." *The Jewish Diaspora in Latin America: New Studies on History and Literature*, 199–217. New York: Garland, 1996.

Nunca más; Informe de la Comisión Nacional sobre la Desaparición de Personas. Buenos Aires: EUDEBA, 1984. Published also in English, with an introduction by Ronald Dworkin. New York: Farrar Straus Giroux, in association with Index on Censorship, London, 1986.

Núñez, Angel. "El circuito gay porteño." *Humor*, January 1993.

———. "El ghetto gay." *Noticias*, July 4, 1991.

———. "La represión sexual en la argentina." *SexHumor*, June/July 1987.

Núñez Noriega, Gullermo. *Sexo entre varones: Poder y resistencia en el campo sexual*. Hermosillo: El Colegio de Sonora; Universidad de Sonora, División de Ciencias Sociales, 1994.

Onega, Gladys Susana. *La inmigración en la literatura argentina, 1880–1910*. Buenos Aires: Galerna, 1969.

Ordaz, Luis. *Florencio Sánchez*. Buenos Aires: Centro Editor de América Latina, 1972.

Paoletti, Mario. "Borges y la ciudad del tango." *Revista de Occidente* 69 (1987): 87–100.

Perlongher, Néstor. *O negócio do michê: Prostituição viril em São Paulo*. São Paulo: Editora Brasiliense, 1987.

Pezzoni, Enrique, and María Luisa Freyre. "El habla de los porteños." *Buenos Aires: Historia de cuatro siglos*, vol. 2, edited by José Luis Romero and Luis Alberto Romero, 377–89. Buenos Aires: Editorial Abril, 1983.

Pile, Steve. *The Body and the City: Psychoanalysis, Space and Subjectivity*. London: Routlege, 1996.

Portantiero, Juan Carlos. *Realismo y realidad en la narrativa argentina*. Buenos Aires: Ediciones Procyón, 1961.

Posse, Abel. *La pasión según Eva*. Buenos Aires: Emecé Editores, 1994.

Potenze, Jaime. "Sara Facio." In *Fotógrafos argentinos del siglo XX*. Buenos Aires: Centro Editor de América Latina, 1982.

Prado, Alejandro del (Calé). *Buenos Aires en camiseta*. Edited by Rudy, with a prologue and notes by Sylvina Walger. Buenos Aires: Ediciones de la Flor, 1994.

Previdi Froelich, Roberto. "América deshecha. El neogrotesco gastronómico y el discurso del fascismo en *La nona* de Roberto Cossa." In *Teatro argentino durante el proceso (1976–1983): Ensayos críticos—entrevistas*, edited by Juana A. Arancibia and Zulema Mirkin, 131–39. Buenos Aires: Editorial Vinciguerra, 1992.

Puig, Manuel. *Estertores de una década, Nueva York '78*. Buenos Aires: Espasa-Calpe Argentina/Seix Barral, 1993.

Rama, Angel. *La ciudad letrada*. Hanover, N.H.: Ediciones del Norte, 1984.

———. *The Lettered City*. Translated and edited by John Charles Chasteen. Durham: Duke University Press, 1996.

Ramírez, Pablo A. "Los que entraron en la historia del deporte." *Todo es historia* 254 (1988): 38–59.

Rep, Miguel. *Y Rep hizo los barrios*. Buenos Aires: Página 12, 1993.

Rivera, Jorge B. *Panorama de la historieta en la Argentina*. Buenos Aires: Libros del Quirquincho, 1992.

Romero, José Luis, and Luis Alberto. *Buenos Aires: Historia de cuatro siglos*. Buenos Aires: Editorial Abril, 1983.

Rosenbaum, Naomi. *A History of Women Photographers.* New York: Abbeville Press, 1994.

Roulet, Elva. *La mujer en la Argentina: Perspectiva histórica y situación actual.* Buenos Aires: Centro de Participación Política, 1986.

Roy-Cabrerizo, Joaquín. "Claves de Cortázar en un libro olvidado: *Buenos Aires. Buenos Aires.*" *Revista iberoamericana* 84/85 (1973): 471–82.

Ross, Stanley R., and Thomas F. McGann, eds. *Buenos Aires: 400 Years.* Austin: University of Texas Press, 1982.

Sabato, Ernesto. *Tango, discusión y clare.* 3d ed. Buenos Aires: Losada, 1968.

Salas, Horacio. "Buenos Aires, mito y obsesión." *Cuadernos hispanoamericanos* 505/7 (1992): 389–99.

Samper Pizano, Daniel. "Mafalda, el foie gras y la oca." In *Toda Mafalda*, by Joaquín Salvador Lavado, 7–17. Buenos Aires: Ediciones de la Flor, 1993.

Sargent, Charles S. "Argentina." In *Latin American Urbanization: Historical Profiles of Major Cities*, edited by Gerald Michael Greenfield, 1–38. Westport, Conn.: Greenwood Press, 1994.

Savigliano, Marta E. *Tango and the Political Economy of Passion.* Boulder: Westview Press, 1995.

——. "Whiny Ruffians and Rebellious Broads: Tango As a Spectacle of Eroticized Social Tension." *Theatre Journal* 47 (1995): 83–104.

Schneider, Judith Morganroth. "Alicia Steimberg: Inscriptions of Jewish, Female Identity." *Yiddish* 9, no. 1 (1993): 92–104.

Scimé, Giuliana. "Sara Facio." In *Contemporary Photographers*, edited by Martin Marix Evans, 310–12. Detroit: St. James Press, 1995.

Scobie, James. *Buenos Aires: Plaza to Suburb, 1870–1910.* New York: Oxford University Press, 1974.

Sebreli, Juan José. "Historia secreta de los homosexuales en Buenos Aires." In *Escritos sobre escritos, ciudades bajo ciudades*, 275–370. Buenos Aires: Editorial Sudamericana.

Sedgwick, Eve Kosofsky. *Between Men: English Literature and Male Homosocial Desire.* New York: Columbia University Press, 1985.

Sharpe, William, and Leonard Wallock, eds. *Visions of the Modern City: Essays in History, Art, and Literature.* Baltimore: Johns Hopkins University Press, 1987.

Shields, Rob. *Places on the Margin: Alternative Geographies of Modernity.* New York: Routledge, 1991.

Shua, Ana María. "La babuela." *El libro de los recuerdos*, 165–81. Buenos Aires: Editorial Sudamericana, 1994.

Sirven, Pablo. *Quien te ha visto y quien TV: Historia informal de la televisión argentina.* Buenos Aires: Ediciones de la Flor, 1988.

Soja, Edward. *Postmodern Geographies: The Reassertion of Space in Critical Social Theory.* London: Verso, 1989.

Somigliana, Carlos. *El Nuevo Mundo. Teatro abierto; 21 estrenos.* Buenos Aires: ADANS, 1981.

Sommer, Doris. *Foundational Fictions: The National Romances of Latin America.* Berkeley: University of California Press, 1991.

Soriano, Osvaldo. "José María Gatica: Un odio que conviene no olvidar." In *Artistas, locos y criminales,* 247–55. Buenos Aires: Bruguera, 1983.

Sosnowski, Saúl. "Alicia Steimberg: Enhebrando pequeñas historias." *Folio* 17 (1987): 104–10.

——. *La orilla inminente: Escritores judíos argentinos.* Buenos Aires: Editorial Legasa, 1987.

Spain, Daphne. *Gendered Spaces.* Chapel Hill: University of North Carolina Press, 1992.

Steimberg, Alicia. *La loca 101.* Buenos Aires: Ediciones de la Flor, 1973.

Szichman, Mario. *A las 20:25, la señora entró en la inmortalidad.* Hanover, N.H.: Ediciones del Norte, 1981.

——. *At 8:25 Evita Became Immortal.* Translated by Roberto Picciotto. Hanover, N.H.: Ediciones del Norte, 1983.

Talesnik, Ricardo. *Teatro: La fiaca. Cien veces no debo* (nueva versión). Foreword by Saúl Sosnowski. Ottawa: Girol Books, 1980.

Taylor, Julie M. *Eva Perón, the Myths of a Woman.* Chicago: University of Chicago Press, 1979.

——. "Tango." In *Rereading Cultural Anthropology,* edited by George E. Marcus, 377–89. Durham: Duke University Press, 1992.

"El temor a la diferencia." *Página 12* 10 (December 5, 1996): 1, 2.

Terrugi, Mario E. *Panorama del lunfardo: Génesis y esencia de las hablas coloquiales urbanas.* 2d ed. Buenos Aires: Editorial Sudamericana, 1978.

Timerman, Jacobo. *Preso sin nombre, celda sin número.* Barcelona: El Cid Editor, 1980. Cover includes *El caso Camps, punto inicial.* Published in English as *Prisoner Without a Name, Cell Without a Number.* Translated by Toby Talbot. New York: Knopf, 1981.

Trentalance de Kipreos, Silvia. "El sentido de la argentinidad en Alberto Gerchunoff." In *Judaica latinoamericana: Estudios histórico-sociales,* 224–33. Jerusalem: Editorial Universitaria Magnes, Universidad Hebrea, 1988.

Trillo, Carlos, and Guillermo Saccommanno. *Historia de la historieta argentina.* Buenos Aires: Ediciones Record, 1980.

Varsavsky, Paula. *Nadie alzaba la voz.* Buenos Aires: Emecé Editores, 1994.

Vila, Pablo. "Tango to Folk: Hegemony Construction and Popular Identities in Argentina." *Studies in Latin American Popular Culture* 10 (1991): 107–39.

Villanueva, Amaro. *El lunfardo.* Santa Fe, Argentina: Imprenta de la Universidad, 1962. Originally published in *Universidad; revista de la Universidad Nacional del Litoral* 52 (April–June 1962): 13–42.

Walsh, María Elena. "Desventuras en el País-Jardín-de-Infantes." Buenos Aires: Editorial Sudamericana, 1993. 13–18. Originally published in *Clarín,* August 16, 1979.

——. *Novios de antaño.* 9th ed. Buenos Aires: Editorial Sudamericana, 1992.

Walter, Richard J. "Buenos Aires." In *Encyclopedia of Latin American History and Culture,* vol. 1, edited by Barbara A. Tenenbaum et al., 480–83. New York: Charles Scriber's, 1996.

Weisbrot, Robert. *The Jews of Argentina: From the Inquisition to Perón.* Philadelphia: The Jewish Publication Society of America, 1979.

Weston, Kath. *Families We Choose: Lesbians, Gays, Kinship.* New York: Columbia University Press, 1991.

Wittig, Monique. *The Straight Mind and Other Essays.* New York: Harvesterwheatsheaf, 1992.

Wolff, Martha, ed. *Los inmigrantes judío: Pioneros de la Argentina.* Buenos Aires: M. Zago Ediciones, 1982.

Women, Culture, and Politics in Latin America: Seminar on Feminism and Culture in Latin America. Berkeley: University of California Press, 1990.

Zago, Manrique, ed. *Argentina, la otra patria de los italianos/Argentina, l'altra patria deglia italiani.* Buenos Aires: Manrique Zago Ediciones, 1983.

Index

police power, 160
popular culture, 122, 135, 157, 159,
165, 166, 167, 169
Posse, Abel: *La pasión según Eva*,
115, 116, 119
postmodern culture, 7, 111, 116, 145
Prado, Alejandro del (Calé): *Buenos
Aires en camiseta*, 50
privatization, 159
Proceso de Reorganización Nacional,
21, 40, 150
prostitution, 39, 56, 68, 102
Protestantism, 105
public sex, 86, 99
public spaces, 56, 58, 60, 61, 64, 68,
97, 98, 102, 103, 105, 106, 114,
116, 117, 131, 145, 190
public transportation, 101, 102, 103,
159, 160, 167, 168
Puenzo, Luis, 128, 174
Pueyrredón (avenida), 135
Puig, Manuel, 12, 15, 128; *El beso de
la mujer araña*, 88; *La traición de
Rita Hayworth*, 127

Quarracino, Monsignor, 89
queer culture, 14, 57, 91, 92, 99, 100,
106, 112, 125, 127
Quino. *See* Lavado, Salvador Joaquin
Quiroga, Juan Facundo, 6, 142

Rabinovich, José, 140, 151; *Tercera
clase*, 139
race, 156
radio, 58, 110, 111, 112, 114, 132,
145, 166
realism, 34, 172
recapitalization, 162
La Recoleta (cemetery), 115
redemocratization, 47, 69, 99, 151,
162, 180
religion, 61
religious cloisters, 101

remasculinization, 187
Rep, Miguel: *Y Rep hizo los barrios*,
74
resistance culture, 129
revolutionary culture, 142
Riachuelo River, 5, 139
Rice, Tim, 113
Rinaldi, Susana, 174, 177, 179
Rio de Janeiro (Brazil), 3, 4, 84, 102
Río de la Plata (region), 4, 5, 11, 49,
56, 135, 184, 185
La Rioja (province), 6
Rivadavia (avenue), 135
romantic love, 57, 61
romantic nostalgia, 54, 64, 66, 73
Rosario (Argentina), 3, 125
Rosas, Juan Manuel de, 1, 6
Ruiz, Chela, 129

Sabato, Ernesto: *Sobre héroes y
tumbas*, 142, 143
Saccheri, Iris, 174
sadomasochism, 53, 61
sainete, 48
Sánchez, Florencio, 34; *La gringa*, 11
San Telmo (district), 136
Santiago (Chile), 4, 102
São Paulo (Brazil), 3, 84, 95, 102, 104
Sarmiento, Domingo Faustino, 142,
143; *Civilización y barbarie*, 6, 87,
115
Scalabrini Ortiz, Raúl: *El hombre que
está solo y espera*, 117
science fiction, 48, 49, 51, 161
self-censorship, 38
Semana Trágica, 137
sensuality, 53
Sephardic Jews, 133
sexism, 56, 67, 69
sexual conformity, 90
sexual discrimination, 103
sexual dissidence, 89, 104, 127, 128,
180